"We shortchange our lives i
instead of 'on top.' Jennifer
miss out on the ultimate Go
Read on to find how you can enter a higher level in your
relationship."

> \- Nancy Campbell, Author of
> *How to Encourage Your Husband*

"...some of the best advice you could ever take... Jennifer
supplies all the information you need to transform your
current marital state into the marriage you both have been
longing for. So *Love Your Husband, Love Yourself,* and reap
more benefits than you ever dreamed imaginable!"

> \- Michelle Kauenhofen
> Author of *Cheer Up!*

"This book is the talk your Mom never had the nerve to have
with you."

> \- Irene's Christian Reviews
> *Goodreads.com*

"In a very discreet and modest way... Flanders not only
shares the Biblical mandate for a wife to meet her husband's
physical needs but also discusses scientific... advantages of
[doing so] on a regular basis."

> \- Good Old Days Farm
> *Mama Loves Books* review

"This is a message openly opposed by our culture and sadly
sidestepped by the Church... I barely got the message [before
marriage] that physical intimacy was part of being a wife. No
one EVER made me feel like it was my PRIVILEGE! Until
now. Thank You!"

> \- Amber C.
> *Amazon.com* review

"...one of the most candid, honest, beautiful books on marriage I have ever read.... I was absolutely fascinated by the research showing the links between the marriage relationship and health. This is the most in-depth book I have read on the subject of Christian sexual intimacy."

- M. McFarland
Amazon.com review

"Even if you have a healthy and happy marriage, following the principles in this book can make it better."

- Joy H.
Reader's Favorite review

"Mrs. Flanders has created a treasure of godly and scientific insight for wives, full of humor, practicality, and encouragement, on so many topics of relevance to Christian marriage. We are so thankful she sacrificed her time and energy to write this book, despite ample reasons to claim her plate was too full for such a project, and I am passing it on to engaged and married women whenever I can."

- Ellen in Madison, WI
Amazon.com review

"This book is AWESOME! Real life, real talk, real situation! It's a marriage cure!"

- Isabelle Mukam Magne
Amazon.com review

"It was very refreshing to have an author directly say that sex is important, it was especially surprising though, to hear it from a Christian author. I would highly reccomend this book to anyone who wonders why their partner has grown distant."

- nesimarie26
LibraryThing.com review

"I count on one hand the number of books that I have read that I would read again, but this has been added to the list."

- Dr. Laura
journeytoasimplelife.com

"This is one of the most outstanding books I have read. It is so honest, candid, wise—and life-changing."

- Bunnysideup
Amazon.co.uk review

"I heartily recommend it to ALL *married* women—young or old, newly married or not."

- mrshuntinak
LibraryThing.com review

"Possibly the MOST important book a woman could read… Jennifer has a way with words that really got down in my heart. It is obvious that she is not just writing about the subject, she has lived it—which makes it so believable and embraceable…I have 11 children and reading that she has 12 and has a "no excuses" attitude motivated me to seek the higher ground… for my husband's sake."

- Mom of 11 in Texas
AboveRubies.com review

"You are never too old to learn. Don't miss this one."

- Blessed Marriage
Amazon.com review

"Get ready to have your socks knocked off and be blessed beyond your wildest dreams… Buy this book for every bride-to-be on your list."

- Sue, in a reader review at
AboveRubies.com

LOVE YOUR HUSBAND
LOVE YOURSELF

LOVE YOUR HUSBAND
LOVE YOURSELF

*Embracing God's Purpose
for Passion in Marriage*

Jennifer Flanders

Prescott
PUBLISHING

Unless otherwise noted, all Scripture references are taken from the NEW AMERICAN STANDARD BIBLE ®, Copyright ©1960, 1962, 1963, 1968, 1971, 1972, 1973, 1975, 1977, 1995 by the Lockman Foundation. Used by permission.

Scripture references marked NIV are taken from the HOLY BIBLE, NEW INTERNATIONAL VERSION ®. Copyright ©1973, 1978, 1984 by International Bible Society.

Scripture references marked AMP are taken from THE AMPLIFIED BIBLE ©1965 by Zondervan Corporation, Grand Rapids, Michigan.

Scripture references marked NKJV are taken from the New King James version, ©1982, by Thomas Nelson, Inc.

Scripture references marked KJV are taken from the authorized version KING JAMES HOLY BIBLE.

ISBN: 978-0-9826269-0-0

FIRST EDITION
(Fourth Printing)

10 9 8 7 6 5 4 3 2 1

For my dearest Doug,
who gives me ample opportunity
to practice what I preach

Contents

PART ONE
Love Him Physically

PART TWO
Love Him Unconditionally

LOVE YOUR HUSBAND
LOVE YOURSELF

Foreword
The Road Less Taken

*"But small is the gate and narrow the road
that leads to life, and only a few find it."*
Matthew 7:14 (NIV)

This is the story of the road less taken.

Are you being herded along the highway of conventional wisdom, jostled by every whim and worry? Are you marching lockstep with hordes of unhappy people to destinations unknown? Are you starting to question where you are going? Why you are going there? And how come everyone seems so miserable along the way?

Then push your way to the edge of the crowd. You may have a bit of a struggle because everyone is packed in so tightly. You may step on some toes. You may get some angry looks as you squeeze by. You may even hear a few harsh words muttered in your direction. Just apologize and keep moving.

Once you break free of the masses, look down the little knoll into the meadow below. Can you see the narrow trail of pushed-down grass cutting through the field of green? Let your eyes follow it until it disappears into the golden wood. Now look at the forest. See the trees as they sway gently in the breeze. Notice the glint of sunshine in the distance, perhaps from a hidden lake, and the little wisp of smoke rising as though from a single chimney.

Turn back around and look at the crowd. Most of the people are expressionless, sullenly tramping along. Some are angry, shoving and elbowing their way forward along the giant conveyor belt that reaches to the horizon. Here and there you see an occasional smile. Your previous companions have moved on and are disappearing into the distance.

Now you face a decision. Do you rejoin the crowd or follow that little grassy trail to see where it leads?

This book is a letter home from someone who took the little grassy trail.

It has been my privilege to hold the author's hand and walk side by side with her along that trail for the past twenty-two years. Nothing you read here is hypothetical. It is all very real. She has lived out daily every single bit of advice she gives. Although it is packed with scientific studies and Scripture references, her book is as much a journal as anything else: a very personal answer to the question, how do you make it all work?

In fact, this book is just the first of a three-part series answering that very question. Each installment is written in the spirit of Titus 2:3-5, which tells older women to encourage younger women to "love their husbands, love their children, and to be *workers* at home." The series gives a detailed description of what each of these three imperatives looks like in a modern context.

This first book deals with successful husband-wife relationships. The second book addresses meaningful parent-child relationships. And the third gives practical advice on managing a home.

When you read these books, you will be challenged to step outside your comfort zone. You will be asked to be more than what you are, maybe more than what you think you can be. As you follow some of the advice, you may find yourself frustrated, skeptical, and possibly a little afraid. From time to time, you may even look back over your shoulder, across the meadow, at the slowly marching crowd and wonder if you made the right decision.

Fear not. What awaits you at the end of the trail is well worth it. I've been there. I know.

Douglas R. Flanders, M.D.
January 8, 2010

Introduction
Where Did We Go Wrong?

*"All we like sheep have gone astray;
we have turned every one to his own way."*
Isaiah 53:6 (KJV)

The only thing worse than being lost is being lost and not knowing it, but that is exactly what happened to me when I attended a holiday home show one December with my dear friend, Wendy.

How were *we* to know *that house* wasn't on the tour? It *looked* like the right place. Hadn't we been told we couldn't miss it—a big, corner spread at the top of the hill, all decked out in white lights and festive garlands? This one certainly fit the description.

Having just moved to the small town of Tyler, Texas, I had no idea what to expect that evening. I never questioned the fact that so many cars lined the street, we had to circle the block twice to find a parking place. We hurried up the walk, wanting to get my six-week-old Joseph out of the night air. The sign on the door read, "Come On In," so that's exactly what we did.

What a surprise!

None of the home shows I'd attended in Dallas had ever served refreshments, but this one did. We could smell the food as soon as we opened the door. Not just punch and cookies, either. This table looked like it was spread for a king.

There was a live band playing upbeat carols in the foyer. And the people there weren't just walking through the rooms looking at the décor—they were sitting around and visiting. *Tyler is the friendliest town*, I thought to myself, *and this is just further proof of it!*

We stepped through the front door onto a wide, marble landing. Steps descended into a huge living area where most of the crowd had gathered. The people seated on the long couches watched as we came in, smiling curiously at us. *Admiring the new baby, no doubt*, I thought as I fell into line behind several ladies who were going to refill their plates. I was glad Joseph was being quiet for the tour.

I forged through the dining room and on into the kitchen, resisting the urge to fix myself a plate. Wendy hung back at the entrance, looking for someone to check our tickets. When she found nobody at hand, a sudden notion that we'd come to the wrong place swept through her mind. Horrified, she slipped the tickets discreetly up a sleeve and resolved to get out of there as soon as she could track down her clueless friend.

I had wandered into the family room and was admiring a mantel arrangement when Wendy caught up with me. Red from embarrassment, she shared her suspicions in hushed tones. We decided we should try to slip quietly out of the house without attracting any further attention to ourselves.

Too late! We'd been spotted by the hostess, who rushed over to greet us. "I don't believe I've met you," she smiled inquisitively. Wendy and I exchanged nervous glances. Too flustered to explain our honest mistake, I just gave her our (first) names, thanked her for her hospitality, and made a beeline for the door.

Outside, we checked the address. Not only were we at the wrong *house*, we were on the wrong *street*.

It was easy enough to understand, in retrospect, how we could have made such a blunder. Our mistakes were myriad: We failed to consult the map provided. We were too busy *talking* to pay attention to where we were *going*. Neither of us can tell our right from our left without pausing to deliberate. We blindly followed the crowd instead of thinking for ourselves. All the tinsel and bright lights distracted us.

Consequently, we had wandered far off course without even realizing it.

I am convinced a similar thing has happened to many women in regard to love and marriage. We may have started the journey with a clear idea of where we wanted to go, but at some point along the way, we stopped consulting the road map. Maybe the lure of materialism distracted us. Maybe the voices of feminism steered us astray. The sexual revolution pedaled a bill of goods that led many far afield; maybe we bought into that. Or perhaps we got caught in that crowd of soccer moms who stay so busy shuffling kids between sports and school that little time is left for anything else.

Whatever the reason, many of us have wandered far off course without even realizing it. When we finally slow down long enough to assess our surroundings, we are plagued by a nagging sense that we somehow wound up somewhere we didn't mean to be. Ever felt like that?

The thing we must remember is that God never intended for us to strike out on our own. He has drawn in His Word a beautiful picture of what marriage is supposed to look like and has given detailed instructions telling how we can get there. Moreover, He has promised to supply everything we need for the journey (Phil. 4:19). We don't even have to pay for the gas!

You probably already know that one of the best things you can do for your children is to love their father. The premise of this book is that *loving your husband* is also one of the best things you can do *for yourself.* Given the one-flesh nature of marriage (Gen. 2:24; Matt. 19:6), it certainly makes sense. When a husband is blessed, his wife likewise benefits. When he is hurt, she also suffers. What affects him affects her, and vice versa, if indeed the two are one.

The virtuous woman, then, acts in her own best interest when "she does [her husband] good and not evil all the days of her life" (Prov. 31:12). Her primary motivation may not be self-serving, but she does in fact gain when he is well treated. That is a nice fringe benefit, don't you think? It's kind of like earning money back on credit card purchases, only at a higher rate than you were spending to begin with. Who wouldn't enjoy *that*?

Men have this concept spelled out for them. The Bible tells us plainly that a husband should love his wife as his own body. "He who loves his wife loves himself; for no one ever hated his own flesh, but nourishes and cherishes it" (Eph. 5:28-30).

Although the Bible doesn't specifically command wives to *love* their husbands—instead, it uses words like *respect* (Eph. 5:33)—it does tell us repeatedly to "love your neighbor as yourself" (cf. Lev. 19:18; Matt. 22:39; Mark 12:31; Gal. 5:14; James 2:8). And what closer *neighbor* do we have than the spouse who shares our bed each night? It is a simple truth, yet one that many wives fail to fully grasp.

So what does this sort of love look like? It is volitional, self-sacrificing, and unconditional. A wife should love her husband with all her being: spiritually, intellectually, emotionally, and physically.

A Christian wife tends to rank such aspects of love in a descending order of importance. In her mind, the primary thing is to love her husband *spiritually*, so she prays for him and encourages him and pushes him to be everything (she thinks) God wants him to be. She may mistake *intellectual* love for a license to teach him a better way to do things, but will feel baffled when her husband accuses her of nagging. *Emotional* love is her forte, so she talks to him and asks his opinion and shares her feelings and tries to draw him into conversation any way she can.

But when it comes to *physical* love, she has a difficult time understanding what all the fuss is about. In her mind, *sex* is just icing on the cake—a little bit is fine, but too much can be nauseating!

Accordingly, many marriage manuals (especially those written by women) save the subject of physical love for last, almost as an afterthought. I believe the topic warrants more attention than that, so I've devoted eleven chapters to discussing the benefits of sex within marriage for both husbands and wives. What's more, I'm breaking with tradition and placing this section right up front—that way, you won't have to skip to the back of the book to read the sex part first (which is what I usually do, since few things reveal more about an author's worldview than what he/she thinks about sex).

As noted by Scott Stanley in the introduction to Tim Alan Gardner's book, *Sacred Sex*:

> We often talk about... three areas—emotional, intellectual, and spiritual—as the essential elements for creating the optimal conditions for physical intimacy. Rarely do we hear the reverse, that physical intimacy has the power to set the stage for the latter three. I'm not suggesting that couples can have great marriages simply by learning to have great sex. But it's clear that we've given far too little attention to something that's so obviously true and indicated all through Scripture: God placed the physical union between husband and wife at the very heart of marriage. When He introduced the first couple to the concept of oneness, physical union was the method He created to make it happen.[1]

Wives often fail to grasp just how central the physical aspect of their relationship *is* for their husband. A man expects that if his wife truly loves him as she professes, sexual expression will be the natural outflow. After all, physical love is so easily *demonstrated*. It's analogous to giving clothing and food to the cold and hungry. Until we address a person's physical needs, our spiritual blessing to "go in peace, be warmed and filled" is utterly useless—just hollow words devoid of meaning (James 2:15-16). James declares that "faith without works is dead" (James 2:26) and challenges us to "show me your faith without the works, and I will show you my faith by my works" (James 2:18). In the same way, many husbands believe that love without sex is dead; for this reason, if you don't make it a priority to love your husband physically, he may have a hard time believing that you love him *at all*.

When a couple embraces God's purpose for passion in marriage, they reap benefits that spill over into every other part of their relationship: "Communication, intimacy, problem solving, teamwork, spiritual growth—every aspect of married life works better when a couple's sex life is practiced according to God's design."[2] When it isn't—when the importance of physical love is overlooked or minimized or ignored altogether—then your husband will be hard-pressed to appreciate *anything else* you do for him.

The problem has plagued marriages since time immemorial: Men and women hold vastly divergent attitudes toward sex. So what else is new? Life would be much easier if couples could get on the same page about this issue. Don't you agree? That's what makes *loving your husband physically* the most logical place to begin our discussion.

PART ONE
Love Him Physically

Chapter 1
Sex: What's In It for Me?

"So Sarah laughed to herself, saying,
'After I have grown old, and my husband is old,
shall I have pleasure?'"
Genesis 18:12 (NRSV)

Sex deserves a lot more attention than it is getting these days.

No, I'm not referring to the shallow act that Hollywood so graphically depicts on the silver screen; I don't mean the topic splashed across those magazine covers in the grocery line; and I'm certainly not talking about the perversion promoted by the pornography industry.

By sex, I mean the consecrated cleaving of a husband to his wife, which God ordained for marital oneness and procreation. It is an act vital not only to the survival of marriage, but to the survival of mankind. Husbands need sex desperately, and—for that matter—wives do, too. But if you are perusing these pages in search of some steamy secrets or titillating techniques, you may as well close the book now and put it back on the shelf. This is not a *"How To"* book, it is a *"Why To"* book.

As far as I can tell, the abundance of low-sex and no-sex marriages that afflicts our society today is not due to lack of know-how, but to lack of desire. Sex in our culture has been so effectively divorced from its intended purpose that it has become, for many women, an empty shell of what it was designed to be. As such, it neither excites nor satisfies, and they can easily live without it, thank you very much. Is it any wonder, then, "that 15 to 20 percent of couples have sex no more than 10 times a year, which is how the experts define sexless marriage"?[1]

Not in the Mood

There are lots of ways to express physical love. A kiss. A hug. A pat on the back. Let's face it—most of us do not have to be talked into *holding hands* with our husbands. But not so for sex. When it comes to the mode of expression that is uniquely reserved for the confines of marriage, many wives require a little convincing.

Consider an item I spotted in the weekend paper a few months back. Kathy Mitchell and Marcy Sugar, authors of *Annie's Mailbox*, devoted an entire column to printing the excuses wives use to get out of having sex with their husbands.[2] With the exception of "Sex is too painful" (a subsequent check-up revealed uterine cancer), most of these were as creative as they were cold and callous, ranging far beyond the timeworn "Not tonight, I have a headache." Mitchell and Sugar, who served as long-time editors of the Ann Landers column, admit the situation reminds them of the farmer who refused to loan his neighbor a rope, claiming he needed it to *tie up his milk*. "Whenever you don't want to do something," they explained, "one excuse is as good as another."[3]

Even women who might ordinarily be interested in sex have a hard time fitting it into their busy schedules. They are simply stretched too thin. Working wives may juggle 40-hour weeks at the office with aerobics classes at the gym, choir practice at church, volunteer commitments at the community center, and laundry duty at home. So-called stay-at-home moms seldom do, but spend their days instead behind the wheel of an SUV, chauffeuring kids to and from ballet lessons, youth orchestra, tennis team, Bible Drill, home-school co-ops, and chess club.

Meanwhile, Dad works overtime to pay off the second mortgage, is on-call every other weekend, and skips dinner three nights a week to coach Little League, attend board meetings, and take Junior to Cub Scouts.

Husbands and wives rarely even see one another anymore. If and when a couple does finally fall into bed together, she is frazzled. How can he want *sex* when all she cares about is *sleep*? Doesn't he ever get tired, too? She has spent her entire day meeting the needs of others. Now she has to give attention to her own needs before she cracks; she must recharge her own batteries before the morrow dawns and the whole cycle starts over again. Hubby will just have to understand.

In his classic book *What Wives Wish Their Husbands Knew about Women,* author James Dobson argues that

> ...if sex is important in marriage, and we all know that it is, then some time [must] be reserved for its expression.... Remember this: *whatever* is put at the bottom of your priority list will probably be done inadequately. For too many families, sex languishes in last place.[4]

From Generation to Generation

I have friends whose mothers gave them the same prenuptial advice they received from their own mothers decades before: *Sex is just something a wife must put up with,* they were warned. As woefully short as such a view falls from all God intended marital oneness to be, at least these gals were encouraged—even expected—to *have* sex with their husbands, however distasteful they found it.

In his first letter to the Corinthians, the Apostle Paul gives a similar admonition regarding a couple's conjugal responsibilities:

> The husband must fulfill his duty to his wife, and likewise also the wife to her husband. The wife does not have authority over her own body, but the husband does; and likewise also the husband does not have authority over his own body, but the wife does. Stop depriving one another, except by agreement for a time, so that you may devote yourselves to prayer, and come together again so that Satan will not tempt you because of your lack of self-control. (1 Cor. 7:3-5)

Sadly, that is *not* the advice many wives receive today, even within the church. I know one young bride who was told that the most loving thing she could do for her new husband was to *deny him physically*, for only then would he learn to die to himself and develop the character of Christ (!). Is it any wonder that such a wife would feel justified, perhaps even obligated, to tell her husband to go take a cold shower?

Such teaching is completely contrary to Scripture. As noted by the 18th century theologian Adam Clarke, neither husband nor wife has "authority to refuse what the other has a matrimonial right to demand. The woman that would [consistently deny sex to her husband] does not love her husband; or she loves someone else better than her husband; or she makes pretensions to a fancied sanctity unsupported by Scripture or common sense." [5]

No More Excuses

For years, I've listened to wives complain about amorous spouses. *He needs to cool off. He needs to understand. He needs to get a hobby. I'm tired. I'm sick. I'm not in the mood.*

Such discussions drive me crazy. I feel like standing on my chair and shouting: *Stop making excuses and sleep with the poor guy!* If we women would spend half the energy having sex with our husbands as we spend coming up with reasons to avoid it, our marriages would be much healthier, our husbands would be much happier, and—as it turns out—we would be much better off ourselves, as well.

Instead of climbing on my soapbox, though, I muster restraint and bite my tongue. If invited to share my opinion, I urge wives to show some compassion, to make sex a priority for their husband's sake. *Somebody else can wash his clothes or cook his meals or clean his house or teach his kids,* I remind them, *but YOU are the only one who can rightfully satisfy your husband's need for physical intimacy.*

This line of reasoning resonates with some women. They begin to recognize their husband's drive for sex as legitimate and God-given, and to respond in kind. As a result, they discover first-hand the far-reaching benefits that flow from such a shift in thinking.

Other women, however, can hear the same arguments and remain unmoved. *My situation is different*, they say, either audibly or to themselves. *My husband is different. It's unreasonable to expect anybody to have sex under my circumstances. I won't do it. Forget it.*

Sex is not a priority for them, and their lives have become far too complicated to consider making it one now. Doesn't conventional wisdom tell us that a man gets more out of sex than a woman does, anyway? Many wives simply do not have the time, interest, or energy to invest in an activity that has so little potential for payback.

Why should I knock myself out for his sake, they want to know. *What's in it for me?*

The chapters that follow will answer that question.

Chapter 2
The Pleasure of His Company

"On my bed night after night I sought him
whom my soul loves..."
Song of Solomon 3:1

One of the things that originally attracted me to my husband—besides his dashing good looks, his brilliant mind, and his love for Jesus—was the fact that he was a *letter-writer*.

I received my first missive from Doug just a few hours after our initial meeting and knew immediately that he was a man after my own heart. It was a simple, hand-written message on a Hallmark card, the first of countless such notes he penned to me over the months that followed.

I saved the whole stack, and it's a good thing I did, because I received precious little written correspondence from Doug *after* we wed. When he didn't even volunteer to scribble a single thank-you note for the wedding gifts we were given, I realized it wasn't *letter-writing* my husband loved—it was *me*.

The dispatches he delivered while we were dating were merely a way to compensate for the fact we could not continually be together. Since he did his deepest thinking in my absence (I wasn't there to distract his attention, but neither was I around to discuss his thoughts), his only recourse was to jot down the things he most desperately wanted to share and save them for later. Letter writing was a slow, shallow substitute for face-to-face communication and was speedily abandoned once marriage granted him unlimited access to a wife who could give immediate feedback.

It was for this sort of *companionship* that God created woman in the first place. The second chapter of Genesis records the whole story:

> Then the LORD God said, "It is not good for the man to be alone; I will make him a helper suitable for him." ...So the LORD God caused a deep sleep to fall upon the man, and he slept; then He took one of his ribs and closed up the flesh at that place. The LORD God fashioned into a woman the rib which He had taken from the man, and brought her to the man. (Gen. 2:18-22)

Do you remember Adam's reaction when he awoke to find Eve standing before him in all her glory? "This is now bone of my bones, and flesh of my flesh; she shall be called Woman, because she was taken out of Man" (Gen. 2: 23). Somehow, when you hear this passage read in unison by a congregation or quoted in monotone during a wedding ceremony, it fails to capture the intense emotional energy Adam must have felt at that moment. I guarantee he said those words *with feeling*.

The Hebrew word for *man* is *'ish*; the word for *woman* is *'ishah*. Can't you just hear the awe and wonder that filled Adam's voice as he breathed it? *'Ishah!* I'll bet he couldn't take his eyes off Eve. Here was the helper he so desperately needed! Bone of his bone! Flesh of his flesh! Better by far than he could've hoped or imagined. Perfectly designed by God to complement and complete him.

"Adam's response was not only one of fanatic fervor, but also one of full acknowledgement that God's provision was everything he needed," observes Tim Alan Gardner in *Sacred Sex*. "He accepted his wife as God's magnificent creation and the fulfillment of his need, the end of his aloneness. And Eve received that gift of total, enthusiastic acceptance from the most important man in her life."[1] Gardner also notes that

> ...the man, who was alone without the woman, and the woman, who was created out of the man, are separate entities until they come together in sexual union.... That is when a man and woman together most fully represent the image of God, which was breathed into them when He gave them life at Creation.[2]

Adam's deep desire for a suitable companion was no accident. God created him in such a way that he would not be whole without a wife. After providing Eve, God blessed their union and declared, "For this reason a man shall leave his father and his mother, and be joined to his wife; and they shall become one flesh" (Gen. 2:24).

This same need for one-flesh companionship is what has driven couples to marry throughout history. "There's something immensely satisfying in being completely known by another person," writes Debbie Maken in *Getting Serious About Getting Married.* "In creating us for marriage, God had something truly divine in mind.... He did not design the vast majority of us to be content without a marriage partner. God designed the spouse-shaped void to be filled by a spouse."[3]

This intense longing for companionship, this deep desire to be "completely known by another person," finds its culmination in a couple's physical union. In fact, a Biblical euphemism for sexual intimacy is "knowing" one another (Gen. 4:1; Luke 1:34 KJV).

As Martha Peace observes in *The Excellent Wife,* God intended for a couple's physical relationship to provide companionship, to protect against temptation, "to be pleasurable, to enhance drawing the husband and wife into a deeply intimate bond, and [to result in] the procreation of children. God gave man these physical desires so that His plan could be carried out."[4]

Time to Reconnect

Think back to when you first met your husband. Didn't you want to spend as much time together as you possibly could? Don't you recall how unsettled you felt whenever the two of you were separated? Wasn't it hard to concentrate on anything but *when will I see him again*? That is the sort of yearning we see described in the Song of Solomon:

> On my bed night after night
> I sought him whom my soul loves;
> I sought him but did not find him.
> I must arise now and go about the city;
> In the streets and in the squares
> I must seek him whom my soul loves.
> I sought him but did not find him.
> The watchmen who make
> The rounds in the city found me,
> And I said, "Have you seen him
> Whom my soul loves?"
> Scarcely had I left them
> When I found him whom my soul loves;
> I held on to him and would not let him go...."
> (Song 3:1-4)

Maybe the desire to spend time with your husband burns more fiercely in your heart today than ever. Maybe it has cooled somewhat over the years. Maybe you've yet to experience such intense longing at all. Regardless of where you find yourself or whence you came, it takes only a little effort to fan the flames of love into a brilliant blaze and to keep those embers glowing brightly.

How? Start by making a firm commitment to *love your husband physically*. Set aside time for sex. Faithfully. Frequently. Fun-lovingly. "Sex is the *consummation* of marriage…. it represents the complete union of husband and wife, it is the physical embodiment of the vows exchanged by a husband and wife on their wedding day."[5] So put everything else on hold, flip that lock on the bedroom door[6] and give your husband your full attention. Don't say you'll find time for sex once things settle down or you finish some project or your baby is sleeping through the night. Do it *now*.

The whole idea of making something a *priority* implies that other things, however pressing, get moved to the back burner while you attend to *this* one. Putting your husband's needs ahead of your own, by definition, means that some of your own needs may go unmet while you focus on fulfilling *his*.

One obvious benefit of making sex a priority in marriage is that it allows a couple to spend time alone with one another. Just the two of you. This self-evident fact should not be undervalued. No matter how busy your life has become, no matter how insane your schedule, when you take time to physically connect with the man you married, you not only enjoy the pleasure of his company for those few private moments, but *you also reinforce the bonds that keep your hearts knitted together even when your bodies are apart*.

The Dutch have a "slang word for sex, *naaien*, which literally means *sewing*," writes Shmuley Boteach. "Two pieces of material are put on top of each other and then attached in a way that will 'keep them secure and fastened to each other long after the sewing is over and the weaver is gone.'"[7] This is exactly what sex does for a married couple: It binds them together. No wonder husbands feel that something is missing when they don't get enough sex.

Certainly Solomon understood this phenomenon, which is why he counseled his son to "rejoice in the wife of your youth…. Let her breasts satisfy you at all times; be exhilarated always with her love." (Prov. 5:18-19) Obviously, this advice presupposes a wife's cooperation, which is not always freely given. According to research done by Harvard graduate Shaunti Feldhahn, most husbands want more sex than they are getting, and their wives don't seem to realize that this is a crisis—not only for the man, but also for the relationship:

> "Why on earth is it a *crisis*? After all, a lot of other legitimate needs get in the way. Like sleep. Isn't sex just a primal, biological urge that he really should be able to do without? Well… no. For your husband, sex is more than just a physical need. Lack of sex is as emotionally serious to him as, say, his sudden silence would be to you, were he simply to stop communicating with you. It is just as wounding to him, just as much a legitimate grievance—and just as dangerous to your marriage."[8]

Too little sex *dangerous*? You may think she is overstating the problem, but I can assure you she's not. That's because, as demonstrated in other studies, physical love serves "both chemically and psychologically to keep a couple's relationship alive.… [S]ex produces oxytocin, a chemical linked with pair bonding that helps to produce strong feelings of affection between couples."[9] And in order "to maintain its effects long-term, the brain's attachment system needs *repeated, almost daily activation* through oxytocin stimulated by closeness and touch."[10]

One of my college friends told me that if a couple puts a bean in a jar every time they make love during their first year of marriage and takes a bean out each time they make love thereafter, they'll never run out of beans. I suspect that in some such instances, the supply of beans might outlast the marriage itself.

Yet this is certainly not true of every marriage. We know couples who would have exhausted their bean supply many times over—lovebirds who continue to act as if they are on their honeymoon even after twenty, thirty, forty years of marriage. What makes the difference? We assume they *still have sex* because they're *still in love*. But that may be backwards thinking. Considering this bonding effect of oxytocin, it may be more accurate to say that they're *still in love* because they *still have sex*.

Never Enough

Ever wonder why men can't seem to get *enough* sex? The conclusions drawn by Swedish researcher Kestin Uvnäs-Moberg provide insight. This study found that males "need to be touched two to three times more frequently than females to maintain the same level of oxytocin...."[11]

As Louann Brinzendine notes in *The Female Brain*:

> The male brain uses vasopressin mostly for social bonding and parenting, whereas the female brain uses primarily oxytocin and estrogen. Men have many more receptors for vasopressin, while women have considerably more for oxytocin. To bond successfully with a romantic partner, males are thought to need both these neurohormones.... When men in love experience the effects of vasopressin, they have a laser-like focus on their beloved and actively track her in their minds' eyes, even when she isn't present.[12]

Isn't that interesting? These findings certainly explain something I've observed in my own marriage. Having been raised in a family that did not do much hugging or kissing—my parents were very loving, but not overly expressive—it was a bit of a shock to find myself married to a man who could not *survive* without such physical expression, and lots of it. His constant touching and patting and pinching and squeezing took a little getting used to, but I eventually learned to just drop whatever else I was doing when he'd sneak up and grab me from behind, in order to respond in kind. I'll confess we have *both* benefited from my learning to relate in a way he appreciates and understands.

Psychologist Sidney Jourard conducted a fascinating study in which he noted the frequency with which couples conversing in cafés casually touched one another over the course of sixty minutes. His findings? "The highest rates were in Puerto Rico (180 times per hour) and Paris (110 times per hour). Guess how many times per hour couples touched each other in the United States? Twice! (In London, it was *zero*. They *never* touched.)"[13]

After reading those statistics, I became much more cognizant of how often I touch my husband while we are talking. In fact, I took the study as a personal challenge. I'll admit I've never gotten *close* to Puerto Rico's 180 times per hour (that's one touch every 20 seconds—I simply can't *count that fast* and maintain a coherent conversation at the same time), but I do usually manage to stay well above the national average.

How about you? What are you doing to show *your* husband how much you love and admire him? Proverbs 27:5 reads, "Better is open rebuke than love that is concealed." Why not begin with a little casual touching over dinner tonight and see where that leads you? You'll get a boost of oxytocin for your effort and may even whet your husband's appetite for dessert.

But don't wait until you're *in the mood* to get started (that's as bad as resolving to begin a diet *tomorrow*—all too often, tomorrow never gets here). The secret to a rich and satisfying sex life lies in responding to your husband's advances—or initiating advances of your own—even when you are *not* in the mood. Willingness must often precede desire. God has wired women in such a way that our *feelings* flow from our *actions*. That's good news for wives with lagging libido: the more sex you *have*, the more sex you *want* to have. Thanks to oxytocin, it's self-perpetuating.

That's good news for husbands, too, since *feeling wanted* is as essential to them as *having sex*. Ninety-seven percent of men rank "feeling sexually desired by their wife" as very important. Three out of four husbands claim that even if they get all the sex they want, they'll feel empty and unfulfilled if they sense their wife is responding "reluctantly or simply to accommodate [her husband's] sexual needs."[14]

Prolonging the Honeymoon

With so much on the line in terms of forging a love that will last, it makes sense to establish a priority of relating to one another physically from the very beginning. Perhaps it was to allow time for this sort of bonding that provision was made in the Old Testament for a man who had taken a new wife to be exempt from all military and other civic duties: "He shall be free at home one year and shall give happiness to his wife whom he has taken" (Deut. 24:5).

Even Alexander the Great, during his expedition against Persia, granted liberty to his soldiers who had married that year to return home and "pass the winter in the society of their wives."[15]

The idea behind such orders was to help preserve and confirm the "love between [newlyweds]. If the husband were much abroad from his wife the first year, his love for her would be in danger of cooling and of being drawn aside to others whom he would meet" along the way.[16]

Even after the first year of marriage, it is vitally important that "love be kept up between husband and wife, and that *everything be very carefully avoided which might make them strange one to another*," for where distance is allowed to grow, an abundance of guilt and grief stands ready to flow through the gap.[17]

In contrast, when warmth and closeness are cultivated in marriage, God's richest blessings begin to overflow. By making it her goal to regularly and selflessly engage in sex with her husband, a wife opens the very floodgates of heaven—and the rewards she reaps go far beyond building a better marriage or enjoying the pleasure of her husband's company. As we shall see in the next chapter, an active sex life packs incredible benefits for a woman's physical health and well-being, as well.

Chapter 3
Health Insurance

"Pleasant words are a honeycomb,
sweet to the soul and healing to the bones."
Proverbs 16:24

I've always trusted Windex to give my mirrors and glass a spotless, streak-free shine, but did you know it also makes a terrific spot cleaner for carpets? My grandmother taught me that trick. Use blue Windex, not green or pink, and try it yourself. It will lift just about any stain except ballpoint pen (for that, you need hairspray).

In the movie *My Big Fat Greek Wedding*, the father of the bride was a firm believer in the powers of Windex, as well. He found uses for that little squirt bottle far beyond routine household cleaning. Burn your finger? Grab the Windex. Get a bug bite? Try some Windex. Spot a pimple? Have more Windex! His daughter considered this just another of her father's quirks and remained skeptical, but his future son-in-law embraced the idea that Windex isn't just for windows. When the time finally arrived to exchange vows, guess whose face was blemish-free?

Many a wife thinks that *sex* is only for special occasions. The very stars of heaven must align for her to consent to it. Wait until the kitchen is clean and the bills are paid and the paper's read and her nails are dry and the kids are asleep and she's in the mood... then she'll consider it.

Other wives realize that sex makes *any* occasion special. Not only that, but *sex is good for what ails you.* Are you stressed? Blue? Sick? Tired? Anxious? Out-of-sorts? Sex can help you feel better in a hurry. And the effect is not just in our heads.

Scientific studies have shown that frequent sex reduces stress, boosts immunity, fights depression, lowers blood pressure, and alleviates pain. It builds muscle, strengthens bone, improves cognition, and sharpens your sense of smell. It protects against stroke and decreases the risk of heart disease, cancer, and a host of other illnesses.

These are real, documented, measurable effects—not mere anecdotal accounts. The list is so long that just reciting it makes me feel like a snake-oil salesman, so let's look at the data:

Sex is an Analgesic

Here's great news for wives who miss out on sex because of too many migraines: *sex provides fast-acting pain-relief.* Just before orgasm, the body's level of oxytocin surges to five times its normal concentration. Higher levels of oxytocin not only reduce the intensity of pain signals that reach the brain (hence, one feels less pain),[1] but also trigger the release of endorphins, which likewise function as an analgesic.

Classified as endogenous (naturally produced) opiates, these endorphins serve to further elevate a person's pain threshold.[2] "As the name implies, they look (in terms of chemical structure) and act (albeit to a much milder and safer extent) like opium, the poppy-derived narcotic that has been used and abused since 4000 BC to relax, sedate, kill pain, elicit pleasurable feelings, and induce euphoria."[3]

Given today's heightened interest in natural remedies and all things organic, this endorphin-mediated relief should really catch on. There is no risk of overdose or adverse side effects; and unlike over-the-counter medications, endogenous opiates won't damage your liver or cause stomach upset. What's more, studies indicate that sex delivers more *rapid* pain relief than do traditional drug therapies.[4]

So next time you feel a headache coming on, skip taking those two aspirin and go straight to bed—but first, invite your husband to join you. Therapeutic sex is not only effective against headaches and migraines, but has also been shown to relieve arthritis[5] and other types of chronic pain, including lower back pain[6]. Since sex prompts the production of estrogen in women, it can even help reduce the discomfort of PMS.[7]

But sex does much more than make us feel better when we are sick. Sex can actually keep us from getting sick in the first place....

Sex Improves Immunity

Dr. Carl Charnetski has spent over 20 years examining the relationship between our nervous and immune systems and how both affect our health and behavior. This field of study, known as psychoneuroimmunology, has turned up some surprise findings which Charnetski details in his book *Feeling Good Is Good For You: How Pleasure Can Boost Your Immune System and Lengthen Your Life.*

As it turns out, the same endogenous endorphins that kill pain and enhance mood can also "improve immune function by producing an antibacterial peptide.... In general, when your body releases endogenous opiates, your immune system is more active, more productive, more lethal, and more protective."[8]

In case it has been a few years since you sat through that high school biology lecture, Charnetski gives a brief review of how this all works:

The fluid-based humoral immune system, utilizing the bloodstream and all mucosal tissue secretions, is comprised of antibodies, the most prevalent of which is immunoglobulin A (IgA). It represents your body's initial defensive counterattack when an antigen attempts to invade.... IgA is most heavily concentrated in the fluids of our most vulnerable places: tears, mucus, saliva, and vaginal and prostatic secretions. It also appears in breast milk.... It not only combats illness but it also deters illness from starting in the first place. When a foreign substance is first detected, IgA rushes in, binds to it, and prevents it from further entering the body.[9]

This is where the research becomes especially intriguing, for IgA production is not just some internal operation our bodies carry on irrespective of our outward behavior. Quite the contrary. Science has demonstrated time and again that our actions and attitudes have a *profound* effect on immune function in general and on IgA production in particular. Among activities shown to increase IgA levels are prayer, music, meditation, laughter, care giving, and faith.[10]

Somehow, I can't believe that any of these findings come as a surprise to God. After all, He is the One who made our bodies in the first place. Certainly He designed them to function in just such a fashion.

It is no coincidence that the activities shown by current research to increase immunity are the *same* activities God's Word has been advocating for millennia:

PRAYER –
- ∞ "Pray without ceasing." (1 Thess. 5:17)
- ∞ "Devote yourselves to prayer." (Col. 4:2)
- ∞ "With all prayer and petition, pray at all times...." (Eph. 6:18)

MUSIC –
- ∞ "Sing praises to God, sing praises; Sing praises to our King." (Psalm 47:6)
- ∞ "Praise Him with trumpet... praise Him with harp and lyre." (Psalm 150:3)
- ∞ "Praise Him with timbrel and dancing; Praise Him with stringed instruments and pipe." (Psalm 150:4)

MEDITATION –
- ∞ "Meditate in your heart upon your bed, and be still." (Psalm 4:4)
- ∞ "...meditate on it day and night." (Josh. 1:8)
- ∞ "...if anything [is] worthy of praise, dwell on these things." (Phil. 4:8)

LAUGHTER –
- ∞ "Rejoice always." (1 Thess. 5:16)
- ∞ "A joyful heart is good medicine...." (Prov. 17:22)
- ∞ "He will yet fill your mouth with laughter." (Job 8:21)

CAREGIVING –
- ∞ "Give to everyone who asks of you...." (Luke 6:30)
- ∞ "Bear one another's burdens...." (Gal. 6:2)
- ∞ "...through love serve one another." (Gal. 5:13)

FAITH –
- ∞ "Trust in the Lord with all your heart..." (Prov. 3:5)
- ∞ "Your faith has made you well." (Luke 17:19)
- ∞ "Without faith it is impossible to please God...." (Heb. 11:6)

But that isn't all. Another item on the list of immunity-boosting activities is *frequent sex* (you knew that was coming, didn't you?). Here again, the Bible has been right on target, all along. As we noted in the last chapter, husbands receive clear instruction in Proverbs 5:18-19: "Rejoice in the wife of your youth... let her breasts satisfy

.

.

you *at all times*; be exhilarated *always* with her love." (*emphasis added*). This command follows a lengthy passage detailing the inevitable consequences of a man's "embracing the bosom of an adulteress" (any woman *not* his wife). Not only will transgressors come to regret such an impulsive act, but they will "groan at [their] final end, when [their] flesh and body are consumed" (Prov. 5:11).

It is certainly sound advice, for if we hope to gain any benefit from the elevated IgA levels that are associated with having sex, we'll need to avoid contracting any sexually transmitted diseases. The studies are all quick to cite *that* caveat. Herein we see the wisdom of God's original plan. The Bible teaches clearly that "each man is to have his own wife, and each woman is to have her own husband" (1 Cor. 7:2). From the beginning, God designed sex to be enjoyed solely (but regularly!) within the confines of marriage, by a husband and wife who remain completely faithful to one another *for life*. Anything that deviates from this pattern cannot rightly be considered "safe sex".

Bearing that in mind, it is interesting to note that *frequent sex* (defined for the purpose of this study as a mere once or twice a week) has been shown to increase IgA concentrations by a full thirty percent.[11] And this beefed-up immunity not only means fewer coughs and colds, but a significantly lower risk for developing certain forms of cancer, as well.

Sex Wards Off Cancer

My husband is glad that I'm committed to doing my part to protect his prostate. Research has repeatedly shown that the higher a man's ejaculation frequency, the lower his risk of prostate cancer.[12] These findings are significant. Prostate cancer is the most common solid tumor malignancy in American men[13] and the third leading cause of cancer deaths in that group.

But what if your husband is among the estimated 219,000 new cases of prostate cancer diagnosed this year?[14] An active sex life can still help. Remember how oxytocin spikes during lovemaking? Laboratory tests have demonstrated that increased oxytocin inhibits the proliferation (growth and spread) of prostate cancer.[15] And once again, God's design for monogamous sex in marriage proves best, since promiscuity can, "all by itself, *raise* a man's risk of cancer by up to 40%."[16] That adds a whole new dimension to Proverbs 18:22, "He who finds a wife finds a good thing, and obtains favor from the Lord," doesn't it?

Lest you think our husbands are the only beneficiaries of frequent sex on the cancer front, statistics show that wives are afforded protection, as well, especially when sex is not separated from its intended purpose of fruitfulness. Research demonstrates that the longer a woman delays having children and the shorter time she spends breastfeeding those children, the higher her risk of getting ovarian cancer, breast cancer, fibroids and endometriosis, possibly due to the fact that "pregnancy and lactation provide a crucial resting period for the ovaries."[17] In *Be Fruitful and Multiply*, author Nancy Campbell details several such studies, including one which revealed that "women who bear their first child before age twenty-two are less likely than others to develop ovarian cancer" and another which showed that "the women with the least breast cancer were those who had the most children and thus a longer breastfeeding experience."[18]

But sex is good for women even when it does not result in childbirth. Oxytocin (released during lovemaking) has the same growth-inhibiting effect on breast cancer as it does on prostate cancer.[19] This is very encouraging news, especially considering the fact that in the United States, breast cancer is the most prevalent carcinoma in women and second only to lung cancer as the leading cause of cancer deaths in women. [20]

I'm not the only one excited about the implications of this report. Shortly after it was published, Nastech Pharmaceutical acquired a patent to market synthetic oxytocin in the form of a nasal spray to be used in the treatment and possible prevention of breast cancer.[21] Of course, *you* know how to boost your oxytocin even without a prescription—so what are you waiting for? Only, make sure you don't stop short. Studies show that women who have sex less than once a month are more likely to develop breast cancer than those who make love more often.[22]

Sex Protects Your Heart

Dr. Michael Phelps, inventor of the PET Scan, once observed, "the first symptom in 40% of patients with heart disease is hard to deal with: sudden death."[23]

That being so, it's good to know that sex not only strengthens the emotional ties that bind two hearts together, as discussed in chapter two, but it also serves to strengthen and protect the heart muscle itself and to keep the entire circulatory system functioning smoothly. By prompting the release of a hormone known as dehydroepiandrostone (DHEA), sex decreases one's risk of heart disease.[24] By simultaneously elevating testosterone, sex lowers one's risk of having a heart attack even further and also reduces the damage done to the coronary muscles when a heart attack does occur.[25]

In 2001, researchers at Queens University examined how sex affects cardiovascular health; they found that "by having sex three or more times a week, [participants] reduced their risk of heart attack or stroke by half."[26]

The mechanism by which these cardio-protective results were realized may have something to do with sex's ability to combat high blood pressure.

Current estimates suggest that almost half of all American adults suffer from either chronic hypertension or prehypertension,[27] putting them at increased risk for heart disease, heart failure, coronary artery disease, atherosclerosis, stroke, kidney failure, and vision problems, including hypertensive retinopathy.[28] Many of those whose measurements fall outside the normal range are not even aware that their blood pressure is elevated.

It might be prudent, then, for all of us to adopt a lifestyle that would help maintain a healthy blood pressure, *before* it becomes a problem or manifests in such serious secondary symptoms.

Do you remember all that coffee shop touching we referenced in the last chapter? Well, frequent touch is good for more than just letting the other café patrons know that *this* dish is taken; touch has a calming effect on blood pressure, as well.

Numerous studies support this claim. One such study, which for three years monitored 24-hour ambulatory blood pressure of married subjects with mild essential hypertension, noted that their blood pressure levels were *inversely proportional* to the amount of spousal contact they enjoyed— that is to say, the more frequently a couple engaged in meaningful touch, the lower their blood pressure remained.[29]

Chronic stress has been implicated as a contributing factor to hypertension, yet physical closeness and touch between married partners has been shown to "lower systolic blood pressure in subjects with job strain."[30] Even when the source of outside stress cannot be stemmed, sex can counteract its negative effects. We will address this in greater detail in chapter four, but the driving force behind these benefits is oxytocin, which, in addition to the other amazing things it does, stimulates sodium excretion from the kidneys,[31] which helps reduce hypertension.

In an attempt to evaluate oxytocin's role in blood pressure regulation, another study demonstrated that greater partner support, as communicated through warm contact, was linked to higher levels of plasma oxytocin and lower baseline blood pressures.[32] This rise in oxytocin confers numerous "cardiovascular health benefits of marriage," whereas "lack of oxytocin activity [promotes] multiple atherogenic factors involving platelet activity, endothelial function, and reductions in vagal tone."[33]

In other words, your heart and circulatory system benefit when you hug and kiss and have sex with your husband, but your cardiovascular health suffers when you try to live without lots of warm physical contact and emotional support.

Sex is Great Exercise

Aside from all these inner workings of our neuropeptides, sex is great exercise. Since it always seems to be on our husbands' minds, and since doctors recommend that we get a minimum of 30 minutes of aerobic exercise five days a week, why not kill two birds with one stone? Get a good cardiovascular workout and make your hubby happy, all at the same time. As noted in Pala Copeland and Al Link's article, "The Health Benefits of Sex:"

> Sex helps increase the blood flow to your brain and to all other organs of your body. Increased heart rate and deep breathing accounts for the improvement in circulation. As fresh blood supply arrives, your cells, organs and muscles are saturated with fresh oxygen and hormones, and as the used blood is removed, you also remove waste products that cause fatigue and even illness.
>
> Lowering your cholesterol is another of the "sex as exercise" benefits. Sex helps lower the overall cholesterol level. Perhaps more importantly it tips the HDL/LDL (good/bad) cholesterol balance towards the healthier HDL side.[34]

As with any exercise program, stick with it consistently and the cumulative benefits to your overall health and appearance will really begin to pay off:

> A vigorous bout [of sex] burns some 200 calories—about the same as running 15 minutes on a treadmill.... The pulse rate, in a person aroused, rises from about 70 beats per minute to 150, the same as that of an athlete putting forth maximum effort. British researchers have determined that the equivalent of six Big Macs can be worked off by having sex three times a week for a year. Muscular contractions during intercourse work the pelvis, thighs, buttocks, arms, neck and thorax.... *Men's Health* magazine has gone so far as to call the bed the single greatest piece of exercise equipment ever invented.[35]

Can you think of a more enjoyable way to get in shape? And if losing weight is your goal, it makes especially good sense to incorporate sex into your workout regimen. As we all know, it's possible to out-eat any exercise program, but with sex, you may no longer be inclined to do so. That is because sex also serves to reduce our appetite for sugary foods.

Sex Reduces Cravings

I recently ran across a curious recipe entitled "Better-than-Sex Cake." Strangely enough, it was included in an old church cookbook, but the parishioner who submitted it up must have spent too much time in the kitchen and not enough time in the bedroom. Why else would she make such an outrageous claim?

As we've already established, sex revs up oxytocin production. Research indicates that oxytocin, in turn, reduces cravings for sweets.[36] (Oxytocin has been shown to curb an appetite for cocaine, morphine, and heroin, as well, making it easier for drug-addicted mice to kick their habits, cold-turkey.[37])

So if your past efforts to lose weight have been promptly derailed by an insatiable sweet tooth, making love may be just the ticket to get you back on track.

And while sex has never completely eradicated my own hankering for chocolate, it has diminished it enough that, even if the aforementioned recipe were made with pure cocoa instead of crushed pineapple, I'd *still* take exception to its name.

Sex Boosts Longevity

Married people, in general, live longer than singles. Moreover, according to studies done by Carl Charnetski,

> Couples in good marriages… are healthier than their unattached peers…. They have more natural killer-cell activity in their immune systems. Cancer doesn't progress as rapidly in their bodies. Good relationships buffer them against a variety of illnesses. Compared with unmarried people, those who have tied the knot also come through hospital stays more successfully. They generally have less serious diagnoses upon admission, stay in the hospital for less time, and are less likely to die while hospitalized. They're also less likely to be placed in nursing homes upon discharge.[38]

So just the fact that you *have* a husband puts you at an advantage as far as length of life is concerned. If you remain sexually active with that husband, so much the better:

> In one of the most credible studies correlating overall health with sexual frequency, Queens University in Belfast tracked the mortality of about

1,000 middle-aged men over the course of a decade. The study was designed to compare persons of comparable circumstances, age and health. Its findings, published in 1997 in the *British Medical Journal*, were that men who reported the highest frequency of orgasm enjoyed a death rate half that of the laggards.[39]

Sex is Good For You

Numerous other studies have been done to explore the salutary effects sex has on our bodies—far too many, in fact, to cite them all here. Among the myriad benefits enjoyed by couples who maintain an active sex life, researchers have made the following observations:

∞ Sex strengthens bones: Sex builds stronger bones and muscles, thanks to increased levels of testosterone and growth hormones.[40] And since lack of exercise, deficiencies in sex hormones, and excesses of cortisol can all contribute to bone loss,[41] an active sex life may even reduce your risk of developing osteoporosis.

∞ Sex enhances fertility: Frequent lovemaking promotes fertility by helping to regulate a woman's menstrual patterns.[42] Likewise, repeated ejaculation (within four to 24 hours) can increase a man's sperm count by more than 200 percent.[43]

∞ Sex promotes better communication: Frequent sex improves a woman's ability to recognize, identify, and communicate emotions,[44] and oxytocin has been shown to sharpen a man's ability to read facial expressions.[45]

∞ Sex protects against stomach ulcers: Research indicates that men who feel unloved by their wives are two to three times more likely to develop duodenal ulcers than those who feel loved and supported.[46]

∞ Sex improves your sense of smell: Orgasm triggers a surge in prolactin, which "causes stem cells in the brain to develop new neurons in the brain's olfactory bulb, its smell center."[47]

∞ Sex facilitates better bladder control: It works to tone the same group of muscles that are responsible for maintaining continence.[48]

As I mentioned earlier, the list goes on *ad infinitum,* but you've got the idea. It was not my purpose in writing this chapter to bore you with a lot of technical jargon, nor do I wish to reduce sex to a purely biological process by stripping it of all romance and mystery. I only hope to stir in you a sense of awe and wonder over God's intricately balanced design for sex in marriage. Did you ever imagine that making love to your husband could so profoundly affect your own health and well-being?

When it comes to proving my original premise that loving your husband is one of the best things you can do for yourself, the evidence is definitely stacked in my favor. But keep in mind that I've merely listed the *known* benefits—an active, healthy sex life likely helps us in other ways we do not yet fully understand.

One thing is clear, though: Sex does much more than just propping up our physical health. Thanks to oxytocin and other neurohormones released during lovemaking, sex has a profound impact on our attitude and appearance, as well, which we shall examine in detail in the next three chapters.

Meanwhile, next time you are feeling a little under the weather, you should seriously consider seducing your husband. That might be just what the doctor ordered.

Chapter 4
Peace of Mind

"...the peace of God, which surpasses all comprehension, will guard your hearts and your minds in Christ Jesus."
Philippians 4:7

Another beautiful day was drawing to a close. Jesus had been standing in a boat to preach while his listeners lined the shore. A gentle, steady breeze had provided refreshment to the followers as they had hung on every word. But now the crowd was dispersing, the wind was picking up, and clouds were starting to accumulate on the horizon. As the sun dipped behind them, it cast a brilliant reflection in reds and yellows and purples upon the Sea of Galilee. Jesus, weary from teaching, lay down on a pillow in the stern of the ship while His disciples weighed anchor and prepared to cross over to the other side.

But those clouds kept moving in. A fierce gale burst upon the ship long before the boat reached its destination. Peter, Andrew, James and John were fishermen by trade and, as such, were accustomed to these sudden changes in weather. "No need to wake the Lord," they agreed, "we can handle this ourselves." They trimmed the sails and allowed the boat to run ahead of the wind while Jesus slept on undisturbed.

Of course, the storm only grew worse, whipping the waves into a fury. The vessel was tossed wildly about, as if it were a child's toy. Breakers crashed violently over the side of the ship. Water poured into the hull faster than they could bale it out. Soon, the panic-stricken disciples began to despair. "Master!" they cried out in terror, "Master! Don't you care that we're about to die?"

Only then did the Savior awake. He rose up and rebuked the wind, commanding the waves, "Peace. Be still." The instant these words left His lips, the wind ceased and the sea became perfectly calm. Turning to His disciples, Jesus asked, "Why are you so afraid? How can it be that you have no faith?"

The disciples were speechless. Still in awe over what they had witnessed, they marveled one to another, "What sort of man is this, that even the wind and the sea obey Him?"

You probably know this story, adapted from Mark 4:35-41, as well as I do. So why have I taken the time to recount it here? Because a similar scenario plays out in our own lives so *routinely*.

Even with Jesus on board, we insist on manning the helm ourselves. When the winds of change begin to blow, when troubles assail us, when sorrows like sea billows roll,[1] we attempt to handle the crisis in our own strength. We ponder and perseverate, unable to concentrate on anything else. Scripture tells us plainly to cast "all your anxiety upon Him, because He cares for you" (1 Peter 5:7), so perhaps we pray. But all too often, we leave the throne of grace with our burden still heavy upon our shoulders, tossing restlessly upon our bed night after night.

Essentially the same thing occurs on a cellular level, as well, in the microcosm of our endocrine system. Some storm arises in the form of a stressful situation to buffet our brain. In response, our adrenal glands secrete a host of hormones, including epinephrine and norepinephrine (also known as adrenaline and noradrenaline) and cortisol (sometimes called "the stress hormone"). This experienced crew immediately launches into action as part of our body's fight-or-flight response. It focuses all its attention on the problem at hand, to the neglect of everything else. Meanwhile, our faithful friend oxytocin lies sleeping, deep within the recesses of our pituitary gland. Never mind that this powerful neurotransmitter has the ability to instantaneously alleviate our anxiety and calm our nerves—cortisol is determined to handle the situation without oxytocin's help.

Yet, during the time that oxytocin lies dormant, great damage can be done. Prolonged exposure to cortisol can do all sorts of awful things to our bodies. It has been implicated in causing or worsening just about every disease described in the previous chapter. Chronic stress can lead to chronic ill health.

An Inexhaustible Supply

The problem is, "you do not run out of stress hormones. Your body possesses the capacity to manufacture them as long as you are under duress." [2] When your toddler turns blue over breakfast, an instantaneous rush of cortisol and adrenaline gives you the energy to leap across the table, snatch him from his seat, turn him upside down, and pummel his back until you've dislodged the donut hole that is stuck in his throat. Even after his color returns and he's breathing easily, your knees still feel shaky and your heart is aflutter. (Trust me. I speak from experience). That is the after-effect of having these stress hormones dumped on your system.

Such chemical reactions are helpful when we are responding to imminent danger, like choking or fire or drowning. When the situation which triggers our fight-or-flight response actually results in our *fighting* or *fleeing*, "the exertion [will help our] physiology return to normal, which [explains] why exercise is a good stress reducer." [3]

Unfortunately, much of the stress we encounter these days is of the protracted rather than the acute variety. The problems that plague many of us have no quick and easy fix. Job strain, overextended schedules, rebellious teens, insurmountable debt, chronic illness, failed marriages—such concerns still unleash a flood of hormones, but we no longer use them to fight or flee. Instead, we fuss or fret or fume. Our bodies continue to churn out the cortisol, but our worrying does nothing to clear it from our systems—if anything, it ratchets production up even further, thus compounding the problem. The end result? Stress hormones build up in our bloodstream and wreak havoc with our health.

In his book *Feeling Good is Good for You,* Dr. Carl Charnetski offers a detailed explanation of the risks associated with a prolonged spike in cortisol, which I quote here at length. These include:

> *High blood pressure and heart disease.* [Hypertension] is the most significant risk factor for heart disease and stroke. A brief blood pressure elevation will pump more blood through your system and help you survive a physical threat. Assuming that it soon returns to normal, you'll probably suffer no long-term damage. But replace a quick battle against a saber-toothed tiger with a drawn-out, messy divorce accompanied by heated accusations, long-simmering acrimony, high-priced lawyers, and crying, confused children, and your tension level and blood pressure will be in the stratosphere for months, not minutes. The increased pressure could force a blood vessel to burst. If the ruptured vessel feeds your heart, you will have a coronary; if the vessel feeds the brain, you will have a stroke.
>
> *Atherosclerosis.* Continued high blood pressure also causes minuscule rips and tears along the interior walls of the arteries. These chinks are ready-made nooks and crannies for cholesterol to lodge in, building up into blood-damming, artery-

clogging plaque…. [Moreover, stress hormones] tend to assist in the production of the type of cholesterol that most likely clings to artery walls (low density lipoprotein, or LDL) and encourage the destruction of artery-cleansing, high-density lipoprotein, or HDL.

Diabetes. How about that rise in blood sugar? Not a problem—in a brief emergency. If you fight or flee, the physical activity will burn off surplus glucose, and everything should be fine. But if you sit and stew in your office cubicle for months on end and don't burn off the extra sugar in your bloodstream, you're essentially developing the primary symptom of diabetes, the fourth leading cause of death in the United States. A stress-filled life, especially if combined with a poor diet and a lack of exercise, is one of the bona-fide risk factors for this disease.

Brain damage, memory loss, and stroke. [Cortisol] kills brain cells, according to research by Robert Sapolsky, Ph. D., a Stanford University biologist who has extensively studied the physiological consequences of stress. Cells that appear particularly vulnerable are located in the brain's hippocampus, an area critical for the formation of memories and one of the parts of the brain that deteriorates in Alzheimer's disease and other memory disorders. The implication is that chronic stress could be a contributing factor in Alzheimer's and other cognitive illnesses.[4]

But the damage done by stress hormones is not limited to physical ailments. "High levels of cortisol are [also] the chief culprits in depression and anxiety disorders."[5] And the fact that "a woman's highly responsive stress trigger allows her to become anxious much more quickly than does a man" puts her at special risk.[6]

Mental Anguish

Why are ladies so susceptible to anxiety and depression? I think for many of us, the problem stems from the pressure we feel—and our subsequent failed attempts—to be *Wonder Woman.* A popular 1970's perfume commercial featured a seductively dressed model singing, "I can bring home the bacon, fry it up in a pan, and never, never let you forget you're a man...." The underlying message was clear: a *real* woman knows how to handle a career, a home, *and* a lover, so if you want to be considered successful by modern standards, you had better excel at all three (and look good doing it).

Yet a woman who wants to have it all faces an impossible task. Biology drives her to do one thing (love a husband and nurture children) even as society demands that she do something else (pursue a career, often to neglect of home and family). Many wives wear "themselves down to the point that ill health and ill temper are the result. The problem is with their notion of a full life."[7] All too often, those of us who try to "do it all" end up being jacks of all trades, but masters of none:

> In fact, there is even a new syndrome ascribed to working mothers called "Hurried Woman Syndrome," a term coined by some in the medical community who listened to women's complaints about their busy lifestyles.... This syndrome has been defined by the symptoms of weight gain, low sex drive, moodiness, and fatigue—all due to the stress caused by trying to do too much, not being able to keep up with it, not feeling very accomplished at any of it, resenting anyone who has any expectations (like husband and children), and ending up feeling hostile and depressed.[8]

This urge to do everything and to please everybody can easily turn into an emotional tug-of-war that lands us on the brink of despair. No wonder anti-depressants are the most commonly prescribed drugs in America right now, with 118 million prescriptions written annually.[9] Yet, "when researchers tested the effect of the six leading antidepressants, they noted that 75 percent of the effect was duplicated in placebo controls."[10] What does that mean, exactly? Is all this medication really necessary? Could we be treating the symptom and ignoring the cause? Does our emotional turmoil have more to do with our life choices than with our brain chemistry? How do we get to the root of the problem?

There was once a time when a whole host of psychosomatic illnesses in women were diagnosed as "hysteria" (a word derived from the Greek word for uterus) and attributed to a "starving womb" (meaning they didn't get enough sex). The recommended course of treatment for this malady was straightforward: if the patient were single, she should marry; if she were married, she should have intercourse.[11] Science has since reclassified many of those diseases, a task that sorely needed to be done. Considering the fact that one physician of the Victorian Era had "cataloged 75 pages of possible symptoms of hysteria and called the list incomplete, almost any ailment could fit the diagnosis."[12]

The same symptoms are seen in patients today, but now we identify them by different names and treat them with psychotropic drugs. I doubt you'd hear many modern physicians advise their patients that the best way to cure anxiety attacks or treat depression is to have sex with one's spouse. But maybe—just maybe—we've thrown the baby out with the bath water.

Help Is On the Way

Life was never meant to be so stressful. Jesus Himself beckons us, "Come unto Me, all who are weary and heavy-laden, and I will give you rest. Take My yoke upon you and learn from Me, for I am gentle and humble in heart, and you will find rest for your souls. For My yoke is easy and My burden is light" (Matt. 11:28-30). Did you notice the Scripture verse at the beginning of this chapter? "And the peace of God, which surpasses all comprehension, will guard your hearts and your minds in Christ Jesus" (Phil. 4:7). Well, *that* is a promise you can take to the bank.

Remember the list of immunity boosters we looked at in the last chapter? We saw that IgA levels are elevated by such activities as prayer and music and meditation—the very things we are commanded in Scripture to do. Conversely, when we examine the things that really rev up the production of cortisol—fear, worry, anxiety, anger, despair, isolation—we find that they are the very things God admonishes us in His Word *not* to do. The Bible repeatedly instructs us:

DO NOT FEAR –
- ∞ "Fear not; I will help thee...." (Isa. 41:13 KJV)
- ∞ "Fear not: for I am with thee...." (Isa. 43:5 KJV)
- ∞ "Do not fear: you are more valuable than many sparrows." (Luke 12:7)
- ∞ "Do not be afraid; I am the first and the last...." (Rev. 1:17)

DO NOT WORRY –
- ∞ "Do not worry about your life...." (Luke 12:22)
- ∞ "...do not worry about tomorrow; for tomorrow will care for itself." (Matt. 6:34)
- ∞ "Do not worry about how or what you are to say...." (Matt. 10:19)
- ∞ "And which of you by worrying can add a single hour to his life's span? If then you cannot do even a very little thing, why do you worry about other matters?" (Luke 12:25-27)

DO NOT BE ANXIOUS –

∞ "Be anxious for nothing, but in everything by prayer and supplication with thanksgiving let your requests be made known to God." (Phil. 4:6)

∞ "...casting all your anxiety on Him, because He cares for you." (1 Pet. 5:7)

∞ "Anxiety in a man's heart weighs it down, but a good word makes it glad." (Prov. 12:25)

∞ "When my anxious thoughts multiply within me, Your consolations delight my soul." (Psalm 94:19)

DO NOT BE ANGRY –

∞ "Get rid of all bitterness, rage and anger..." (Eph. 4:31 NIV)

∞ "Put them all aside: anger, wrath, malice, slander, and abusive speech...." (Col. 3:8)

∞ "Be quick to hear, slow to speak and slow to anger; for the anger of man does not achieve the righteousness of God." (James 1:19-20)

∞ "A fool always loses his temper, but a wise man holds it back." (Prov. 29:11)

DO NOT LOSE HOPE –

∞ "Why are you in despair, O my soul? And why have you become disturbed within me? Hope in God, for I shall again praise Him for the help of His presence." (Psalm 42:5)

∞ "Let us hold fast the confession of our hope without wavering, for He who promised is faithful." (Heb. 10:23)

∞ "Hope deferred makes the heart sick, but desire fulfilled is a tree of life." (Prov. 13:12)

∞ "...show this same diligence to the very end, in order to make your hope sure." (Heb. 6:11 NIV)

DON'T BE A LONER –

∞ "But if we walk in the light, as he is in the light, we have fellowship with one another." (1 John 1:7 NIV)

∞ "Let us consider how to stimulate one another to love and good deeds, not forsaking our own assembling together, as is the habit of some, but encouraging one another...." (Heb. 10:24025)

∞ "God sets the lonely in families...." (Psalm 68:6 NIV)

∞ "Two are better than one, because they have a good return for their work: If one falls down, his friend can help him up. But pity the man who falls and has no one to help him up!" (Ecc. 4:9-10 NIV)

∞ "Do not forsake your own friend or your father's friend.... Better is a neighbor who is near than a brother far away." (Prov. 27:10)

Fear. Stress. Anxiety. Hopelessness. Depression. Isolation. Anger. All boost our production of cortisol. All are weapons Satan uses to defeat us. Do you think it a coincidence, then, that God advises us to cast off such negative behavior and thought patterns?

Like the seed which falls among thorns, our lives can become so overgrown by the cares and concerns of this world that we fail to yield that crop the Holy Spirit has worked so diligently to cultivate: "love, joy, peace, patience, kindness, goodness, faithfulness, gentleness, and self-control" (Gal. 5:22). In place of this delectable harvest, we reap nothing but grief when we allow distress, distraction, and despond to entrap our hearts and minds in their coiling tendrils. And since stress prompts the release of cortisol, which itself leads to more stress, the whole thing becomes a vicious cycle.

But all hope is not lost: We need not remain entangled in such a snare, because cortisol is essentially deactivated in the presence of oxytocin. The parasympathetic nervous system, which stimulates the release of oxytocin, runs completely counter to the sympathetic nervous system, which is responsible for the production of cortisol. This explains why "you cannot be stressed and happily content at the same time."[13]

Although "stress cranks up the sympathetic engine, the reverse is also true: Parasympathetic activity turns the sympathetic motor off and pulls the key out of the ignition. A high degree of activity in one system [shuts down] the other."[14] And while cortisol elevates blood pressure and kills brain cells, putting our hearts and minds at risk for strokes and myocardial infarcts, oxytocin quite literally serves to protect—or guard, if you will—those same hearts and minds, thus propagating a sense of calm and peace which truly does surpass all understanding (see Phil. 4:7).

Fighting Depression

Did you know that as women, we are four times more likely to struggle with anxiety and depression than our male counterparts?[15] Why do you suppose that's true? Is there something in our constitution that makes us more sensitive to stress in general? If so, then it would stand to reason that the additional responsibilities we take on by becoming wives and mothers would further compound the problem. The Bible even reminds us that a "woman who is unmarried... is concerned about the things of the Lord, that she may be holy both in body and spirit; but one who is married is concerned about... how she may please her husband" (1 Cor. 7:34-35).

Yet the duties associated with getting married or giving birth do not plunge most of us into the depths of despair. Why? Because our Heavenly Father is infinitely wise and good. He promises: "My grace is sufficient for thee: for My strength is made perfect in weakness" (2 Cor. 12:9 KJV). He fortifies us for the task at hand and, from the beginning, has designed our bodies to work in such a way that the very process of fulfilling our obligations to husband and offspring triggers the release of an extremely effective, natural antidepressant which serves to buoy our spirits, relieve our anxieties, and quiet our nerves.

Can you guess the name of this miracle substance? It's oxytocin, and a mother gets a burst of it each and every time she nurses a baby, cuddles a toddler, or hugs a teen. A woman who quits her job to stay at home and raise a family may end up with a smaller savings account than her career-minded peers, but she'll gain infinitely more in terms of the longer-enduring riches of love, appreciation, and mutual respect that grow from time spent bonding with her family. In the process of giving her little ones the attention they crave, she benefits herself as well, both physically and emotionally.

In the same way, a wife who cheerfully tends to her husband's very basic need for physical affection and loving admiration will not only boost *his* oxytocin levels, but will see a five-fold increase in her *own*. Sex effectively serves as a booster shot to inoculate her against all the damaging effects of long-term stress and elevated cortisol, *including* depression and anxiety. Research indicates that the "release of oxytocin due to [sex also] reduces stress and neurotic tendencies."[16]

But recent studies have indicated that oxytocin is not the only mechanism by which sex fights depression, and herein lies another benefit of embracing God's purpose for passion in marriage: A wife whose husband does not use a condom during sex is less subject to depression than one whose partner does. While scientists don't fully understand why this is the case, they speculate that "prostoglandin, a hormone found... in semen, may be absorbed in the female genital tract, thus modulating female hormones."[17] Interestingly, "male perspiration [also has] a surprisingly beneficial effect on women's moods. It helps reduce stress, induces relaxation, and even affects the menstrual cycle."[18]

These findings are nothing less than awe-inspiring. Do you see what a beautiful system of checks and balances God has built into our bodies? Is it not humbling to consider how thoroughly He has provided for our every need? Studying such things causes me to marvel at God's wisdom and to trust in His goodness all the more fully. I can emphatically affirm with David, "I am fearfully and wonderfully made: marvelous are Thy works; and that my soul knoweth right well" (Psalm 139:14 KJV).

Relieving Stress

Of course, sex works wonders for men, as well as women. So making it a priority to regularly relieve tension and stress through an active sex life is a wonderful way for a wife to minister to her husband, while benefiting herself at the same time. As Providence would have it, men and women differ in their response to stress just as surely as they differ in their drive for sex.

This is a particularly important concept for women to grasp. Men have an uncanny ability to enjoy sex no matter how burdened they become with deadlines, difficulties, or disasters. It's as if they had some internal switch that allows them to instantaneously shift their focus from problems ahead to pleasures at hand. A man's sex drive is often *even stronger* during stressful situations. In fact, for many men, the more stressed they are, the more sex they want (and need).

Amy Gardner elaborates on this fact in her husband's book, *Sacred Sex*:

> Men are…compartmentalized. They can separate out their sexual thoughts and desires from the rest of their day. A husband can walk into a house full of screaming kids, a ringing phone, and a barking dog, and he'll still be thinking, *Tonight is going to be one exciting rendezvous.* Short of being comatose or in a full body cast, a man's sexual desire is largely unaffected by external factors.[19]

This is *not* true of most women. Women are opposite. Stress completely shuts us down. Problems distract us, demanding our full attention. Anxiety causes our sex drive to plummet. As author Louann Brizendine notes in her book, *The Female Brain*, "the reason [behind this phenomenon] may be that the stress hormone cortisol blocks oxytocin's action in the female brain, abruptly shutting off a woman's desire for sex and physical touch."[20] Brizendine goes on to explain:

> Sexual turn-on [for a woman] begins, ironically, with a brain turn-off. The impulses can rush to the pleasure centers and trigger an orgasm only if the amygdala— the fear and anxiety center of the brain—has been deactivated. Before the amygdala has been turned off, any last-minute worry—about work, about the kids, about schedules, about getting dinner on the table— can interrupt the march toward orgasm.[21]

This situation presents a conundrum: sex can help relieve our worries, but worries can prevent our enjoying sex, if—and that's a big *if*—we can be persuaded to participate at all. Sex is as much a discipline of the mind as it is an expression of the body. It requires *focus*. It may seem like a mean trick, but that is how our bodies are designed (and, I am convinced, for good reason).

Pray First

Scripture demands married couples to "stop depriving one another" (1 Cor. 7:5). Do you think God didn't realize just how much stress you were going to be under, way back when that verse was written? I assure you He did, yet He still issued the command. And it does apply to *you*. Are you too distracted to enjoy sex? Have too much on your mind?

If there is too much on your mind to enjoy sex, then there is too much on your mind. You've got to do something about it. Try keeping a notepad in your nightstand drawer. You can use it to jot down those thoughts that are vying for your attention: Additions to your grocery list. Plans for the weekend. Errands for tomorrow. Ideas for a project. Mind, your husband won't want to wait while you inscribe volumes (again, I speak from experience)—so just jot down enough information to jog your memory *later*, so as to give him your full attention *now*.

But what if you're plagued by weightier concerns than remembering a dental appointment or not forgetting to buy eggs? That lump in your breast. Lay-offs at work. Your daughter's new boyfriend. Black mold in your basement. Some distractions cannot easily be relegated to a sticky-note and forgotten. So how *does* a wife take her mind off such troubles long enough to enjoy lovemaking? What can be done to bridge the gap and keep everyone happy?

Early in our marriage, my husband and I settled upon a solution to this quandary that works beautifully: We always *pray* together before we have sex (which keeps *me* happy), and we *have sex* as often as we can (which keeps *him* happy). Given his strong drive, this system has kept us faithfully on our knees for over twenty years now.

Marriage counselor and national speaker Dr. Tim Alan Gardner made the same discovery and advocates the practice in his book *Sacred Sex:*

> [Husbands], if you want to do something that your wife will find sexy and sensual, try this simple act of foreplay: Pray with her. I don't mean saying grace before dinner, nor do I mean asking God to bless Grandma and Grandpa and your dog Skippy. I mean *really pray with her.* Bring before God your fears, your failures, your hopes, and your dreams. And pray for your wife, for the challenges and demands she faces each day, for her worries, for her strength. Then thank God for her beauty, her charm, her

friendship, and her faithfulness. And praise God for giving you the privilege of sharing in His beautiful gift of sexual intimacy with her. It might sound crazy, but praying together opens doors to intimacy that you never even suspected were there.... Praying together simply and profoundly deepens the intimacy that will in turn deepen the sexual experience when it occurs.[22]

In my own marriage, the more I learn and understand about sex, the more I appreciate the fact that God put it on our hearts from the outset to begin love-making with prayer. As we've already seen, God's word commands us to cast our cares at the foot of the cross. Since a woman's body cannot achieve climax when her mind is preoccupied with other concerns, having sex after prayer serves as sort of a pop-quiz to determine whether she's really surrendered those burdens or not. Further, since it is no easier to enjoy sex when you are angry than when you are anxious, this system also ensures that you "let not the sun go down upon your wrath" (Eph. 4:26 KJV).

The bottom line is: Obedience equals blessing. Am I saying that a person who tries faithfully to live a life in accordance with Holy Scripture will never have problems? No. Jesus Himself tells us, "These things I have spoken unto you, that in Me ye might have peace. In the world ye shall have tribulation: but be of good cheer; I have overcome the world" (John 16:33 KJV). There is great assurance in the knowledge that God is in control:

∞ "Greater is He who is in you than he who is in the world." (I John 4:5)
∞ "The LORD is my light and my salvation; whom shall I fear? The LORD is the strength of my life; of whom shall I be afraid?" (Psalm 27:1 KJV)
∞ "Who shall separate us from the love of Christ? Shall trouble or hardship or persecution or famine

or nakedness or danger or sword? …No, in all these things we are more than conquerors through Him who loved us." (Rom. 8:35-37 NIV)

∞ "'For I know the plans I have for you,' declares the LORD, 'plans to prosper you and not to harm you, plans to give you hope and a future. Then you will call upon me and come and pray to me, and I will listen to you. You will seek me and find me when you seek me with all your heart.'" (Jer. 29:11-13 NIV)

∞ "And we know that God causes all things to work together for good to those who love God, to those who are called according to His purpose." (Rom. 8:28)

Does this all sound too good to be true? *Wish I could believe it,* you may be thinking, *but I guess I just don't have enough faith.* Maybe you know it in your head, but don't feel it in your heart? As it turns out, canoodling your husband can help in that department, as well.

Building Trust

That's because the release of oxytocin actually stimulates trust. Some fascinating studies have been done to demonstrate this link. In Swiss experiments with nasal spray, investors who had first inhaled oxytocin offered twice the amount of money to a stranger posing as a financial advisor as the group that got a placebo.[23]

> From an experiment on hugging, we also know that oxytocin is naturally released in the brain after a twenty-second hug from a partner—sealing the bond between the huggers and triggering the brain's trust circuits…. Touching, gazing, positive emotional interaction, kissing, and sexual orgasm also release

oxytocin in the female brain.... Estrogen and progesterone dial up these bonding effects in the female brain, too, increasing oxytocin and dopamine.... These hormones then activate the brain circuits for loving, nurturing behavior while switching off the caution and aversion circuits. In other words, if high levels of oxytocin and dopamine are circulating... the skeptical mind [shuts] down."[24]

Thus, the same sort of solace that our spirits find in our relationship to Christ can be felt in our bodies through a godly marriage. Think back to that storm on the Sea of Galilee. Those panic-stricken disciples were able to relax once they'd glimpsed the mighty power that Jesus wields over all of creation. In the same way, I can rest in the knowledge that the same God is at work in my innermost being, calming the storms, quieting the seas. Thus flooded with joy, my whole heart sings:

> Be still, my soul! Thy God doth undertake
> To guide the future as He has the past.
> Thy hope, thy confidence let nothing shake
> All now mysterious shall be bright at last.
> Be still, my soul! The waves and winds still know
> His voice who ruled them while He dwelt below.[25]

So go ahead. Sing. Pray. Cast your cares upon Jesus. Delight yourself in the Lord, and take delight in the husband He has given you while you're at it. God has already made provision for the peace your heart desires. All you must do is co-operate with His plan.

As we will see in the next chapter, when you embrace God's purpose for passion in marriage, you will find rest— not only for your soul, but for your body as well. Just how long has it been since you've gotten a decent night's sleep, anyway?

Chapter 5
Sweet Dreams

"When you lie down, you will not be afraid;
When you lie down, your sleep will be sweet."
Proverbs 3:24

"Right *now?* You can't be serious. I just walked through the door. I'm *exhausted.* Can't I sit down and rest a minute? It's been a long day. I'm worn out. *Frazzled*, I tell you. Besides, we haven't eaten. Shouldn't we have dinner first? *Boy!* Am I *beat!* Maybe we could just save it for tomorrow. Or better yet, the weekend!"

Some conjecture there must be something in wedding cake that affects a bride's libido, causing her sex drive to plummet. Whether a groom's notion of matrimonial bliss is wildly unrealistic or whether a wife just feigns interest long enough to get a ring on her finger, I don't know. But the disconnect between expectations and reality happens frequently enough that the cake hypothesis has been proffered as a possible explanation.

For me, it was not *cake* but *a baby* in my belly that brought about the change. I conceived two weeks into our honeymoon and felt as if I'd been buried under a ton of kryptonite. Never in my life had I experienced such overwhelming fatigue. It still amazes me how incubating a baby can so completely sap a woman's strength. It is physically draining.

I could barely keep my eyes open even while standing at the blackboard teaching business calculus to undergrads. You can imagine what a struggle it was for me to stay awake once I'd crawled under the covers at home, frisky husband or no. I was thrilled to be pregnant, but no longer excited about participating in the deed that got me that way in the first place. From sun-up to sundown, all I could think about was *sleep*. It seemed the only thing *he* ever thought about was *sex*. Both of us spent our days counting the hours until we could climb back into bed, but our ideas of what should happen once we slipped between the sheets differed dramatically.

Is he blind? I would bristle, *Can't he see how tired I am?* As a new bride, I should have been basking in my husband's attention and returning his affection in a spirit of love and enthusiasm. Instead, I wasted an inordinate amount of time and energy dodging his advances and trying to weasel out of my conjugal duty.

Something similar seems to be going on in chapter five of the Song of Solomon (verses 2-3), as Rob Bell notes in his book *Sex God*:

> Later… it appears that this couple is married. He comes to her at night. "Open to me…my darling… my head is drenched with dew, my hair with the dampness of the night…"

> …She responds, "I have taken off my robe— must I put it on again? I have washed my feet—must I soil them again?"

> What's interesting about her words is that they translate from the Hebrew language, "I have a headache."

> This is the awkward, real-life stuff that happens every day in relationships. She's tired, and getting out of bed right now seems like such a hassle. It's been a long day, she's exhausted. Her reaction is, "Anytime but now."[1]

Clearly, even a king does not always receive the respectful accommodation he expects, much less the enthusiastic response he desires.

In her marriage manual, *The Proper Care and Feeding of Husbands*, Dr. Laura Schlessinger addresses this very situation. She tells wives frankly:

> It is your *obligation* to keep yourself healthy and fit so that you can be involved with your husband. You can't do the "I am tired" bit every day and have your husband just accept that this important, intimate part of his life is simply going to be controlled by your whim. It is your obligation not to be tired all the time. So take a nap, eat more protein, take your vitamins. What kind of thing is that to pull on him? What if he said, "I'm too tired and I'm not going to work anymore"? You have obligations to each other, and one of them is not to be constantly tired. That is not an acceptable excuse....[2]
>
> It's one thing to have a tiring, stressful day— or even week. It's another thing to allow outside activities, no matter how seemingly important, to routinely get in the way of obligations to the roles created by holy vows, moral obligations, and love.[3]

Tim Gardner draws a similar conclusion in his book, *Sacred Sex*. He urges wives to consider how fatigue may be damaging or even destroying their sex lives: "If you are frequently too tired to put any energy into a dynamic sex life with your husband, you must ask yourself [why]. Are you overcommitted? [Are] your kids overcommitted? Sex with your husband should not be the undone errand on your to-do list. You need to drop something else."[4]

Unfortunately, neither Dr. Laura nor Mr. Gardner had penned their sage advice back when I was a young bride. Nor did any of the godly wives or older women with whom I was personally acquainted offer a candid warning about how vital a need sex is for a man, newlywed or no. I was destined to learn these lessons the hard way. So instead of embracing God's purpose for passion in marriage from the outset, I made sex a point of contention.

In my pregnancy-induced stupor, I interpreted my husband's romantic overtures as selfish and insensitive. He (rightly) leveled the same accusations against me. If he had little regard for my needs, I had absolutely none for his. For someone supposedly dead on her feet, I certainly put up a good fight. But it was a battle I couldn't win.

Contrary to my suspicions, my husband was *not* blind. Although I may have felt sluggish, I was apparently nimble enough in my efforts to elude him that he quickly discerned the truth: I was *not* "too exhausted for sex", no matter how fervently I argued otherwise. So he chased and cajoled and seldom gave in—a fact I found terribly irritating at the time, but for which I am profoundly grateful in retrospect. All that energy I had poured into trying to persuade him to forgo sex in favor of sleep had been expended unnecessarily—or at least misdirected.

But what of those rare occasions when my avoidance tactics *worked?* Skipping sex may have allotted more time for shut-eye, but it was not the kind of deep, satisfying slumber I so desperately craved. Rather, it was fitful and uneasy. We'd both toss and turn, feeling guilty for going to bed angry. So even when I got *my way*, I didn't *win.* I only succeeded in making us both miserable.

Our marriage might not have survived had we continued in that vein. The fatigue of my first trimester melted into the distraction of my second and weariness of my third. The blessed event of our baby's birth was followed by long months of sleep deprivation and midnight feedings. I poured so much of myself into meeting the needs of my new son that I felt justified in marginalizing the needs of my husband. *After all,* I reasoned, *I am sacrificing* sleep *for the sake of our child. It won't hurt Doug to make a few sacrifices, as well.*

This way of thinking is, of course, very unwise. Let me warn you to never use your children, no matter how young and needy they are, as an excuse to neglect your relationship to their father. You were his wife before you were their mother.

I eventually learned that, regardless how consuming the demands of motherhood become, I must reserve enough energy to nurture my marriage by regularly devoting my full attention to my *husband's* needs, particularly in the area of physical intimacy. But, alas, that realization was not immediately forthcoming....

Our firstborn had neither weaned nor learned to sleep through the night when I got pregnant again. Nine months later, exhaustion took on a whole new meaning as I spent my days chasing after an active toddler and my nights trying to soothe a colicky newborn (and doing neither very adeptly). Soon I was pregnant again. Then again. And again. In fact, I have been either pregnant or nursing—or both—for over twenty years now. Had my husband been forced to wait until I felt well rested to enjoy sex on a regular basis, he would likely have been driven to the jumping-off place.

But God in His mercy showed us a better way.

Never Enough

The conflict we faced early in our marriage was nothing new. All couples have to strike a balance between sex and sleep (and everything else in life). The question is, what do we do when we reach an impasse?

He can't go to sleep until he gets a little sex, but she can't think of sex until she gets a little sleep. Is that so unreasonable? The Bible acknowledges our need for sleep. From the very beginning, we see that God built circadian rhythms into all of creation: "And there was evening, and there was morning, one day.... And there was evening, and

there was morning, a second day…. And there was evening,
and there was morning, a third day…" (Gen. 1:5, 8, 13). The
LORD Himself rested on the seventh day, establishing yet
another pattern for us to follow.

The Psalmist tells us: "It is vain for you to rise up
early, to retire late, to eat the bread of painful labors; for He
gives to His beloved even in his sleep" (Psalms 127:2). Even
amid the myriad cautions against laziness and sloth in the
book of Proverbs, we find such balancing promises as: "The
fear of the LORD leads to life, so that *one may sleep satisfied,*
untouched by evil" (Prov. 19:23, *emphasis mine*).

Science, too, has shown how vital sleep is to our
physical and mental health and well-being. Without adequate
sleep, the natural process by which our body repairs damaged
cells is thwarted, our immunity is compromised, and we are
more apt to get sick.[5] "Deep sleep… triggers the release of the
human growth hormone—a substance necessary for physical
development and a healthy immune system."[6]

Also while we sleep, our body restores to the brain
"some of the substances depleted during waking hours, and
[does] repair work on vital proteins and amino acids"[7]
Furthermore, "[sleep enables] the brain to process and store
information from the day,"[8] which may help explain why a
lack of sleep impacts our mood, making us "grumpy and
muddled; similarly, clinical studies have shown that [an
effective] way of treating depression is simply to help the
sufferer to sleep better."[9]

Sleep deprivation can cause memory lapses, decreased
concentration, and hallucinations; people who suffer from
lack of sleep may also experience psychotic episodes "which
may or may not disappear after the person has returned to a
normal sleeping schedule."[10]

Everybody needs sleep. Yet in our fast-paced, non-
stop, late-night society, many of us have a hard time getting
enough of it. "The average American now gets ninety minutes
less shut-eye per night than she did a century ago."[11]

Our lives are hectic, our schedules crammed with continuous activity, our thoughts preoccupied with consuming responsibilities. Does this describe you? Long after your head hits its pillow, is your mind still spinning (a sign of anxiety)? Or perhaps you drift off easily enough, but wake up in the middle of the night and can't get back to sleep (a marker for depression)? You drag yourself out of bed in the morning feeling even tireder than when you crawled into it the night before. The resultant sluggishness can cause you to fall even further behind in your work, creating even deeper anxiety, which deprives you of even more sleep the following night. It is a vicious, vicious cycle!

According to the American Insomnia Association, over 20 million Americans suffer from chronic insomnia (defined as poor sleep every night or most nights for more than six months).[12] One in ten has trouble falling to sleep or staying asleep *routinely.* Is it any wonder that in 2005, the last year for which statistics are available, over 42 million prescriptions for sleeping pills were filled—up 60 percent since 2000.[13] This, despite the fact that such medications are often addictive and can cause rebound insomnia upon discontinuation more severe than it was to start with.[14]

Even over-the-counter sleeping aids threaten serious side effects including prolonged or severe drowsiness, forgetfulness, and confusion, meaning you still feel dazed even after you are supposed to wake up.[15] Prescription sleeping pills have been linked to an increased risk for skin cancer[16] as well as to such bizarre behaviors as sleep-driving, sleep-eating, and sleep-sex. People under their influence have awakened to find themselves in a different location than where they went to bed, having apparently driven there themselves, or they've discovered groceries missing from their refrigerator (like an entire cooked chicken, picked to the bone!) with no recollection of having eaten them.[17] As for sleep-sex, if you're going to make love when you're only half-awake anyway, why not skip the medication and just let sex produce the soporific effect? You'd be better off in the long run.

Health experts claim that *sleep is the sex of the twenty-first century.*[18] It is continually on our minds. We can't get enough of it. Perhaps we even fantasize about it. Sleep may be "the new sex", but that doesn't warrant tossing out "the old sex" altogether. Sex is an effective antidote to insomnia, so it needn't be an either/or proposition. Why not enjoy both to the fullest?

Unexpected Benefits

Back in the early years of my own marriage, somewhere in the midst of our ongoing conflict over sex versus sleep, I began to hear that still, small voice. The Holy Spirit was at work, pricking my conscience, stirring my soul, plaguing my mind with a single nagging thought: By trying to finagle my way out of sex, wasn't I ignoring God's express command for husbands and wives to "stop depriving one another" (1 Cor. 7:3-5)?

How could I rationalize violating such a clear directive? Surely God was no more interested in my *excuses* than my husband was. After all, He knows my limitations even better than I do. Did my depleted energy level somehow nullify His injunction? Did my exhaustion exempt me? Does weariness *ever* justify disobedience? The more I studied the matter, the more convicted I became that *God expects me to cooperate with His purpose, whether I need a nap or not.*

At first, that's all it was: Cooperation. Having recognized that my attitude toward sex was wrong, I confessed my sin to God and determined in my heart before Him that I would never again withhold from my husband what was rightfully his nor use it as a way to control or manipulate him.

Mind, I didn't bother to tell *Doug* about this commitment right away. Although I was sincere in my resolve, I didn't want him testing it, taking advantage of it, or otherwise holding it over my head. Still, it didn't take him long to realize *something* was up when I inexplicably began responding to his advances instead of resisting them.

Admittedly, I was initially driven by a sense of duty rather than delight. I would sometimes even pray (silently), "God, I'm only doing this to be obedient to *You*, not because I have any desire for *him* right now." Not optimal, but it was a step in the right direction—a step which God has honored and blessed more abundantly than I ever would have imagined possible.

Do you remember how in chapter two we said that putting your husband's needs ahead of your own might mean that your needs go unmet for a time? Well, such was my expectation when I finally surrendered in the area of bedtime routines. I was already fatigued. By the end of the day, I had *nothing left to give* (or so I thought). The idea of habitually putting my husband's need for sex ahead of my own need for sleep threatened to cast me into a terminal state of exhaustion. I fancied myself moving zombie-like through life, eyes propped open with toothpicks, dead on my feet. A real martyr.

But my fears were completely unfounded. Irrational, even. My husband wasn't asking me to leap buildings with a single bound. The poor guy just wanted to make love! To *me*! To whom else could he righteously turn? How utterly selfish it would have been for me to keep putting him off.

The Bible tells us plainly, "Whoever seeks to keep his life will lose it, and whoever loses his life will preserve it" (Luke 17:33). As long as my number one priority had been providing for my own welfare, *nobody's* needs were getting met, including my own. But the LORD is faithful. Once I began to pour myself into meeting *Doug's* needs, God lavishly supplied *mine* as well. That's because the same principle was at work here as is described in Prov. 11:24-25: "There is one who scatters, and yet increases all the more, and there is one who withholds what is justly due, and yet it results only in want. The generous man will be prosperous, and he who waters will himself be watered."

I discovered that responding to my husband's sexual advances required less energy than resisting them. The difference in bedtimes was negligible, especially if you factor in the time saved by getting straight to business instead of playing cat-n-mouse all evening. Rather than *losing* sleep as a result of putting my husband's needs first, I *gained*. And I didn't just sleep longer. I slept better.

What's more, I felt more energetic upon waking. In fact, I found that by investing in my marriage in this manner, I reaped huge dividends in the end and multiplied my strength manifold. Like loaves and fishes, when I freely and joyfully gave myself to my husband, despite the overwhelming fatigue I felt at the time, God took that gift and stretched it in amazing ways, so that I was able to accomplish much more than I ever imagined, and to feel great doing it.

Finally, it dawned on me: God does not command me to have sex with my husband *in spite* of my exhaustion, but *because* of it.

Sex Recharges Your Batteries

People who know me often marvel over my organization, my stamina, and how much I accomplish in a 24-hour day. *How do you do it?* They want to know. *What kind of vitamins do you take? Where do you find the energy? What's your secret?*

I usually answer such inquiries with a slight shrug of my shoulders and a sheepish smile. "It's all by the grace of God," I assure them. And I mean it with every ounce of my being. I firmly believe that the LORD *equips* us to do whatever He *calls* us to do. He is one hundred percent faithful to "supply all [our] needs according to His riches in glory in Christ Jesus" (Philippians 4:19). Moreover, His "grace is sufficient... [for His] strength is made perfect in weakness" (2 Cor. 12:9).

But I also acknowledge that God can by grace lead us to practical solutions for our earthly problems, and so I've pondered my friends' questions carefully. How *do* I do it? What *is* my secret? Certainly drawing on God's strength through regular Bible study and prayer helps sustain me. Such discipline is also central to prioritizing wisely.

The vitamin question makes me laugh. Don't we all wish it were as easy as popping a pill? Honestly, up until a couple of years ago, I was never very faithful about taking a daily supplement, although I made more of a concerted effort to do so whenever I was pregnant.

As for accomplishments, the fact that I don't watch television (only an occasional video) is key to my getting much more done than I might otherwise. And I also multitask: reading while riding my stationary bike, crocheting while traveling in the car, tutoring math while I nurse the baby, and the like.

But when it comes to energy levels, my secret may surprise you. I truly believe that for me, the revitalizing force in *that* department is a direct result of having made sex with my husband a genuine priority: I don't just *say* that sex is important to me; I *show* it, by making myself available to him, whenever, wherever. By so doing, I have proved that the Word of God is true:

> Whoever sows sparingly will also reap sparingly, and whoever sows generously will also reap generously. Each man should give what he has decided in his heart to give, not reluctantly or under compulsion, for God loves a cheerful giver. And God is able to make all grace abound to you, so that in all things at all times, having all that you need, you will abound in every good work. (2 Cor. 9:6-9 NIV)

I am grateful that God taught me this truth early in my marriage. As a bonus, I've found that sex recharges my batteries much more efficiently than would the same amount of time invested in any other activity, including sleep.

Try it yourself. Start responding to your husband cheerfully, generously, *hilariously*. An active sex life makes a great front line of defense against insomnia, anxiety, and chronic fatigue. So let lovemaking become a *real* priority in your marriage. The oxytocin released by doing so will reduce stress and boost relaxation.[19] You will soon find yourself falling asleep faster, staying asleep longer, and awaking refreshed, rejuvenated, and reenergized.[20]

Chapter 6
A Happy Home

"You will be happy, and it will be well with you.
Your wife shall be like a fruitful vine within your house,
Your children like olive plants around your table."
Psalm 128:3-4

As I mentioned in the preface to this book, one of my favorite pastimes back when we lived in Dallas was frequenting home shows. This may have been, as one friend suggested, my way of escaping the fact that at the time my husband and I were ourselves living in a miniscule apartment, together with a growing brood of small children. My friend couldn't imagine how supremely happy we were in those modest surroundings, despite the fact we could sit at our dinner table and retrieve milk from the refrigerator, answer the back door, or switch on the bathroom light—almost without leaving our seats.

The truth is that I enjoyed walking through other people's houses because doing so gave me such grand ideas for decorating my own. We were blessed with an accommodating landlady who let us paint walls, hang curtains, add shelves, and plant flowers to our heart's content, so our little hole-in-the-wall became more pleasant, warm, and inviting with every home tour we attended.

In reality, our humble abode bore little resemblance to the lavish residences we toured. The sum total of our living space would have fit into one of their walk-in closets with room to spare. But our home was characterized by a spirit of love and joy that I suspect was lacking in at least one of the sprawling mansions we visited.

What makes me think so?

A sign in the master bedroom told me as much.

Lifestyles of the Rich

This bedroom wasn't just a bedroom; it was an entire wing of the house. "Master Suite" or "Owner's Retreat," the tour guide called it. I can remember it vividly even now. Such opulence you wouldn't believe.

An exquisite Persian rug covered the floor and felt lush beneath our stocking feet (visitors had been asked to remove their shoes at the door). The walls were adorned with priceless works of art—all original oil paintings or signed and numbered prints. Two overstuffed armchairs flanked the marble fireplace, a gleaming silver tea service perched atop an antique tray table between them. A beveled mirror in an ornate frame hung above the mantle to camouflage the high definition television built into the wall behind it. (Two more TVs were hidden behind his-and-her vanity mirrors in the master bathroom, each equipped with a set of earplugs, so she could watch her HGTV and not be bothered by his ESPN).

Beyond the fireplace, a chaise lounge stood in front of floor-to-ceiling plate-glass windows through which we could see a pristine blue granite pool shaded by potted palm trees and bordered by well-tended beds of trailing lantana, bright impatiens, and fragrant gardenias. Atrium doors in the master bedroom opened onto a wide veranda that overlooked the pool, granting the couple easy access for late-night dips in the attached Jacuzzi.

Of course, the focal point of any bedroom is the bed, and theirs was no exception. Centered on the wall opposite the fireplace was an enormous reproduction of something straight out of *Princess and the Pea.* It was so high that a stepstool was needed—and provided—just to climb into it. Four massive mahogany posts supported an ornately carved canopy that brushed the ceiling. Heavy curtains of silk brocade hung at each corner. The thick mattress was buried beneath a sumptuous duvet, its topmost edge folded back to reveal smooth satin sheets beneath, and the towering headboard was fronted by ranks of ruffled, tucked, and tufted pillows and bolsters in an array of complementary patterns, textures, and designs.

It was at this point that I identified, upon closer inspection, the telltale sign that something in this home was amiss. There, standing prominently at the head of that army of cushions, was a small needlework pillow bearing the sentiment,

NOT TONIGHT, DEAR
I HAVE A HEADACHE

Keep in mind that everything (else) about this room whispered romance: A pile of logs crackled in the fireplace. Sweet violin music wafted through the speaker system. Scented candles flickered on the nightstand. And that luxuriant bed beckoned, "Come. Drink your fill of love until morning."

It was enough to quicken the pulse of any husband still in possession of half his senses—but all for naught.

Should the pitiable man dare *think* of approaching his wife with tender words or ardent hopes, *The Pillow* stood sentry, ready to quench his passion with icy water. What a cruel, cruel trick! What a slap in the face!

Not tonight. Not tonight. Not tonight. Did the heartless wife *hide* the cursed thing on that rare occasion she was in the mood?

Not tonight. Not tonight. Not tonight. Did her husband's heart lift when he noticed it missing?

The Corner of a Roof

The book of Proverbs speaks of such a home as this. It tells us unequivocally, "Better is a little with the fear of the LORD than great treasure and turmoil with it. Better is a dish of vegetables where love is than a fattened ox served with hatred" (Prov. 15:16-17). And again, two chapters later, it declares, "Better is a dry morsel and quietness with it than a house full of feasting with strife" (Prov. 17:1).

Whence does all this strife and tension and turmoil come? I'm convinced that in many instances, the root source is a wife's negativity. Proverbs 21:9 tells us: "It is better to live in a corner of a roof than in a house shared with a contentious woman." When most of us hear that verse, we picture an embittered, demanding nag who is impossible to please. That sort of faultfinding person might be described as being *actively* contentious, and we'll discuss why and how we should guard against those kinds of destructive attitudes in chapter 15. But for the purposes of the present discussion, I want to focus on the flip side of this problem: that of being *passively* contentious.

You see, a wife does not have to continuously harp on her husband in an irritating voice to be a thorn in his side. In fact, she can be absolutely insufferable without ever opening her mouth at all. How? By practicing the art of *manipulation*. She can sulk and pout or cry and carry on until she gets her own way or—what's worse—she can simply withhold sex until her husband gives in to her demands out of sheer desperation. *This* is contention in its most insidious form, for her husband has no recourse. He must either capitulate or be driven mad.

If you routinely put off your husband's sexual advances, if you insist that he wait until some remote time when you are "in the mood" before you give him what he so desperately desires, then you are *by definition* being contentious. A good synonym for the verb "to contend" is "to resist," which is precisely what you are doing when you refuse to have sex with your husband. According to the Bible, a man would be better off inhabiting a corner of the roof— exposed to what? Scorching heat? Gale-force winds? Torrential rain? *Anything* would be more tolerable than sharing a house with a contentious, resistant, vexing wife.

So, I beg you—for the sake of your husband, for the sake of your children, for the sake of your home—please do not allow a lagging libido to limit the frequency with which you make love to your husband. Otherwise, you may exchange what could have been heaven-on-earth for something far inferior.

The Heart of a Home

But my guess, since you are reading this book, is that robbing your home of joy was never your intent. None of us sets out to make our family miserable. Nevertheless, sometimes, somehow, the happy homes we envision fail to materialize. Instead of a haven of rest, our homes begin to feel more like "an incubator for stress."[1] How does this happen? And what can be done about it?

Have you ever seen that little acrostic definition of JOY: Jesus–Others–You? This is a great starting place for anybody who deeply desires a happy home. True contentment comes not through selfishly manipulating circumstances to ensure one's own happiness, but through selflessly pursuing the happiness and well-being of others. When we put others' needs ahead of our own, we model Christ's love to everyone around us. By serving our family, we are in actuality serving Him. Jesus explains this concept to His disciples in Matthew 25:37-40:

> Then the righteous will answer Him, "Lord, when did we see You hungry, and feed You, or thirsty, and give You something to drink? And when did we see You a stranger, and invite You in, or

naked, and clothe You? When did we see You sick, or in prison, and come to You?"

The King will answer and say to them, "Truly I say to you, to the extent that you did it to one of these brothers of Mine, even the least of them, you did it to Me."

Paul urges us to adopt the same attitude we see in Christ: "Do nothing from selfishness or empty conceit, but with humility of mind regard one another as more important than yourselves; do not merely look out for your own personal interests, but also for the interests of others" (Phil. 2:3-4). Likewise, after washing the disciples' feet, Jesus commanded them to follow His example in serving one another, promising that, "If ye know these things, *happy* are ye if ye do them" (John 13:17, *emphasis added*). Elsewhere, Jesus tells His followers, "*Happy* are those whose greatest desire is to do what God requires; God will *satisfy* them fully!" (Matt. 5:6 TEV, *emphasis added*).

It is true. There is great joy to be found by living a life poured out for others. Not only does such commitment bring the eternal satisfaction of knowing that one is living in obedience to Scripture, but there are immediate benefits that result from selfless living, as well. This is particularly true of a husband/wife relationship.

The Hindus have a beautiful proverb which states: "When the one man loves the one woman and the one woman loves the one man, the very angels leave heaven and come and sit in their house and sing for joy."[2] It is more than a lovely sentiment. The Bible itself exhorts us to cast off our sinful, selfish ways, "since we are surrounded by so great a cloud of witnesses" (Heb. 12:1 NKJV), and it specifically implores wives to give deference to their husbands, "because of the angels" (1 Cor. 11:10).

Solomon believed that "the way of a man with a maid" (Prov. 30:19) was something too wonderful to understand. The Living Bible translates the phrase, *the growth of love* between a man and a woman. And guess what? The world *still* marvels at this. They should know we are Christians by our love (John 13:35). Our homes should be spilling over with such love.

The day a wife decides to stop keeping score, the day she joyfully begins to meet her husband's needs instead of stalling until he meets hers, the day she exchanges her feelings of contempt and bitterness and resentment for an attitude of love and admiration and gratefulness—*that* is the day that happiness will begin to permeate her home and infect all who live there. It ceases to matter whether the husband ever responds in kind (although, more often than not, he will), because she is not choosing selflessness in an effort to manipulate him or to act the part of a martyr or to guilt-trip him into thinking of someone besides himself. She is simply living in obedience to God's Word and is finding her joy in Him.

Stop and Smell the Roses

We're all familiar with the old adage: "If *Mama* ain't happy, ain't *nobody* happy." Well, in our family, we have another saying: "If *Dad*'s on edge, we're *all* on edge."

A woman's attitude may set the tone for the entire family, but her husband's temperament affects the household, as well. Fortunately for everyone involved, God has given a wife the unique ability to rid her home of conflict and tension, should she choose to use it. That power hinges on her responsiveness to her husband.

Here's a novel idea: Instead of cooking up excuses to skip out on lovemaking, try giving your husband as much sex as he asks for. Make it your goal to never turn him down. I guarantee this will have a huge impact on his attitude and demeanor. Initiate sex yourself once in awhile. Such treatment makes for happy husbands, and that happiness will soon overflow, affecting all other aspects of your life together.

This formula not only produces happier homes, but possibly cleaner homes, as well. Those sprawling mansions with the lavishly appointed master suites? They probably had maids to help keep them immaculate. But for those of us who live in the real world of dirty laundry and bathtub rings, meeting your husband's sexual needs may even inspire him to pitch in and help with the housekeeping.

As Jeff Feldhahn notes in the book *For Men Only*: "A recent study by famed marriage psychologist John Gottman found that men who do more housework have both happier marriages *and* better sex lives." Feldhahn admits, "Picking up the broom or doing dishes after a hard day on the job isn't exactly... well, what you were thinking when you were thinking you couldn't wait to get home! But as Gottman found, this kind of sacrificial support can often be more impressive than a dozen roses."[3]

My question is: Which came first, the chicken or the egg? Is it really that men who do housework get more sex? Or do men who get sex do more housework? Experience has taught me that when I make it a priority to meet my husband's needs first, he is *way* more interested in helping around the house... without my even asking!

And, yes, I'm far more impressed by my husband's doing dishes, sweeping floors, or changing diapers than I am by store-bought bouquets. Such selfless gestures are the kind of foreplay that *really* grabs my attention. And my unconditional willingness to get physical with him, *whether he has helped with the chores or not*, is something he deeply appreciates. This cycle of responsiveness (as opposed to resistance) is one of the most characteristic and indispensable components of a happy, contented home.

It's often the smallest acts of love that make the biggest difference. Josephine March must have realized this fact, for in *Little Women* she tells her sister Amy, "I wish it was as easy for me to do little things to please people as it is for you. I think of them, but it takes too much time to do them, so I wait for a chance to confer a great favor, and let the small ones slip; but they tell best in the end, I fancy."[4]

How many wives are guilty of passing up little opportunities to show love to their husbands? They may promise to make up for it over the weekend, or at the end of the month, or on their next anniversary, but in the meantime, they let slide countless chances to confer affection, little realizing that it is the love shared in these snippets of time that "tells best in the end."

I once heard a speaker suggest to a women's group that a wife should plan occasional romantic interludes for her husband with the same forethought she would invest in preparing a gourmet meal: She should light candles, play soft music, perfume the sheets, wear a new nightie—give him a real feast for his senses. The speaker reasoned that if a wife made sex extra-special in this way, her husband would be content to wait longer between trysts.

I probably don't have to tell you that this speaker was a woman. Clearly, that is exactly how women think. *Wow! I really outdid myself tonight! That should tide him over for at least a week or two!*

Let me warn you, if you haven't figured it out already, this is *not* how the minds of most men work. They think, *Wow! That was great! Let's do it again tomorrow night!*

I thought the five-star dinner analogy was very apropos, though. How many guys do *you* know who could get full on an artful arrangement of a silver-dollar-sized pork medallion sprinkled with fresh rosemary and flanked by three green beans and a curled carrot shaving—especially if they haven't eaten in days? If it has to be either/or, I think most men would choose a steady diet of meat and potatoes over a sporadic sampling of gourmet delicacies.

"One good time of sex will make a man thankful...for a while. But if you turn him down the next five times when he approaches you, he'll think about the five rejections, not that one special night," warns Kevin Leman, "You can't just 'try' sex in marriage; it has to become a way of life."[5]

If it does, if sex really becomes "a way of life" in your marriage, if you make it an integral part of your routine interactions with your husband, then you will begin to reap benefits you never imagined. One such benefit is a happy, tranquil home, remarkably free of tension and strife.

A Little Peace and Quiet

Science has shown us that love ramps up the production of oxytocin. Since oxytocin causes relaxation and fearlessness in both males and females,[6] it is easy to see how love in general, and physical love in particular, can exert such a becalming effect on all our senses. But the wonderful thing is that this effect appears to be contagious.

Visitors to our home frequently comment on how peaceful and tranquil it is. Although I am always pleased to receive these compliments, in the beginning such statements puzzled me, for the walls of our house echo and are usually ringing with lively music, infectious laughter, and animated conversation. *Peaceful?* I'd wonder to myself. *Are they not hearing what I'm hearing?* But I eventually came to realize that these guests weren't referring to the noise level; they were talking about the atmosphere. And, indeed, our home normally *is* filled to overflowing with love and joy and peace.

Have you ever been in a room where the tension felt so thick you could cut it with a knife? Sometimes, an entire *house* can feel that way, with every member of the family living in a perpetual state of anger or unrest. It isn't a pleasant place to be.

Interestingly, humans aren't the only creatures who work themselves into such frenzied states. Rats do the same thing, and scientists who study them have made some fascinating discoveries about group dynamics. They have found, for instance, that taking "a single rat injected with oxytocin" and placing it in a cage full of anxious rats will cause the whole lot of them to chill out.[7]

The increased oxytocin not only serves to calm and reassure the injected rat, but it indirectly acts on all the stressed-out rats around her, producing the same soothing effect.

> [Oxytocin] strongly affects your mind and behavior…. It creates feelings of calm and a sense of connection, so it actually shapes how you view the world. The whole universe looks like a better place when you feel tranquil and loving…. The more you nurture and connect with others, the more responsive your body and brain become to it. This makes it an unusual neurotransmitter. Compare it with substances like alcohol or caffeine. The more you use them, the greater the quantity you require to obtain the same effect. Oxytocin is the opposite. The more you give and nurture, the more strongly you respond.[8]

Do you see where I'm going with this? Remember how sex produces a five-fold increase in your circulating levels of oxytocin? That much oxytocin goes a long way toward calming your nerves and exerts an indirect calming effect on the nerves of everyone around you.

In the book *Being a Woman*, Toni Grant notes that "a woman without serenity seems hardly a woman at all; she is nervous, high-strung, all 'bent out of shape' and utterly impatient."[9] Author Debi Stack agrees. In *Martha to the Max*, she writes:

> Saying "I can't help it; this is just how God made me" when we're snippy, judgmental, or unloving is a cop-out. Our heavenly Father did not design His daughters to stomp through life irritated and impatient, to cut down people with criticism and conditional love, or to

sacrifice our health for half-baked projects that won't last anyway. [10]

She's right. God wants us to be chaste and respectful, "with the imperishable quality of a gentle and quiet spirit, which is precious" in His sight (1 Peter 3:1-4).

But how do we change from one to the other?

The Gospel of Luke provides a clue. It tells a story of two sisters, Mary and Martha, who beautifully illustrate the difference between a heart at rest and a heart distressed. When Jesus and his disciples visited their village,

> Martha opened her home to him. She had a sister called Mary, who sat at the Lord's feet listening to what he said. But Martha was distracted by all the preparations that had to be made. She came to him and asked, "Lord, don't you care that my sister has left me to do the work by myself? Tell her to help me!"
>
> "Martha, Martha," the Lord answered, "you are worried and upset about many things, but only one thing is needed. Mary has chosen what is better, and it will not be taken away from her" (Luke 10:38-42 NIV).

Sometimes we must make a choice. Will we spend our time and energy focusing on people or possessions? On our spouse or our stuff?

Although I can readily relate to Martha, I make a conscious attempt to behave more like Mary. It's not that there's anything intrinsically wrong with wanting your home to be clean, orderly, and aesthetically pleasing. The problem arises when *that* goal takes precedence over relationships. If my efforts to create a lovely home cause me to alienate everyone who lives there, what does it profit? If my determination to have things look a certain way causes me to snap at anyone who thwarts my progress, I can be sure that

I've failed to make the *right choice*. I've neglected the *one essential*.

In so many marriages, the wife stays busy, busy, busy, tending to all the items on her to do list, often to the detriment of her relationship to her husband. She is missing the one thing that is truly needful. Given the choice, don't you think *your* husband would choose an attentive, admiring wife over dust-free furniture and a spotless sink?

Silk Embroidery and Secret Codes

I sometimes think back on the little "headache pillow" which first caught my eye during that luxury home tour so long ago. I am sorry to report, that wasn't the only time I've noticed such a hateful thing being used to accessorize an otherwise beautiful bed. In fact, I've seen so many—*too many!* —"Not Tonight" pillows over the years that I've completely lost count. (There's obviously a bigger market for needlepoint excuses than I realized.)

Every time I spotted a new one, I felt an intense urge to showcase a drastically different "message" on my own bed. I admired the exquisite needlework, but wanted *my* pillow to say something along the lines of *"Tonight and Every Night"* or *"I'm Ready When You Are"* or maybe even *"Bring It On"*.

Two things prevented my acting on this impulse. First was the knowledge that our parents, children, friends, and houseguests might consider it in poor taste for us to adorn our bed with such a straightforward reminder of why we share it. Second was the fact that, regardless how earnestly I searched, I could never find a store that even *sold* pillows with such sentiments stitched upon them. *Go figure!*

Still, it was an idea that refused to die. Although I could sidestep the second issue by sewing the pillow myself, the first concern still presented a problem. How could I phrase what I wanted to say in a way that others wouldn't find offensive or embarrassing?

The solution came to me unexpectedly about ten years ago when my husband and I were at a Sunday school class dinner. One of the other couples in attendance knew about the commitment Doug and I had made early in our marriage to always pray together before having sex, so when we tried to slip away from the party early, they couldn't resist teasing us a bit.

"Are you guys going home to *pray?*" they called to us across the parking lot.

Doug answered back with a grin, "Well, we've already prayed together *once* today, but we might decide to pray again."

"You know what they say," the couple laughed. "You can never pray too much!"

And there I had it… the sentiment I would stitch on my pillow.

If you were to visit our home today, you would find a spacious master suite, complete with plush Persian rug and four-poster bed. The dust ruffle, duvet, and a mound of pillows were custom-made by me in complementary colors, textures, and patterns. And there in the center of it all, you would find a beautiful little velvet cushion, hand-embroidered with silk ribbon roses and tiny glass beads. To the rest of the world it simply says, "You can never pray too much." But to my husband, who can decipher my secret code, it sends another message entirely.

To him, it clearly reads, "You can never have too much sex… and I'm ready when you are."

Chapter 7
The Fountain of Youth

"They drink their fill of the abundance of Your house;
and You give them to drink of the river of Your delights.
For with You is the fountain of life."
Psalm 36:8-9

It came time recently to renew the inspection stickers on our family vehicles, so my husband took them in, one after the other, to be serviced. With three down and one to go, he drove over to the junior college to exchange cars with our daughter who was a student there at the time. Bounding up the steps to the student center, Doug tracked her down, gave her a hug, traded keys, and left. As soon as he was out of sight, Beth's friends came rushing over to question her.

"Who was that *adorable guy?*" they all wanted to know.

Bethany frowned, obviously puzzled. "You mean my *dad?*"

Her friends were incredulous. "Your *dad?*" they chorused in unison. "No way! We thought he must be your *boyfriend!*"

They bantered back and forth awhile before one of them asked, "Just how old *is* your dad, anyway?"

Beth answered, and they all resolved to get a better look when Doug returned. But even upon closer inspection, they insisted he looked much younger than his forty years. And do you know what? They were absolutely right.

When Bethany later related the conversation to her father, his head swelled noticeably. He strutted around the house like a peacock for weeks on end and worked the story into as many conversations as possible, however tangential the connection.

I'll tell you straight up that I've never been mistaken for one of my sons' sweethearts, but a few nearsighted folks *have* asked on occasion whether Bethany and I were sisters.

The fact that neither my husband nor I smokes, drinks, or frequents tanning salons undoubtedly keeps us from looking ten years older than we really are. But what could possibly make a person appear ten years younger than their actual age? What's the secret of a perpetually youthful appearance? Wouldn't we all like to know?

Nip and Tuck

We live in a society that is obsessed with youthful beauty. Like Dorian Gray,[1] it seems that some would barter their very soul to stop the march of time.

> The mania to appear young is proverbially associated with the United States, where many people go to extreme lengths to maintain the appearance of youth—trying to buy their way into the ranks of the superyoung, as it were, by paying thousands of dollars to plastic surgeons to snip away wrinkles from their faces and suction out fat from their bodies. The cost of cosmetic surgery has dropped drastically since 1990, with the result that many more people than ever before are going under the scalpel in an effort to cheat time.[2]

Over 11 million plastic surgery operations, both invasive and non-invasive, are performed in the US annually.[3] It is a lucrative business: Americans spend over 12 billion dollars a year on cosmetic procedures,[4] the four most common being liposuction, breast augmentation, eyelid surgery, and face-lifts (in that order).[5]

For those who would rather avoid the risks associated with surgery, there is the 33 billion dollar weight-loss industry:

> According to the federal government, 25 percent of American men and almost 40 percent of American women are trying to lose weight.... Whether the advertisements are for pills or the latest fad diet, millions of dollars are spent each year to get us to use a product that promises to change our bodies. Of course, this advertising statistic doesn't even touch on those who go the route of exercise, where another $5 billion a year is spent on home workout equipment... and $8 billion more (some estimates are double that) spent on health club memberships.[6]

Once the excess weight is off, we are faced with the exasperating problem of saggy, baggy skin. From his observations of the "superyoung," those people who age most gracefully, David Weeks concludes that:

> The most conspicuous clues to a person's age are to be found in the skin.... The onset and severity of facial wrinkles are affected by a number of factors, notably prolonged ultraviolet exposure, smoking, diet and sleeping habits.... The most deleterious factor, undoubtedly, is continual exposure to strong sunlight.
>
> There can be little doubt that some form of moisturizing is essential for middle-aged skin to retain its suppleness and healthy glow: the skin's oil ducts slowly dry up as part of the aging process, and unless those natural oils are replenished, the skin will become cracked and sore. However, many of the superyoung reported that inexpensive moisturizing

lotions were just as efficacious at doing the job as exclusive products with famous names....[7]

The "market for anti-aging skin care products begins at approximately 25, with more than half of the dollars spent on facial skin care attributed to anti-aging products."[8] Here again, the dollars add up: Of $70 billion spent annually on cosmetics,[9] $20 billion goes for creams, lotions, serums, and ointments which promise to turn back the hands of time, vanishing wrinkles and restoring youthful facial skin.[10]

Women, especially, feel an enormous pressure to maintain their youth and beauty. Katha Pollitt summarizes the situation succinctly:

> Today I am urged on every side to fight the encroaching decay of my person with large investments of energy, time, and money. I should slather my face with makeup by day and collagen cream by night. I should take up aerobic dancing and resign myself to 1,200 calories a day for life. I should dye my hair. Advertising, which features no female who looks one minute over twenty-five, tells me this, and so do women's magazines, which treat beauty care and dieting as a female moral duty....[11]

Further complicating matters is the fact that some of those things we do to ourselves in pursuit of youth and beauty are counterproductive. Brown fat may look better than white fat, as the saying goes, but sun-worshippers and tanning-bed patrons often wind up with "the leathery, deeply lined skin of 70-year-olds while they are still in the prime of life;" similarly, "a lifetime of heavy make-up use may [actually] accelerate facial aging—an ironic side-effect of overenthusiastic attempts at self-beautification."[12]

The Bible warns that physical beauty is fleeting. "Charm and grace are deceptive, and beauty is vain [because it is not lasting], but a woman who ...fears the Lord, she shall be praised" (Prov. 31:30 AMP). "Imagine having the kind of beauty that doesn't need to be 'propped up' by artificial means, a beauty that doesn't merely last a few years and then fade with age, a beauty that will be cherished and appreciated for a lifetime," writes Leslie Ludy in *Set-Apart Femininity.*[13] It is such a beauty that Scripture promotes in passages like the following: "Your adornment must not be merely external— braiding the hair, and wearing gold jewelry, or putting on dresses; but let it be the hidden person of the heart, with the imperishable quality of a gentle and quiet spirit, which is precious in the sight of God" (1 Pet. 3:3-4).

While outward beauty should never be our primary goal, there certainly is nothing wrong with wanting to look our personal best. So we must strike a balance. What about you? Do you see fine lines and deepening crevices staring back at you when you look into a mirror? Are you bothered by them? What would you be willing to do to slow or reverse the signs of aging? How much would you be willing to give in order to look, say, ten years younger?

Ten years is about all a plastic surgeon can promise. Even the most experienced and skilled surgeon cannot make a 50 year-old look 20 again. I've noticed that several anti-aging skin care regimens claim they'll take ten years off your appearance—just try their products for six weeks and judge for yourself! Likewise, books abound which pledge to teach us how we can look ten years younger by changing the way we dress or how we style our hair. Evidently, ten years is the magic number.

One cosmetic survey found a full 45 percent of women believe that looking ten years younger would help them feel more confident.[14] Thirty-six percent of the female respondents in another survey said they would give up an all-expense-paid trip to Europe in favor of taking a decade off their appearance.[15] We've already seen the kind of money people spend on surgical procedures, diet plans, and skin lotions in an attempt to set the clock back the same amount of time. But what would you say if I told you there is a way you can look ten years younger that is inexpensive, effective, and *enjoyable*?

An Easier Way

Bypass the Botox. Cancel the chemical peels. Forgo the fat injections. According to a 10-year study of 3500 people ages 18 to 102, there is a much easier way to retain your youthful appearance, and it won't cost an arm and a leg, either. Dr. David Weeks, the neuropsychologist from the Royal Edinburgh Hospital who conducted this study, "concluded that genetics were only 25 percent responsible for how young we look—the rest is down to behavior."[16]

As I poured over his findings, I was reminded of an article I had read years earlier, while still in my teens. In it, a dozen actresses of advancing years shared the "beauty secrets" that kept them looking young. These women were all gorgeous; the 25 percent of their appearance determined by genes had certainly given them a huge head start on being beautiful. Even so, most of them cited the sort of personal practices one would expect: I eat right, I drink lots of water, I do sit-ups, I sleep eight hours a night. Two of the answers, however, were surprising enough that I have never forgotten them. One of the celebrities—I believe it was Jerry Hall—said that her secret for looking good was washing her hair only once a week (a time-saving practice I immediately adopted myself). The other actress, who really was much older than her apparent age, insisted the thing that kept her looking young was "lots of sex".

The funny thing is, this last actress was spot-on. Years before David Weeks had even commenced his research, she'd hit upon the same conclusion. That conclusion is this: The "superyoung"—those folks whose appearance belies their age—"enjoy a robust sex life, significantly higher than average for their age group in terms of quantity and quality, usually in the context of a loving relationship."[17] In fact, "a vigorous sex life, Weeks says, [is] the second-most important determinant of how young a person look[s]. Only physical activity prove[s] more important than sex in keeping aging at bay."[18] "Both men and women who reported having sex on average four times per week... looked approximately 10 years younger than they really were, according to volunteer raters."[19]

But beware. "The sex doesn't work without a good relationship."[20] The same study showed that promiscuity—having casual sex with different partners—does not slow the aging process, but accelerates it. Cheating can actually cause premature aging from worry and stress.[21]

Why does sex within a committed relationship have such a pronounced influence on how young we look? For starters, sex "pumps oxygen around the body, boosting the circulation and the flow of nutrients to the skin."[22] But a clearer, more radiant complexion and smoother skin is only one advantage to meeting your husband's physical needs. Another "positive cosmetic benefit" linked to sex is "healthier hair (thanks to increased estrogen production)".[23] Additionally, "sex strengthens your bones and, when done right, can become a great cardio workout that can markedly tone your muscles."[24] Not to mention, "if you're worried about wrinkles—orgasms even help prevent frown lines from deepening."[25]

Every time you have sex with your husband, it triggers the release of a small amount of Human Growth Hormone (HGH), which helps "reduce fatty tissue and increase lean muscle in various parts of the body, giving it a more youthful appearance."[26] A product of the anterior pituitary gland in the brain, HGH "may actually help treat the blueprint of aging, keeping the cells in as healthy a state as possible."[27] Doctors and nutritionists alike tell us how important antioxidants such as vitamins C and E are to our diet, since they help to limit the damage done to our DNA by free radicals. Human growth hormone goes one step further by helping already-damaged DNA repair itself prior to cell division; thus, HGH acts not only to

> ...prevent biological aging, but to significantly reverse a broad range of the signs and symptoms associated with aging.... People with age-related deficiency of HGH become fat, flabby, frail, and lethargic, lose interest in sex, have trouble sleeping, concentrating, remembering things, tire easily, and in general, lose their zest for life. With HGH, all these so-called signs of aging are reversed. HGH appears to be the silver bullet of life extension.[28]

Another hormone that factors into our overall health and appearance is DHEA (dehydroepiandrosterone). DHEA promotes sexual excitement and *increases* in response to it. According to Theresa Crenshaw, author of *The Alchemy of Love and Lust*, "DHEA may be the most powerful chemical in our personal world. It helps balance the immune system, improves cognition, promotes bone growth, and maintains and repairs tissues, keeping your skin healthy and supple. It may also contribute to cardiovascular health and even function as antidepressant."[29] This anti-depressive action is beneficial to our appearance, as well, because "when you feel better, you look better."[30]

If You're Happy and You Know It

One thing that does more for a woman's appearance than any make-up or perfume or designer dress she can put on... is a smile. I don't mean the fake-y grin that some women glue on their faces but don't feel in their hearts. I mean an honest-to-goodness, genuine expression that starts in your innermost being and goes all the way up to your eyes. Such smiles are infectious. And the women who wear them look radiant. They positively beam. Put one on yourself anytime you'd like an instant face-lift—it's faster, easier, safer, less expensive, and far more natural looking than any surgical procedure—and much more attractive than that knot of wrinkles stationed permanently between so many wives' carefully arched and tinted brows.

"Who and what you are is reflected in your face," Debi Pearl reminds us. "Does your husband see you as a happy thankful woman? Does he smile when he looks at you, amused at the cheerful little grin on your face and the totally delightful things you think and say...? Learn to charm him with your mischievous 'only for him' grin."[31]

Just as a soft answer turns away wrath (Prov. 15:1), so a heartfelt smile disarms those who encounter it. Keep one on your lips at all times. Let it be the first thing your husband notices when he awakes in the morning, the last thing he sees before he drifts off at night: "Any time your eyes meet or your hands touch, let it be a reminder to smile and offer a word of gladness."[32] As Baroness von Schrader explained to Maria, "There's nothing more irresistible to a man than a woman who is in love with him."[33] Your joyful countenance will communicate loving admiration and will make you exceedingly beautiful in the eyes of your mate.

But you don't always *feel* like flashing hubby a smile, you say? You think it's insincere, maybe even hypocritical, to smile when your emotions don't warrant it? Well, think again.

In his book *Feeling Good is Good for You*, Carl Charnetski advises, "Whether or not you have reason to do so, smile frequently. The nerves connected to your face's smile muscles project right into parts of the brain that help determine mood. Send a signal to your brain that you're happy, and voila! You *are* happy."[34]

Author Malcolm Gladwell confirms this observation in his phenomenally popular *Blink*, wherein he cites some fascinating research on the interplay between expressions and emotions. In one experiment, participants were asked to watch cartoons either while clenching a pencil between their teeth (thus forcing a smile) or while gripping the pencil with their lips (thereby preventing a smile). Interestingly, the smilers found the cartoons much funnier than the non-smilers.[35]

Another study demonstrated that "expression alone is sufficient to create marked changes in the autonomic nervous system."[36] Researchers discovered when they spent long periods frowning, they felt terrible. Merely furrowing the brow, protruding the lower lip, and turning down the corners of the mouth was enough to produce intense feelings of sadness and anguish. Likewise, by simply gritting their teeth and flexing their facial muscles into a scowl, they could actually generate anger—accompanied, even, by an elevated heartbeat and sweaty palms!

"These findings may be hard to believe, because we take it as a given that first we experience an emotion, and then we may—or may not—express that emotion on our face," Gladwell notes. "What this research showed, though, is that the process works in the opposite direction as well. Emotion can also *start* on the face. The face is not a secondary billboard for our internal feelings. It is an equal partner in the emotional process."[37]

A Confidence Boost

If youth is not a stage of life but a state of mind, sex has the power to brighten our disposition and shave years off our self-image. Love may be blind, but the way we are seen by those we love will largely determine how we see ourselves. This is especially true of husbands and wives. The knowledge that our spouse still finds us attractive is a huge confidence booster.

My husband said something to me several years ago that really drove this concept home. We were on a cross-country road trip at the time. Doug loves to travel—we all do, in fact—so he'd taken a couple weeks off work, loaded the family into our 15-passanger van, and embarked on a 6,000 mile tour of the West Coast. As you might imagine, traveling with so many little ones in tow necessitates frequent potty breaks. During one such stop, while our older children queued up with their little partners outside the restroom doors, I took advantage of the peace and quiet to phone my mother. The kids were soon back, noisily piling two-by-two into the van, so I slid out the passenger side door to continue my conversation outside. Doug, who was pumping gas at the time, noticed me leaning over a nearby newsstand with my backside turned toward him, but since he hadn't seen me get out of the van, he did not at first recognize me as his wife. Instead, as he laughingly admitted once we were back on the road, the exact thought that crossed his mind was, *"Gee, that gal looks just like a heavy-set version of Jennifer!"*

When I later told this story to a couple of friends, they were appalled. They couldn't believe Doug admitted to thinking such a thing, nor could they understand why I didn't take offense. I tried to explain that I found my husband's confession reassuring. He was actually *shocked* to discover that the overweight woman who reminded him of me really *was* me—a fact which lets me know that what his brain normally perceives is something quite different than what his eyes take in. Our bathroom scales leave little doubt that Doug's gas-station impression was accurate: I *really am* "a heavy-set version" of the girl he married. But thankfully, that is not what registers whenever he looks at me and *knows it's me*; he sees instead the slim young bride who met him at the altar so many years ago. Now, why on earth would I consider that revelation insulting? I find it rather endearing (which is not to say I didn't *immediately* swear off sweets and start exercising more—blind love is a wonderful thing, but there's no sense testing the limits!).

Of course, communicating love and acceptance goes both ways. Sending the message to your husband that you still find him attractive, appealing, and completely irresistible is one of the most priceless gifts you can give him, especially as he enters middle age and begins to question such things. Let your actions prove to him that he has not lost his sex appeal! Such assurances will build him up and inspire him, while "an ongoing perception that [you don't] desire him would translate into a nagging lack of confidence, withdrawal, and depression."[38]

My husband recently finished re-reading Majorie Rawlings' 1939 Pulitzer Prize winning novel, *The Yearling*, aloud to our family. The book is full of character studies, but I was especially impressed by the contrast between Jody's faultfinding mother and the fun-loving Grandma Hutto. What different responses the attitudes of these two women elicited from the men and boys with whom they had contact! His ma's constant criticism made Jody feel as if he could do nothing right, whereas when he was around Grandma Hutto,

> ...it seemed to Jody he could bring in a panther single-handed, in return for her approval.... She drew gallantry from men as the sun drew water. Her pertness enchanted them. Young men went away from her with a feeling of bravado. Old men were enslaved by her silver curls. Something about her was forever female and made all men virile....[39]
>
> "Bless her old soul," Boyles said. "Why I say 'old soul' I don't know. If a man's wife was as young-hearted as Grandma Hutto, why, living'd be a feast."[40]

Aren't those last lines downright convicting? Would your husband consider life with you a feast or a famine? Do you smile or scold? Enchant or enslave? Harvard University graduate Shaunti Feldhahn examines the connection between a wife's approval and a husband's performance in her book, *For Women Only*. After personally interviewing over one thousand men nationwide, she reports on what she's learned: "You know that saying 'Behind every good man is a great woman?' Well, that is so *true*. If a man's wife is supportive and believes in him, he can conquer the world—or at least his little corner of it. He will do better at work, at home, everywhere. By contrast, very few men can do well at work *or* at home if their wives make them feel inadequate."[41]

One of the most effective ways a wife can express loving approval of her husband is to respond to him sexually. "Sex is energizing for a man. It builds his confidence and boosts his overall sense of well-being," writes psychologist Kevin Leman. "If he's in an unfulfilling job, he gets the strength to keep on doing what he's doing because he knows that there is a purpose for his work…and a willing wife waiting as a reward at the end of his long day."[42] A husband who is sexually fulfilled "will take on his life work with an unmatched vigor and purpose."[43]

Jeff Feldhahn addresses this same topic in *For Men Only*, a companion volume to his wife's *For Women Only*: "Men are powerfully driven by the emotional need to feel *desired* by our wives, and we filter everything through that grid…. If we feel our wife truly wants us sexually, we feel confident, powerful, alive, and loved. If we don't, we feel depressed, angry, and alone."[44]

To think that we as women have the ability, the power, the *opportunity*, to make or break our husbands in terms of confidence! Former Chairman and CEO of General Electric, Jack Welch writes in his autobiography that this kind of confidence "gives you courage and extends your reach. It lets you take greater risks and achieve far more than you ever thought possible… It [provides] opportunities and challenges for people to do things they never imagined they could do…."[45]

This observation is well documented. Scientific studies have demonstrated the link between a wife's physical expressions of love for her husband and his subsequent success in business:

> A German group of psychologists, physicians, and insurance companies cooperated on a research project designed to find the secret to long life and success. They made a surprising discovery. The secret? Kiss your wife each morning when you leave for work! The meticulous German researchers discovered that men who kiss their wives every morning have fewer automobile accidents on their way to work than men who omit the morning kiss. The good-morning kissers also miss less work because of illness and earn 20 to 30 percent more money than non-kissers. How do they explain their findings? According to West Germany's Dr. Arthur Szabo, "A husband who kisses his wife every morning begins the day with a positive attitude." How would your husband's attitude change in your home for the evening if you greeted your spouse when he got home with a hug and a kiss? Over time there would probably be some tangible results.[46]

Did you catch that? "Good-morning kissers earn 20 to 30 percent more than non-kissers"? That's a significant chunk of change. So send your husband off with a kiss each morning and give him a good reason to hurry home after work every night. If smooching can bestow such measurable financial benefits, just think what sort of pay-raise *regular lovemaking* might translate into!

Of course, there's more to life than earning a paycheck. All work with no play makes Jack a dull boy. Fortunately for us, sex is not only great for our appearance, our health, our peace of mind, and our earning potential, but as we shall see in the next chapter, it's good clean fun, to boot.

Chapter 8
Good Clean Fun

*"Marriage is to be held in honor among all,
and the marriage bed is to be undefiled."*
Hebrews 13:4

As much as I would like to sympathize with the parents of picky eaters, most of the feeding problems I have encountered with my own children have tended to toward the opposite extreme. My kids would eat *anything*. I've caught little ones gleaning used chewing gum from beneath restaurant tables, licking smashed gummy bears from the soles of their shoes, and ingesting bugs, worms, or other slimy substances they've found buried in our flowerbeds. *Yuck!* Surely it would be better if they were just a *little* more discriminating in their tastes.

I remember one such incident as if it happened yesterday, although it has been a good fourteen years now. My third-born was about four at the time. One afternoon as I stood at the kitchen sink washing up the lunch dishes, I saw him come through our back door munching on a suspicious looking bread roll. Not recognizing it as anything I'd ever brought home from the grocery story, I was compelled to ask, "David, where on earth did you get *that*?"

At this, my son smiled broadly, his little eyebrows shooting up in excitement. He hurriedly swallowed the bite in his mouth and answered proudly, "*Molly* brought it home. It's *good*!"

Understand: *Molly* was the name of our *dog*. So what my little boy was telling me, between mouthfuls, was that this shaggy, smelly mutt had been digging through our neighbors' garbage cans (again), found some tasty morsel they'd tossed out—*how many days ago?*—and carted it home for dinner, tail wagging, saliva dripping in anticipation, whereupon she was accosted by my tenacious preschooler, who wrestled the bun away from the dog in order to finish it himself. Now doesn't *that* sound appetizing?

What made it worse was the fact I had served him a hot, nutritious meal just half an hour earlier—which might actually have satisfied his hunger had he not been in such a rush to get back outdoors and play. Moreover, our pantry and refrigerator were both full of fresh, delicious food that would have been his for the asking.

Feasting at His Banquet Table

When it comes to sex, the world generates a staggering amount of rubbish. In fact, it's *worse* than trash: it's poison. And you don't have to go digging through back alley dumpsters to find it, either. Romance novels now account for more than half of all mass market fiction sold.[1] Many women's magazines are just as smutty: a person cannot make it through the check-out line at a grocery store without being inundated with images and article teasers that are the diametrical opposites of modesty and discretion. Hollywood continuously pushes the envelope in an attempt to normalize perversion. And thanks to the easy access of Internet porn, the most toxic waste of all can be pumped via our computers and cell phones into the privacy of our own homes.

Our society has been stripping sex of its intended purpose for over fifty years now. "Do you like its *new* attitude toward sex?" asks author Mary Pride:

> Look at the ads in magazines, in the stores, on TV and billboards. Is this a noble picture of women,

for our bodies to be used to sell everything from jeans to toothpaste? Think about the flood of pornographic materials, which oozes wider and more loathsome every year.... Consider also how this attitude has undermined marriage. Many husbands no longer look at their wife as the mother of their children, but as their legal mistress. Is it surprising that they divorce their wives whenever someone better-looking comes along?[2]

No, it's not surprising at all; it's a logical progression. We have shifted the focus of sex from marital unity to self-gratification, from procreation to recreation. In so doing, we have diminished it gravely. The Bible warns against becoming "callous" or giving oneself over "to sensuality for the practice of every kind of impurity with greediness" (Eph. 4:19), yet that is exactly what our society has done.

Describing the slippery mores of the sexual revolution, columnist Cal Thomas observes:

> Millions of young men bought [Hugh Hefner's] religion of sex as love, without marriage and commitment, and the fiction that it could be indulged in without physical, emotional, and cultural consequences. As men began to believe they could, and should, seek sexual pleasure outside marriage, women at first reacted by participating in this newfound "freedom." More recently, women have begun to experience the pain that comes with disease, unwanted pregnancies, abortions, easy divorce, and the poverty of the greatly diminished lifestyles that often accompany single motherhood, not to mention reduced self-esteem and the feeling that they have been "had."
>
> That God might have been aware of the physical ailments, emotional distress, spiritual consequences, and pain that are caused by sex outside

of marriage, and thus wished to spare those He loves from such things by establishing rules of conduct to safeguard us, apparently never occurred to Hefner.[3]

Some folks become addicted to sexual garbage in their desperate search for some way to spice up jaded love lives, yet they ignore the fact that a sumptuous feast of wholesome delights has already been prepared by our Heavenly Father. When couples scoff at God's purpose for passion in marriage and seek instead the empty thrills this world dangles before their eyes, it is as if they were leaving a heavily laden banquet table to wrestle a moldy crust of bread away from some mangy mutt. Why would anyone in his right mind *do* that?

"Sex is to be fun, for sure," writes Tim Gardner in *Sacred Sex*, "But if we make fun the measuring stick by which we judge our sexual relationship, then we'll fall prey to the law of diminishing returns. And we'll never find true passion."[4]

Satan has no power to create. He is only able to corrupt. And that is exactly what he has done for countless couples in the area of sex. In her book, *The Way Home*, Mary Pride includes an entire chapter devoted to "The Joy of Un-kinky Sex." She warns:

> Kinky sex is not a glittering toy we can fondle without harming ourselves. It does not proceed from the mouth of God, but from the *Deep Throats* of the world. It abases women and casts contempt on our beautiful ability to bear and nurse children. It endangers children, as the line of puberty means nothing where kinky sex is concerned. It places men under temptation to pervert themselves with men, by turning them on to homosexual styles of coupling that do not require a female partner."[5]

I once heard a professed-Christian insist that anything goes between two consenting adults, as long as they are married to one another. That is a lie straight from the pit of hell. Scripture teaches that "marriage is to be held in honor among all, and the marriage bed is to be undefiled; for fornicators and adulterers God will judge" (Heb. 13:4). We are "to be wise in what is good and innocent in what is evil" (Rom. 16:19). If marriage were a license to indulge in whatever perversions suit our fancies, if it were truly impossible to defile the marriage bed, then there would be no need to include in Holy Scriptures an admonition not to do so.

In regard to such things, Jesus sets an even higher standard in the New Testament than the Old Testament law laid down. He calls us to remain pure not just physically, but mentally as well. There is never an appropriate context for entertaining impure thoughts or lustful fantasies. Said Martin Luther, "You can't stop the birds from flying over your head, but you can stop them from nesting in your hair."[6] Husbands and wives must exercise vigilance and self-restraint in this area, even after the wedding vows are exchanged. The Bible makes this clear in the following passages:

- ∞ "Let love be without hypocrisy. Abhor what is evil; cling to what is good." (Rom. 12:9)
- ∞ "But I say to you that whoever looks at a woman to lust for her has already committed adultery with her in his heart." (Matt. 5:28-29 NKJV)
- ∞ "For as he thinks within himself, so he is." (Prov. 23:7)
- ∞ "Finally, brethren, whatever is true, whatever is honorable, whatever is right, whatever is pure, whatever is lovely, whatever is of good repute, if there is any excellence and if anything worthy of praise, dwell on these things." (Phil. 4:8)
- ∞ "Be ye holy; for I am holy." (1 Pet. 1:16 KJV)
- ∞ "And do not be conformed to this world, but be transformed by the renewing of your mind, so that you

may prove what the will of God is, that which is good and acceptable and perfect." (Rom. 12:2)

Why would anyone want to tamper with perfection, anyway? Perverting God's design is, well, perverse! Simply stated, married sex is good, clean fun. "Great sex and purity are inseparable," write Eric and Leslie Ludy in their book, *Meet Mr. Smith.*[7] "If we approach sex with a selfish attitude, we will never experience Great Sex as God intended it to be.... It's only when we selflessly lay down our lives for our spouse and allow sex to be an outflow of that sacrificial love that we truly experience the amazing satisfaction of physical intimacy in all its glory."[8]

Read the Song of Songs and note the abandon with which Solomon and his bride relish one another. God intended for sex to be immensely satisfying and delightfully wholesome—and not one of Satan's substitutes can hold a candle to the pleasures that await a couple willing to fully embrace God's original design.

Only on the Weekend?

Standing in the checkout line at Hobby Lobby one afternoon recently, I noticed the customer behind me was buying a wall plaque. I smiled when I spotted the sentiment written across the top of it. It read: "Life is too short to go fishing...."

I can certainly agree with that! I mused, slightly surprised to think anyone would want to hang a sign on their wall that said so. Although I have fond memories of fishing with my grandpa as a child, I have little desire to bait a hook now that he's gone. My husband shares this opinion, so I knew he'd appreciate the quote. Thinking I might buy a duplicate plaque for him, I glanced back in search of a price tag. That's when I noticed the *other* half of the sign. The message on the plaque actually read, "Life is too short to go fishing *only on the weekend*!"

I nearly laughed out loud when I realized my mistake. That last little phrase changed the meaning entirely, didn't it? I wonder, though, how many husbands would argue that life is too short to *have sex* only on the weekend. I wonder how many wives would be inclined to agree.

"Hollywood depictions of sex… lead many couples to expect that all they need for a fulfilling sexual relationship is moonlight, a soft breeze, and the right background music," note authors Henry Cloud and John Townsend in *Simple Secrets of a Great Marriage*. "The movies never show the couple five years later, fifty-hour workweeks busier, forty pounds heavier, or any of the other eventualities that make for real life. In reality, sustaining a sexual connection in your marriage takes focus, attention, and work—but the effort is worth it in the end."[9]

If you are as busy and overworked as most of the women I know, carving out more time for sex is probably not high on your priority list. But it should be. The idea of "taking a little vacation every day" lends itself beautifully to more frequent lovemaking, especially if a couple isn't attempting to pack a month's worth of romance into a single encounter.

"Someone once asked Somerset Maugham if he wrote on a schedule or only when struck by inspiration. 'I write only when inspiration strikes,' he replied. 'Fortunately it strikes every morning at nine o'clock sharp.'"[10]

This anecdote, related by Steven Pressfield in *The War of Art*, could apply just as readily to lovemaking as to writing. Should married couples have sex on a schedule, or only when they're in the mood?

Waiting for the mood to strike is fine, as long as you make certain it strikes with predictable regularity. Otherwise, you should go ahead and get started without it. "Most of us think that attitude must change before behavior changes," notes researcher Carl Charnetski. "That's true, but the inverse works too. If you force yourself to behave in a way that's out of synch with how you actually feel, your brain won't long be able to tolerate the incongruity. It'll change your attitude to come into accordance with your behavior."[11]

"There's a secret that real writers know that wannabe writers don't," Pressfield points out in his book, "and the secret is this: It's not the writing part that's hard. What's hard is sitting down to write."[12] Likewise, for countless couples, it's not the physical intimacy part that's hard. What's hard is finding time for it—which is why, I say, you should never underestimate the value of a "quickie".

There are few things I find more refreshing than a long, luxuriant soak in a hot tub. Add a plush towel for my neck, some classical music, a couple of candles, and a good book, and I'm set. But what would happen if I decided that, unless I have at least an hour to devote to such a bathing ritual, I just won't bathe at all? I'd eventually get to smelling so bad that my friends and family would shun me. So instead, I content myself most mornings with a two-minute rinse in the shower. A bubble bath is nice, but it certainly isn't the only way to get clean.

The same principle applies to our sex lives. The notion that a quick romp is cheap sex is a lie Satan propagates to make wives feel justified in denying their husbands, despite the fact that this excuse doesn't hold water. When it comes to making love, it's far better to take advantage of fleeting moments of time as they present themselves, than to miss out completely while you wait for a large block of free-time that never materializes. A wife's willingness to be available to her husband, regardless of time constraints, assures him of her commitment to meet his needs and to make sex a priority in their marriage. This willingness is key, whether it *immediately* leads to lovemaking or not, as one author wisely observes:

Have you ever been putting on your mascara when your husband came up behind you and cupped your breast? Have you ever slapped his hand away with a curt, "Not now!"

Why *not* now?

How long does it take to caress a breast? Ten seconds? Twenty seconds? Can you really not give your husband that amount of time?

I know what you're thinking: *You don't understand.... If I let him touch my breast, I'll be on my back looking up at the ceiling in 10 seconds flat. My clothes will be thrown all over the floor, my hair will get messed up, and I'll have to redo my makeup. Then I'll be late for work.*

...But many times your husband just wants a quick feel. So next time surprise him by turning around and getting a quick feel of your own.

There's a huge difference between a wife who slaps a man's hands away and one who giggles mischievously, even engaging in one or two minutes of light petting, only to whisper in his ear, "This feels so delicious, but unfortunately, I really do have to get ready for work. Let's save it for tonight, when you'll get all you want and more." The second woman will have fulfilled her husband, even while staying clothed and keeping her hair in place. The first wife will have deflated her husband and eroded his masculinity, all for the sake of 60 to 90 seconds.

That's a costly minute.[13]

"What attracts men to women is their femininity," according to radio personality Laura Schlessinger, "and femininity isn't only about appearance, it's also about behaviors. Looking womanly and behaving sweetly and flirtatiously are gifts wives give to their husbands. This gift communicates that the husband is seen as a man, not just a fix-it guy, the bread-winner, or the sperm donor."[14] A woman's sincere admiration and respect for her husband has the "singularly magical ability... to transform deflated men into heroes and warriors" writes Dr. Laura; women have the power "to not only create life in their wombs, but to sustain that life force in the husbands."[15]

I'm not saying you should *reluctantly submit* to your husband's sexual advances; I'm saying you should *enthusiastically welcome* them.

"There's a big difference," pastor Tommy Nelson explains. "I had a man say to me one time, 'You know, whenever I make love to my wife, I feel like I'm a bee circling an inert flower to pollinate it. There is no response in her whatsoever.' A man doesn't want a wife who is just being a good Christian martyr."[16]

No, he's hoping for a bit more excitement than that.

A Tiger in Bed

"During an early counseling session," writes Tim Alan Gardner, director of The Marriage Institute, "I asked [my counselee] Karen to describe her image of a woman who thoroughly enjoys sex, is 'a little wild' in bed, and occasionally initiates sex." Gardner recalls her response:

> She described that sort of woman as "single, loose, immoral, a seductress" and added that such a woman would be "provocatively dressed." Karen might have been describing that divorced woman who's been on the prowl at [her husband's] office.
>
> My response to Karen surprised her. "Actually, the woman I was describing is a married, middle-aged mom who's a committed follower of Christ."
>
> "That can't be," Karen told me. "It doesn't fit."[17]

But Karen was mistaken.

Devout Christian wives who enjoy sex really *do* exist; apparently, there are a bunch of them. "Seemingly every year," reports Wendy Shalit in *A Return to Modesty*, "another study announces that married women are more orgasmic than single women." She writes:

> At first I wonder, Do I really need to know this detail? But then I read on and I am transfixed…. A University of Chicago survey of 3,432 Americans ages 18 through 59 found that monogamous married couples reported the highest sexual satisfaction, while singles and marrieds who have multiple partners registered the lowest…. After surveying 100,000 women, *Redbook* magazine found that the most strongly religious women were 'more responsive sexually' than all other women."[18]

Does this surprise you? It shouldn't, if you stop and think about it. What did we say in chapter four must happen for a woman to achieve climax? She must first set aside her worries. She must relax. She must completely entrust herself to her partner.

The "circumstances most conducive to female sexual arousal and satisfaction are hard to come by in the impersonal, sex-act-driven landscape of the hookup culture," writes Carol Platt Liebau in *Prude*. "As Pfizer learned when it tried to create the female equivalent of Viagra, female sexuality isn't as much of a biological as it is a mental matter, and an emotional one." She continues:

> Fear and stress, for example, inhibit women from reaching orgasm. Obviously, it's much easier for a… woman to be comfortable and relaxed with a trusted partner who cares about her as an individual, not primarily as a sex object—and is therefore

interested in enhancing her sexual satisfaction, rather than being exclusively focused on his own. Such partners are found not in quick, furtive hookups or meaningless one-night stands, but in the context of a committed relationship like marriage....

Indeed, the trust factor may be why women in monogamous relationships enjoy vastly superior sex lives than the 'liberated' girls who are engaging in sexual activity with a variety of males."[19]

Marriage has always been the best context for both sexes to experience physical oneness, but it might surprise you to learn just how much attention has traditionally been given to the pleasure *a wife* derives from conjugal relations. Wendy Shalit explains:

> Any cursory acquaintance with ... the Torah's commandment of *onah* (the husband's obligation to his wife) will reveal that the ancients developed elaborate systems out of a concern over satisfying female desire.... Hence, in Judaism, there is the husband's sexual obligation to his wife: before he goes away on a journey, after she returns home from the *mikveh*, and so forth. As Maimonides elaborates:
> 1. The conjugal [women's sexual] rights mentioned in the Torah are obligatory upon each man according to his physical powers and his occupation. How so? For the men who are healthy and live in comfortable and pleasurable circumstances, without having to perform work that would weaken their strength, and only eat and drink and sit idly in their homes, their conjugal schedule is every night; for the laborers, such as tailors, weavers, masons, and the like, their conjugal schedule is twice weekly if their work is in the same city, and once a week if their work is in another city; for the donkey drivers, their

schedule is once a week; for the camel drivers, once in thirty days....

2. A wife may restrict her husband in his business journeys, so that he would not otherwise deprive her of her conjugal rights. Hence he may not set out except with her permission. Similarly, she may prevent him from exchanging an occupation involving a frequent conjugal schedule, for one involving an infrequent one.[20]

Imagine for a moment that your husband comes home from work brimming with news of a promotion. Honestly, now: Do *conjugal schedules* even enter into your conversation? "Oh, honey! They'll give you a fifty percent pay raise, ten weeks vacation, and a company car? That's terrific! But wait... it means I'll only get sex *twice a week*, and not *every night*? Tsk! Tsk! Then you'd better turn it down."

When I read those last few sentences aloud to get my husband's reaction, he sniggered, "Right. Like that would ever happen!"

If you can't imagine a woman even thinking in those terms, it may be because you are confusing *drive* with *desire*. "There are actually two different types of desire," Jeff and Shaunti Feldhahn tell us. Whereas "men have more testosterone-type hormones linked to 'assertive' sexual desire, women have more estrogen, which is tied to what is called 'receptive' sexual desire.... This doesn't mean she doesn't want it, or won't enjoy it once it's happening, but just that seeking it out isn't usually on her mind."[21] The bottom line? Although men may be more apt to *pursue* sex, that doesn't mean they're better able to take *pleasure* in it.

In fact, the exact opposite may be true, although female enjoyment typically takes longer to unfold. The "swift roll in the hay" that is so helpful in curbing your husband's sexual appetite may be insufficient to completely satisfy your own. "Speed has its place between the sheets," writes Carl Honoré in *In Praise of Slow,* "But sex can be so much more than a sprint to orgasm. Making love slowly can be a profound experience. It can also deliver fantastic orgasms."[22]

Especially, it would seem, for a woman who lets her husband take his time. While men undergo a refractory period after climax, women can keep right on going. "Rarer and the result of more refined longing as they are," Jonathan Margolis explains in *O: The Intimate History of the Orgasm,* "women's orgasms, with their satisfying multiple muscular contractions, are an infinitely bigger and more expansive experience than the sensation men have when they ejaculate."[23]

Yet such pleasure is still just a side effect, not the end-goal, of embracing God's purpose for passion in marriage. Couples who set as their chief objective a heightened enjoyment may find that the attendant performance-anxiety prevents them from reaching it at all. Solomon warns in the book of Proverbs, "Do not weary yourself to gain wealth, cease from your consideration of it. When you set your eyes on it, it is gone. For wealth certainly makes itself wings like an eagle that flies toward the heavens" (Prov. 23:4-5). In the same way, sensational orgasms may elude lovers who pursue sex for no other reason.

God had a much higher purpose than pleasure in mind when He created sex. It may well be an enjoyable pastime, but it is also *far more.* As we'll see in the next chapter, if a couple wishes to fully experience oneness as God originally intended, then they must not divorce sex from fruitfulness,[24] for those "who live [only] for pleasure, delighted by the attractive package, throw the gift away—in this instance of sex, the great gift of life itself."[25]

Chapter 9
Baby Showers

"Behold, children are a gift of the LORD,
The fruit of the womb is a reward."
Psalm 127:3

I love Garage Sales. Yard Sales. Tag Sales. Estate Sales. Call them what you may, the chance to rummage through another person's junk in search of treasure has always been a thrill for me.

As a young wife and mother living on school loans while my husband completed his medical training, it was a matter of necessity. Just as God provided manna in the wilderness for the children of Israel, He used such second-hand sales to sustain our growing family throughout those lean years. I was able to clothe our children, furnish the house, build a library, and complete our Christmas shopping—all for cents on the dollar.

Even now that finances are not so tight, I still enjoy a good sale and will stop at any that look promising. Thus I found myself, a few years back, hiking up an asphalt driveway to ruffle through a rack of baby clothes.

The homeowner eyed my bulging, pregnant belly and enthused, "Well, you've certainly come to the right place! We've got everything you need for a new baby."

Fingering the frilly pink dresses, I replied, "Maybe not... I'm having a boy."

"Ah, well," he apologized, "then we can't help you. Ours was a girl." He continued to make small talk as I browsed through the household items. "So, is this your *first?*"

I love it when folks ask me that question. It flatters me to think that perhaps I look young for my age. And I love to see people's reactions when I tell them, "No, actually, this is my *tenth* [or *eleventh* or *twelfth*]."

The homeowner's response to this revelation did not disappoint. His eyes grew large. He pretended to clean out an ear with his pinkie. He asked me to repeat myself. Then, satisfied he had heard me right the first time, he swore under his breath and said, "Well, you really must love your husband—and you obviously don't care about the consequences!"

This was an astute observation. The fact is, I *adore* my husband, and I am *delighted* by the consequences.

Children are a Blessing

No discussion of the benefits of sex would be complete without the mention of children. Having babies is one of the most obvious outcomes of embracing God's purpose for passion in marriage. Sex, after all, was designed with procreation in mind: Marital intimacy and reproduction. "The two shall become one flesh" (Mark 10:8; Gen. 2:24). "Be fruitful and multiply" (Gen. 1:22).

In the course of doing research for this book, I read through countless articles enumerating the various advantages of having an active sex life. Would you believe that not a single author included *babies* on his list of benefits? One scholar expounded at length on "the scientific reasons for having sex." You would think that reproduction would certainly make *that* list, yet it ran completely below the radar.

If I were to ask you to itemize the scientific reasons for eating, you might mention the fact that some people eat to fight boredom, to ease loneliness, or to be sociable, but surely you wouldn't overlook the fact that most folks eat because they need nourishment. They're hungry. The whole reason our bodies even *feel hunger* is to make sure we all tend to this basic, universal need. And the defining "scientific reason" God even created sex was to provide a pleasurable, convenient way for mankind to reproduce. It has been the standard means of propagating the human race throughout all of history. Those other things—heart health, cancer protection, longevity, mental stability, stress relief—are wonderful fringe benefits we enjoy as a result of embracing God's design for sex, but they are not the end-goal in and of themselves.

The Bible bears this out. Malachi 2:15 states, "Has not [the LORD] made them one? In flesh and spirit they are his. And why one? *Because he was seeking godly offspring.* So guard yourself in your spirit, and do not break faith with the wife of your youth" (NIV, *emphasis added*). God designed sex so that we'd produce children, pure and simple. Throughout Scripture, fertility is viewed as a great blessing; infertile women felt humiliated by their barrenness and considered it a terrible curse. The Lord bestowed great favor upon Israel when He promised to "love you and bless you and multiply you; [to] bless the fruit of your womb and the fruit of your ground, your grain and your new wine and your oil, the increase of your herd and the young of your flock..... You shall be blessed above all peoples; there will be no male or female barren among you or among your cattle" (Deut 7:12-14).

In Genesis we read, *"Be thou the mother of thousands of millions, and let thy seed possess the gate....* Can you imagine attending a wedding where families and friends offered [that] blessing to a new bride?" asks Doug Phillips, founder of Vision Forum and father of eight:

> Yet these words of encouragement, once offered to Rebekah on the advent of her marriage to

Isaac (Genesis 24:60), beautifully communicate the heart of God's command to Christian husbands and wives that they be exceedingly fruitful and raise children who will influence all of culture and society for the glory of God.

There is no escaping the fact that the Bible is dogmatically pro-child. Scripture declares unapologetically that the birth of many children is a source of blessing, that a key reason for marriage is to bring forth many children for the glory of God, and that parents should actively seek such blessings.[1]

Sadly, this is not the vision[2] shared with most young lovers in their prenuptial counseling sessions. All too often, children are depicted as an unnecessary stress and strain, something best avoided for the first five or six years of marriage, at least. That's the advice my husband and I received before our wedding from almost every married couple we knew—advice, I am grateful to report, that was entirely outstripped by the refreshingly different viewpoint we found in Mary Pride's *The Way Home.* This inspiring book made motherhood seem the most noble, fulfilling, delightful undertaking imaginable, and I could hardly wait to get started. Herself the mother of nine, Mrs. Pride was speaking from experience when she wrote:

> Don't you enjoy holding a sweet, warm little baby and watching him contentedly nurse at your breast? Don't you treasure that first little smile as your baby drinks you in, the most important person in his world? Isn't it satisfying to make a yucchy little bottom all clean and sweet, and can't you laugh at your offspring's gooey face, innocently awash in carrots and rice cereal? Doesn't it make you feel special that God has trusted you to nurture and protect this tiny morsel of helpless humanity?

As the baby grows, a nurturing mother shares the excitement of those first wobbly steps. She thrills to those baby lips calling, "Mama." A downy head pillowed on her shoulder; little fingers trustingly curled around her thumb; happy giggles when she tickles her toddler—what queen can buy these pleasures?[3]

King Solomon, who was as wealthy in wisdom as he was in material possessions, considered children an invaluable asset, as evidenced by his writings: "Like arrows in the hands of a warrior so are the children of one's youth. How blessed is the man whose quiver is full of them" (Psalm 127:4-5). Commenting on this passage in their book *Start Your Family*, Steve and Candice Watters quip:

This is one psalm we have yet to hear adapted into a contemporary praise chorus—perhaps due to the prevalence of suburbanites who aren't inspired by images of warriors with fistfuls of arrows. But just think how motivated people would be to start their families earlier if the psalm had this contemporary equivalence: "Like a thousand shares of Google stock are children born in one's youth."[4]

Thanks, but No Thanks

Yet few people think in such terms. What other blessing of God is met with more disdain than the blessing of a fertile womb and the children that proceed from it?

Most of us would agree the gift of *vision* is a blessing. Sadly, blindness does exist, but it isn't a condition many of us would choose of our own free will. If we are fortunate enough to possess good eyesight, we cherish it. If it is not keen, we wear lenses to correct it. If it becomes cloudy, we undergo surgery to restore it. As we grow older, we grieve the loss of accommodation that accompanies advancing years. Imagine how horrendous it would be to live in a society that treated eyesight as ours treats fertility, a society that tied thick blindfolds on themselves to keep from seeing too early, then willfully gouged out their own eyes once they'd seen quite enough. Unthinkable? Yet such behavior would be comparable to the measures we take to limit fertility through the use of contraception and elective sterilization.

"The Bible teaches us to approach sexual intimacy and the possibility of conception with awe and reverence," write Sam and Bethany Torode. "The womb is the place where God forms new life in His image, not a frontier to be arrogantly invaded and conquered.... Pregnancy is not a disease—why vaccinate against it?"[5]

I once heard someone compare having "unprotected" sex to playing Russian roulette. "Do it often enough," he warned, "and you'll eventually blast your brains out." The analogy did not set well with me. It somehow did not seem right to equate a beautiful bouncing baby with a bullet to the head. Procreation is an activity that results in God's blessings, as children are repeatedly called throughout Scripture. Russian roulette is a fool's game that shows complete disregard for life. Perhaps a better analogy might be dropping coins into a slot machine: *Deposit frequently enough, and you may eventually hit the jackpot!*

A couple's fertile years provide a window of opportunity, a window that may close far sooner than they expect. "Remarkably few women realize in their 20s that their fertility begins a decline at age 27 that quickens after 35 and plummets after 40. And how many men even think about their fertility beginning to dwindle starting at age 35?"[6] The term *birth control* is actually a misnomer; it leads us to believe that we can just as easily *make* a baby as we can *prevent* one, when in reality this is simply not true.

Sam and Bethany Torode point out that contraception might "be compared to binging and purging. It promises to satisfy our appetite for sex while ignoring its created purpose."[7] When a person who loves to eat but doesn't want to get fat makes a habit of gorging on food then forcing herself to vomit, she not only robs her body of the nutrients it needs to function properly, but she eventually loses the ability to keep anything in her stomach even when she wants to. In the same way, couples who like to have sex but don't want to have babies will go to great lengths to enjoy the former without risking the latter. Many sacrifice their health and squander their fertile years trying to avoid pregnancy, only to discover that when they *do* decide to try for a baby, they are no longer able to conceive at all.

It is foolish to assume that because I am fertile today I will be tomorrow. We can't count on the blessing of fertility lasting forever, any more than we can count on always being able to run the 100-yard dash in fourteen seconds. I believe that once we start looking more realistically at our fertility, seeing it as a fragile and special blessing which many people will never have and which everyone eventually loses, we will have a higher respect for babies.... If I don't want a baby today, but do tomorrow, I may find when tomorrow comes that I have already missed my only chance.[8]

The thought of forever missing out on motherhood seems tragic to me, but I am admittedly in the minority. According to a recent report from the Pew Research Center, "only 41 percent of Americans now view having children as 'very important' to a successful marriage, down from 65 percent in 1990."[9] Modern society seems much more concerned with acquisition than procreation. Couples still want the big house, but they aren't so interested in having lots of children to fill it; thus, we see smaller families living in larger homes: "No longer are the bedrooms crammed with bunk beds and toy chests. The suburbs, once a haven for flourishing families, now boast spacious dwellings with three and more bedrooms filled with exercise equipment, computers, and craft supplies."[10] In fact, in the United States today "there are more *televisions* per household than there are children!"[11]

Danielle Crittenden laments that too many couples "talk about marriage as if it were some sort of theoretical domestic labor arrangement" and treat children as "nothing more than a codicil to the arrangement, an add-on option to a marriage like a leather interior and digital compass in a new car, and not the fundamental reason why men and women join together for a lifetime,"[12] She goes on:

> A woman will not understand what true dependency is until she is cradling her own infant in her arms; nor will she likely achieve the self-confidence she craves until she has withstood, and transcended, the weight of responsibility a family places upon her—a weight that makes all the paperwork and assignments of her in-basket seem feather-light. The same goes for men. We strengthen a muscle by using it, and that is true of the heart and mind, too.... For it's in the act of taking up the roles we've been taught to avoid or postpone—wife, husband, mother, father—that we build our identities, expand our lives, and achieve the fullness of character we desire.[13]

Sam and Bethany Torode echo this sentiment in their excellent little treatise on birth control called *Open Embrace*:

> ...some wives and husbands try to sever the procreative dimension [of sex] from the unitive. They imagine that by refusing the "burden" of children, they can achieve a better partnership, a higher intimacy. The problem here is that their partnership was *designed* for raising children, and any so-called intimacy which is deliberately closed to new life is

merely a collaboration in selfishness. Children change us in a way we desperately need to be changed. They wake us up, they wet their diapers, they depend on us. Willy-nilly, they knock us out of our selfish habits and force us to live sacrificially for others; they are the necessary and natural continuation of the shock to our selfishness which is initiated by marriage itself.[14]

Of course, "we don't create children—God does," the Torodes remind us, "they are a gift only He can bestow. As married persons, our part is to remain open to children, by becoming one flesh and refusing to compromise that union." By way of clarification, they add,

> This is not to say that every time a couple makes love, they should be trying to conceive—after all, conception is possible for only a few days of a woman's cycle and impossible during times such as pregnancy and after menopause. But every time husband and wife come together, they ought to do so in earnest, in an open embrace, withholding nothing from each other—including their fertility.[15]

"Children," note Steve and Candice Watters, "give parents an up close and personal opportunity to welcome little ones in Christ's name and then humble themselves to become like children on a regular basis. In the process, they can experience the joys of seeing life through fresh eyes."[16] Jesus himself taught, "Whoever receives one such child in My name receives Me" (Matt. 18:5). And do you remember His reaction when He discovered His disciples were turning young ones away? Jesus told them unequivocally, "Let the little children come to Me, and do not forbid them; for of such is the kingdom of heaven" (Matt. 19:14, NKJV).

It took a long time for the disciples to receive Jesus' message about children. Jesus had just spoken to them about embracing children in the previous chapter and yet [here] they are still pushing the children away! How sad it is that those who confess Jesus as their Lord do not have the same heart that He has about children. Instead, they do everything in their power to stop the children coming.[17]

Enjoy Them While You Can

Our family was standing in the buffet line at a local cafeteria one afternoon recently when I realized we had become the topic of conversation between two older women who were in line behind us. As is my habit in such situations, I immediately pricked up my ears to listen without turning to look at them, so they wouldn't realize I was eavesdropping.

They were still counting heads when I tuned in. Traditionally such a headcount is followed by an "Oh, how sweet" or an "Aren't they well behaved?" But this time, I heard one of those grannies groan, "Goodness *gracious*! I'm glad it's *them* and not *me*. I only had two kids, and I wish I didn't even have those!" Saddened by these words, I grieved silently for the circumstances that would so embitter a woman against her own offspring.

Fortunately, her comments were an aberration from the norm, particularly from older generations. Much more commonly, we feel a hand on our shoulders and turn to see some white-haired gentleman who smiles and tells us how happy it makes him to see our large family or how much he has enjoyed observing our interactions. Some are fondly reminded of their own upbringing, when having lots of children was more common. Others sympathize, remembering the effort and energy they had invested in raising their own brood of children years earlier. All are quick to admonish us, "Savor every minute, because they'll be grown before you know it!"

Many times, though, we turn to see a wistful look in the eyes of an elderly couple who tell us how *blessed* we are, and how they wish now they'd had more children than they did. If only they could do it over again, they would have a houseful, they assure us. It is a widespread sentiment, as evidenced by a letter sent to Nancy Campbell, editor of *Above Rubies* magazine, which she quotes in her thoughtful book, *Be Fruitful and Multiply*:

> I am a registered nurse, and many older people whom I've cared for are now in their eighties and nineties and were having their families during The Depression. They were a generation who tried hard to limit their family size. I've held so many old, frail hands and listened to so many sweet souls tell me how they regretted not having more children. It is such a common thread, and it is so typical of our enemy. First he tricks people into not letting God bless them with a big family, then when they are old, he torments them with their error.[18]

What a *privilege* it is to conceive children. What a blessing to cooperate with God's divine plan. Yet cooperating is something few couples aspire to do. Many consider their fertility a nuisance or a curse; they do whatever it takes to counteract it. Some go so far as to sterilize themselves in their determination to triumph over this Unwelcome Side Effect of Sex. Others trade closeness for condoms, spontaneity for spermicides. Even "Natural Family Planning" denies the wife intimacy at precisely the point in her cycle when she would most desire and enjoy it—which hardly seems natural at all. What was designed to be the ultimate expression of love and warmth between a husband and wife becomes a cold, slimy struggle with bulky diaphragms, smelly creams, and ovulation predictors. It's little wonder that many wives would like to avoid the whole messy affair.

Since the majority of couples would rather spare themselves the permanency of surgical procedures, the hassle of contraceptive devices, *and* the inconvenience of abstinence during fertile times, many resort to using the Pill or the Patch. Hormonal contraceptives make all other solutions a thing of the past. Besides, they're so easy. Our problems are solved! Now couples can enjoy spontaneous, skin-to-skin sex and still not risk unwanted pregnancy!

But what of the *other* risks?

Life and Death

When my husband was in medical school, he discovered in one of his course textbooks seven full pages describing in detail the known adverse side effects associated with oral contraceptive use. That volume is now outdated and no longer in our library, but a quick search through the current *Physician's Drug Handbook* shows that hormonal birth control still puts a woman at increased risk for a whole host of medical problems, including heart attacks, strokes, liver tumors, blood clots, gall bladder disease, migraine headaches, depression, hypertension, edema, constipation, diarrhea, nausea, vomiting, loss of vision, weight gain, urinary tract infections, yeast infections, jaundice, acne, skin rashes, thyroid problems, high blood sugar, subsequent miscarriage of future pregnancies, and congenital anomalies (birth defects) in future babies,[19] to name just a few, as well as "temporary infertility after discontinuation of treatment."[20] Add to this the fact hormonal contraceptives often act as an abortifacient—consistently blocking *implantation*, but not always preventing *fertilization*—and the risks associated with their use become lethal.[21]

When Doug showed the original list to me, I was shocked. It was harrowing to think a woman might unknowingly compromise her health or unintentionally endanger her offspring in an attempt to avoid pregnancy. My husband felt the same way, so together we began a crusade to educate the masses. We photocopied that entire section from his medical text and started passing it out to all the family and friends we knew who were using or considering using the Pill.

Admittedly, our methods of disseminating this information might have been more effective had we used a little tact and diplomacy. We probably should've argued less and prayed more. But the dangers were so grave, the decisions so imminent, and the message so urgent that we never paused to consider what might be the best way to deliver it.

As it was, our campaign repeatedly met with either apathetic indifference or open hostility. "If the Pill were really *that* unsafe," some argued, "then doctors wouldn't prescribe it." What we tried to explain, but could never quite communicate, was the idea that society's attitude toward children and "unplanned" pregnancies made assuming such risks acceptable.

Consider, for example, the current standard of care for cancer patients. Everyone on the planet knows that chemotherapy leaves you feeling as sick as a dog. It saps your strength. It makes you nauseous. Your hair falls out. Yet doctors still prescribe it, and cancer patients still submit themselves to such treatment routinely. Why? Because they consider the alternative (letting the cancer grow unchecked until it kills them) completely unacceptable.

Our culture is willing to assume the high risks associated with hormonal contraceptives, because the alternative (conceiving and carrying a baby until it is time to deliver) is seen as something to be avoided at all costs. These days, an unplanned pregnancy is about as welcome as a cancer diagnosis. Abortionists treat unborn babies precisely as surgeons treat malignant tumors. They even use the same language, referring to that precious developing child as "a mass of tissue". As long as this is our attitude toward babies, doctors will continue to prescribe the Pill, regardless of the risks.[22]

If, however, we reject the notion that children are a burden and instead affirm with Scripture that they are a blessing, then the prospect of going to such hazardous extremes to avoid having a baby becomes incomprehensible.

Milk and Honey

When God rescued the Israelites from slavery in Egypt, miraculously parting the Red Sea and leading them to the very edge of the Promised Land, they balked. He promised to go ahead of them, to throw their enemies into confusion, to send hornets to drive the pagan inhabitants out of Canaan (Ex. 23:23-30). Yet rather than taking God at His word and placing their full trust in Him, the Israelites heeded the report of ten faithless men who claimed the land was full of unconquerable giants. "We're as grasshoppers in their sight!" these spineless spies exaggerated. "Surely we will be utterly destroyed, our wives and children enslaved. It is too great a risk" (see Num. 13:30-33).

Joshua and Caleb alone pleaded with their brethren not to shrink back. "The land which we passed through to spy out is an exceedingly good land.... [D]o not fear the people of the land, for they will be our prey. Their protection has been removed from them, and the LORD is with us" (Num. 14:9). But instead of heeding this advice, the Israelites rebelled. They changed course, opting to remain in the desert, where they lived for forty years until the generation who doubted had completely died off.[23]

Yes, God still loved them. Yes, He still led them. Yes, He supplied their needs. They ate the manna. They pitched their tents. They drank from the Rock. But they died never knowing what they had missed.

Every couple who meets under a wedding canopy today faces a similar situation. Perhaps they'll tell you how

God brought them together. Their meeting was miraculous. The timing was perfect. Yes, theirs was a match made in heaven. So here they now stand, pledging life and love to one another, eager to enter the Promised Land of marriage.

They sense that God has untold treasures He longs to pour out upon them, blessings overflowing. Sex is one such blessing. And—the Bible makes it clear—children are another. These two blessings originally went hand-in-hand (and what God has joined together, let no man put asunder).

Yet few young couples stand at the altar alone. Most are surrounded by a chorus of well-wishing family and friends, whose intentions are good, but whose advice often isn't.

"Don't burden yourselves with a baby right away," they caution. "Get to know one another first. Make sure your marriage is going to last. Wait until you finish school. Wait until you are established in your career. Wait until you own a house. Wait to have kids until you can better afford them."

Like those pessimistic spies, they try to drown out the voices of any who would tell them differently.

The fact that this is almost universally the advice newlyweds receive is enough to make even the most stouthearted take pause. Are children *really* a blessing? Maybe that was true in an agricultural society, but in a technological one? Maybe those verses in Psalms are no longer culturally relevant. Maybe we *shouldn't* start our family right away.

And so they wait.

And wait.

And wait.

Some may eventually accept their 1.6 children with grateful hearts, but others will wake up one morning and realize they have waited too long. They may regret ever having listened to the naysayers who convinced them that children are a burden, a distraction, a hassle. But it's too late.

Their weary bodies collapse in a barren wilderness, their eyes never having seen the land that flows with milk and honey.[24]

Our Father Knows Best

One of my all-time favorite movies is *The Sound of Music* starring Julie Andrews and Christopher Plummer. In my opinion, that film has everything: a compelling story, beautiful music, spectacular scenery, faith, love, honor, courage, action, and humor. Our family spent three weeks backpacking Europe several years ago, and I read *The Story of the Trapp Family Singers* and taught our kids the lyrics of "My Favorite Things" before we ever left home. (I also tried to convince them to wear matching lederhosen for our tour of Salzburg, but they politely declined. *That*, they insisted, would be going too far.)

As is normally the case, the book contained all sorts of details that were never mentioned in the movie. Did you know, for instance, that when the Trapp family was crossing over the border into Switzerland, Maria was newly pregnant? Not only that, but she was afflicted with a severe kidney infection and hypertension at the time. A specialist in Germany had recommended they abort the baby, "since there was no chance he would be born alive."

The Trapps refused, so the doctor prescribed a strict diet and complete bed rest for Maria: She must keep "absolutely quiet—no excitement—the blood pressure is very high," he told them.[25] As Providence would have it, however, this diagnosis came only days before Georg refused his naval commission from the Nazis, his grown son rejected a surgical post with the Third Reich, their musical children turned down an invitation to sing for the Fuhrer's birthday, and the entire family was forced to flee Austria.

The remainder of Maria's pregnancy was far, far from restful. Looking back on it, she remarks:

118

Many years later I happened to learn about planned parenthood and birth control to guard against unwanted children. I must say, [our baby] had not been exactly planned for that very moment, and as far as being wanted is concerned, I would have gladly said many times, "Oh, won't you please be so kind as to wait for just six months." Yes, many times on the flight, on the boat, on the bus, on the stage. But thousands of years ago God assured us—it's in the Book—"For My thoughts are not your thoughts, nor your ways My ways." So if there is any planning to be done, why don't we let Him do it? Looking back now, I know that He chose the only right moment for Johannes' arrival. The predictions of the doctor in Munich proved beautifully wrong, and Johannes promises to be a fine American boy.[26]

Statisticians tell us that "close to a third of all pregnancies in marriage are unplanned. In the nine months they have to make course corrections, however, many of these couples come to realize that God has a better sense of timing than they do," Steve and Candice Watters suggest. "Maybe the unplanned pregnancies that seem the most ill-timed in the moment are actually God's way of weaving into crowded lives and tightly orchestrated timelines a better plan that He conceived before the world began."[27]

God can be trusted. God *should* be trusted. But putting the decision in His hands necessitates our willingness to abide by what He decides, to have faith that He knows best. We can choose to believe that children are a blessing and act accordingly, accepting what He sends with grateful hearts. Or we can listen to modern society, which tells us children are a burden and inconvenience.

Scripture clearly teaches it is the LORD who opens and closes the womb (see Gen. 20:18; 29:31-32; 30:22). Just because a couple decides not to use birth control does not mean they will have a dozen children—or even one. We know couples who haven't had a single child despite years of trying, and others who have never used contraceptives throughout their marriage and still wound up with only one or two. I've heard it said, "God gives His best to those who let Him choose." Nowhere is that truer than in the area of family planning.

Compound Interest

An influential theologian of the Reformation, Joseph Hall recounts the time when a great man visited his home. Upon being introduced to Hall's children, oldest to youngest, the guest remarked, "These are they that make rich men poor," to which Hall straightway replied, "Nay, my lord, these are they that make a poor man rich; for there is not one of these whom we would part with for all your wealth."[28]

We've discussed at length how married couples benefit from having an active sex life. We've seen how their obedience to the injunction, "stop depriving one another" brings great blessings. But it is worth noting that when a couple enthusiastically embraces God's *full* purpose for sex in marriage—in both its unitive and *procreative* aspects—when they open their hearts and homes to the blessing of children, these dividends are multiplied exponentially. And this is true for just about every area we've discussed:

∞ Togetherness: "Children draw their mother and father closer," notes George Barna in *Revolutionary Parenting*. "This is not only through the act of procreation, but through the years of teamwork that the parents jointly venture into while striving to raise [their children].[29] I agree. The love and admiration I felt for my husband as a spouse, great though it was, increased manifold when he became the father of my children. I still enjoy watching him teach and train and interact with our preschoolers, adolescents, teens, and adult children, but there is something so specially endearing about the way he cuddles and cootchy-coos our babies that it makes me glad we still have one in the house to draw that tenderness out of him.

∞ Healthy Living: We've already noted that childbirth and breastfeeding decreases a woman's risk of breast, ovarian, and uterine cancer.[30] Interestingly, studies have also demonstrated a link between parenting and longevity: mothers and fathers who take an active role in raising children live longer than non-care-giving parents.[31]

∞ Peace of Mind: Despite the old joke that insanity is hereditary (you get it from your kids), raising children is actually very good for our mental health and stability. Shouldering responsibility is an effective antidote for depression. Parenting turns our focus off ourselves and onto others, thus providing a higher purpose for living.

∞ Youthful Beauty: In enumerating the benefits to having lots of children, Mary Pride writes, "While other women are having hot flashes and growing moustaches and experiencing all the other delightful effects of early menopause, you will sail serenely along with your youthful complexion (although maybe not a youthful waistline!)."[32] Perhaps that explains why it's so hard to differentiate mothers from daughters in all those portraits of large families we see in home schooling magazines.

∞ Happy Homes: Seeing the world through the eyes of a child not only keeps you young, but fills your home with a sense of wonder, excitement, and awe over each new discovery. Something about the energy and enthusiasm of children is contagious, and their presence infuses a home with love and joy and happiness.

∞ Better Sleep: Okay, okay—so having kids probably means you sleep *less*, not more. But, hey! Nine out of ten ain't bad!

∞ Spontaneous Lovemaking: Being open to pregnancy frees a couple to have sex virtually whenever, wherever they want. No frantic search for a misplaced diaphragm when hubby makes his move in the shower. No mad dash to the drugstore when you forget to pack the condoms for your camping trip. And no need to compensate for the fact that the Pill reduces a woman's already flagging libido[33] even further.

∞ Marital Stability: Having babies—and lots of them—is protective of your marriage. Each child a couple has reduces their risk of divorce by 20 percent.[34] Sociologists tell us "the strongest predictor of marital stability is the presence of small children in the home."[35] Also, the older a couple is when their last child leaves home, the better chance their marriage will survive. "The 20-year marriage is more vulnerable to the disruptive effects of the empty nest syndrome than the 30-year marriage."[36]

∞ Social Security: Contrary to what "Zero Population Growth" proponents will tell you, demographic declines cause deeply troubling problems for societies world-wide. "Having fewer people can wreak havoc on an economy, creating both a labor shortage and a shortage of buyers," notes Gene Edward Veith in a *World Magazine* article entitled "Population Implosion."[37] That's why some countries, like Germany, are paying couples to procreate.[38] "A government with a shrinking population faces a small military and fewer taxpayers. Dwindling populations have always signaled cultural decline, with less creativity, energy, vitality on every level of society."[39]

∞ Experience and Expertise: Having a family broadens our circle of influence. Raising children "adds immensely to the contribution [a couple is] able to make later in life in the workplace, the church, and the community," note Steve and Candice Watters. "It's the stuff of parenting that directs and motivates their productivity, and in many cases, it's the catalyst that gives them something significant to contribute."[40]

This last point—the idea that the attitudes we hold toward sex and family have a significant effect on our scope of influence—is one that deserves more discussion. In chapter 11 we will look at how "loving your husband physically" lends credibility to your testimony, especially as viewed by those who know you best: your kids. But if your home is to ever be the beacon of light that God intends, your marriage must not only *survive*, it must *thrive*. And, as we will see in the following chapter, sex can help it do just that.

Chapter 10
A Firm Foundation

"For no one can lay any foundation
other than the one already laid, which is Jesus Christ."
1 Corinthians 3:11 (NIV)

Few things do more for the curb appeal of a house than good landscaping. Have you ever noticed that? You can take a run-down little shanty, surround it with a well-manicured lawn, some neatly trimmed shrubs, maybe a few terra cotta pots brimming with geraniums, and it is miraculously transformed into something truly charming. Add a wisteria vine to shade the porch and a bright bed of day lilies, and folks won't even notice that the paint is peeling and the front steps sag.

Conversely, let the grounds go to pot around some stately mansion, and it won't look so stately anymore. Without plentiful water and vigilant care, the lush grass will give way to patches of dusty, bare earth, the fragrant flowers will wither and die, and unsightly weeds will choke out everything else. When a tangled hedge hides the windows and brambles bar the path to the front door, a home that once seemed warm and inviting begins to look inhospitable and foreboding.

Eventually, such neglect starts to affect the house itself. Mortar crumbles where clinging vines stray from their trellises, cracks appear on walls and ceiling as soil washes out from under the foundation, fallen limbs and dead branches damage the roof, granting easy access to rodents and rainwater to wreak further havoc inside.

You see, good landscaping is vitally important for a house's well-being. It does much more than make a home look pretty—it helps to keep it structurally sound. The shrubs and trees planted right next to the walls of a house actually serve to hold the dirt in place, thus guarding against erosion. Professional landscape designers even refer to such elements as "foundation plantings" and are careful to choose hearty specimens that add beauty to a home while simultaneously affording protection to its underpinnings.

Sex Beautifies and Protects

Sex does exactly the same thing for a marriage that landscaping does for a house. It serves to beautify your relationship to your husband, but just as importantly, it protects the very foundation of your marriage. Think about that next time you admire a beautiful yard in your neighborhood or spend the afternoon puttering around in your own flowerbeds. "God intended the union of man and wife to be inexpressibly sweet, satisfying beyond words," author Elizabeth Handford reminds us, "But the entering into that garden of mystery and wonder is through the door of a wife's submission. There is great joy beyond that gate! For your own sake, enter in."[1]

Sex makes a marriage all the more lovely. It takes what is already wonderful—the affection shared by a husband and wife—and adorns it and enhances it and transforms it into something that is truly sublime. Psychologist Kevin Leman observes:

> You can be married without having any sex at all. You can still talk over dinner, celebrate the holidays, and—if you adopt—raise children. You can buy each other anniversary gifts, share intimate conversations, and even, in an emergency, share

toothbrushes or bring an urgently needed roll of toilet paper.

But something would be missing.

A good sex life colors your marriage from top to bottom. It takes the humdrum and boring out of all the daily things you do for each other.

Think about it: 90 percent of life is filled with mostly boring stuff, like changing dirty diapers, cleaning up countless spills, paying the bills, filling the gas tank....

Into the world of obligation and responsibility, God has dropped something absolutely fabulous into our laps. At the end of the day—and sometimes at the beginning—when our work is done and the kids are in bed and we're home from work, we can touch each other and kiss each other and pleasure each other in such a way that the world feels like it is light-years away. We're transported to another place and removed to another time, and it's a glorious feeling indeed.[2]

This is not to imply that the physical element is what a couple's relationship should be *based* on. A marriage, like life in general, should be built upon the Lord Jesus Christ if we expect it to endure. "For no other foundation can be laid, which is Jesus Christ" (1 Cor. 3:11). Nevertheless, sex does play a vital role in safeguarding the integrity of a husband and wife's commitment to one another, and we would all do well to keep that in mind. Sex not only beautifies, it also protects.

Physical intimacy "promotes marital harmony. The stresses and strains become more manageable when a couple is having sex regularly."[3] In fact, an active sex life at home serves to significantly reduce, if not completely eliminate, one of the most onerous tasks any husband must face—that of keeping his heart and mind pure despite the countless snares the Enemy has laid for him in our sex-obsessed culture.

In his book, *Better Love Now*, pastor Tommy Nelson reminds us "Satan knows when there is a sexual problem in a relationship, and he knows how to make the most of it."[4] He continues:

> "How can you avoid an affair? ...Have good sex. Especially for men, having good sex pretty much takes the excitement out of the thought of an affair. Most men are not looking for a bikini model and exotic lovemaking; they just want to have passionate and fulfilling sex. Make this a regular part of your marriage, and you will go a long way toward preventing an affair."[5]

Helping couples avoid temptation was undoubtedly one of the goals Paul had in mind when he penned First Corinthians, declaring that a husband's body was not his own but belonged to his wife, and vise versa. Even if a couple should decide to refrain from sex for the purpose of devoting themselves to prayer, the verses that follow caution them to keep such periods of abstinence brief, "so that Satan will not tempt you because of your lack of self-control" (1 Cor. 7:5).

Theologian Adam Clarke expounds upon this same passage:

> Some have rendered the words ["render due benevolence"], not inaptly, the matrimonial debt, or conjugal duty—that which a wife owes to her husband, and the husband to his wife; and which they must take care mutually to render, else alienation of affection will be the infallible consequence, and this in numberless instances has led to adulterous connections. In such cases the wife has to blame herself for the infidelity of her husband, and the husband for that of his wife. What miserable work has

been made in the peace of families by a wife or a husband pretending to be wiser than the apostle, and too holy and spiritual to keep the commandments of God![6]

Solomon addresses the topic of marital intimacy in the book of Proverbs, where husbands are commanded to "rejoice in the wife of your youth. As a loving hind and a graceful doe, let her breasts satisfy you at all times; be exhilarated always with her love. For why should you, my son, be exhilarated with an adulteress and embrace the bosom of a foreigner?" (Prov. 5:18-20). Note that the word translated *satisfy* here literally means to be *satiated*. "In other words, the husband is so satisfied with [his wife's] love that no one else would even get a second glance from him."[7] Of course, it is well nigh impossible for a husband to "embrace the bosom" of his wife and to "let her breasts satisfy [him]," if every time he approaches her, she slaps him away. Such a reaction is dishonoring and disheartening to a husband, and selfish and shortsighted of the wife.

In a book Vicki Farris co-authored with her daughter, *A Mom Just Like You*, we are reminded that:

> Sexual intimacy is a precious gift from God, and it sets the marriage relationship apart in its complete unity and openness. Of all God's precious gifts, this is the one your husband can legitimately share with no human being on earth besides you. Of all your husband's needs, this is the one that only you have the right and privilege to meet. Furthermore, of all his needs, this is the one that should never be set aside. There are too many women out there who are willing to pick up your slack, and even godly Christian men can fall. You can be a very effective antidote to temptation, and I guarantee your husband will appreciate it tremendously, if you show interest in

him physically and delight in your physical relationship with him.[8]

If more wives lived by this principle, our marriages would be much stronger, our families much healthier, and our homes much happier. In fact, society in general would benefit immensely if unmarried women would stop saying yes to sex with their boyfriends, and married women would stop saying no to sex with their husbands. Single guys might not favor such a change in the status quo, but married men would undoubtedly consider it a vast improvement. "One of the most loving and holy things you can do in marriage is to pursue your husband sexually.... Want a husband who goes to sleep with a smile on his face, thinking, *I've got to be the happiest guy in the world?* ...Then learn to be an extravagant lover. It will set your marriage and his satisfaction in cement."[9]

One-Track Mind

That last quote is from Kevin Leman's *7 Things He'll Never Tell You.* On the back cover of this book there appears a short quiz, the final question of which is:

How often does a man think about sex?
    A. As much as you
    B. 10 times as much as you
    C. 33 times as much as you
    D. Every day but April 15
    E. Only on days that end in the letter Y.

According to Dr. Leman, the correct answer is (C).[10] I'm not sure where he got his information, but the actual numbers may be much higher than that.

For years, I've likened a man's drive for sex to his need for food. Your husband's desire for sexual intimacy is as legitimate and God-given as his physical hunger, I tell wives.

You wouldn't dream of suggesting that he just wait for the weekend to *eat*. Why starve him sexually? But Mike Farris, president of Patrick Henry College and father of ten, goes even further. He insists, "For men, sex is like breathing."[11] When I first saw this quote I thought it a gross exaggeration, but when I showed it to my husband he assured me Farris had not overstated the case at all.

And perhaps he hadn't.

According to a study cited by Louann Brizendine in *The Female Brain*, "85 percent of twenty- to thirty-year old males think about sex every fifty-two seconds."[12] *Every fifty-two seconds?* How is that even possible?

Perhaps the extreme frequency with which men think about sex has something to do with the fact that, "for most of their adulthood, [men] produce ten to one hundred times as much testosterone [the sex-drive hormone] as females do."[13] That much testosterone is hard to ignore, as Dr. James Dobson explains in *What Wives Wish Their Husbands Knew About Women*:

> When sexual response is blocked, males experience an *accumulating* physiological pressure which demands release. Two seminal vesicles (small sacs containing semen) gradually fill to capacity; as maximum level is reached, hormonal influences sensitize the man to all sexual stimuli. Whereas a particular woman would be of little interest to him when he is satisfied, he may be eroticized just to be in her presence when he is in a state of deprivation. A wife may find it difficult to comprehend this accumulating aspect of her husband's sexual appetite, since her needs are typically less urgent and pressing. Thus, she should recognize that his desire is dictated by definite biochemical forces within his body, and if she loves him, she will seek to satisfy those needs as meaningfully and as regularly as possible.[14]

Dobson is correct in noting that a woman's drive is "typically less urgent." In contrast to the once-a-minute rate at which sex enters a man's mind, most women think about sex only once a day[15]—and I suspect for many of them that single thought revolves around, "How am I going to talk him out of it *tonight?*"

I've heard it said that if God had given women the same sex drive as men, none of us would ever get anything accomplished. But if He'd given men the same sex drive as women, the human race would have died out long ago. Why the discrepancy? Is this God's idea of a practical joke? No, I believe He wired us this way to provide balance, and to give both husbands and wives the recurrent opportunity to think of the other first.

The Bible tells us, "Do not merely look out for your own personal interests, but also for the interests of others" (Phil. 2:4). Note that this verse says, essentially, "Consider others." It does not say, "Make sure others consider you." Wife, it is not your responsibility to demand that your husband meets your needs. Put him first, and don't worry if that seems unfair. "Give, and it will be given to you... good measure—pressed down, shaken together, and running over. For by your standard of measure it will be measured to you in return" (Luke 6:38). God is fully capable of teaching your husband to reciprocate without any help from you, save the shining example that your own loving behavior toward him provides.

"Does that mean that I'm expected to have sex, even when I'm not in the mood, just because *he* wants it?" This was a question Laura Schlessinger once fielded on her popular radio program. Her reply to this caller was laudable: "I took a deep breath and answered, 'Most of the time, yes.' She was horrified and likened my response to a call for some form of slavery. I reminded her that she expected [her husband] to go to work and earn money to support the family even on days he didn't feel like it."[16]

Remember in chapter five when I talked about nursing my newborns on demand? Don't you think that there are times when the baby wakes up hungry at two in the morning that I wish I could just stay asleep?

But I *don't*. I sacrifice my own rest for the baby's sake, because I know I am the only one in the house who can breastfeed him. If I don't do so, he goes hungry.

In the same way, I'm the only one in the house—yea, the only one in the *world*—who can rightfully make love to my husband. What message would I send to *him* if I persistently claimed to be too tired for sex? How is it, he would wonder, that I can repeatedly drag myself out of bed, exhausted, at obscene hours of the morning to tend to the needs of my baby, but cannot spare even fifteen minutes for my husband?

How, indeed!

Another of Schlessinger's listeners offers the following advice by way of compromise:

> If you are not really interested in having sex at a certain time but your husband is, say something to the effect of, "Come on, big guy. Show me what you got. Let's do it just for you." Then tell him to skip the foreplay on you and just do his thing. Be extra enthusiastic and active…. You might even find that you yourself are more interested in having an orgasm than you thought!
>
> But remember, do it with enthusiasm…. What's worse than rejection is a begrudged spreading of the legs so [you] can get it over with and go to sleep. How is a man supposed to feel like he is pleasuring his wife with an attitude like that? The most pleasure a man can get from sex is to know he is pleasing his wife.[17]

Does this sound distasteful to you? Too much of a hassle? Then know this: If you are not willing to so minister to your husband's needs, then your refusal betrays a woeful lack of love for him. Moreover, you are in direct disobedience to Scripture. You put your husband in a hopelessly vulnerable position. He is completely at your mercy. Either you gratify his God-given appetite for sex, or you force him to do without completely. There is no middle ground. If he attempts to find release apart from sexual union with his wife, he is in sin. This is by no means justification for a man to give in to temptation—and he must one-day answer to God for any moral failings in this area—but a frigid wife who callously chooses to ignore his plight is by no means blameless in such a situation.

Women seem to have a double standard when it comes to hormones. They use "PMS" as an excuse for everything from exhibiting a permanently crabby attitude to committing premeditated murder. Many a wife expects her husband to make all sorts of allowances for fluctuations in *her* hormones—he must walk gingerly around on eggshells for weeks at a time—yet she shows no sympathy whatsoever for the anguish that her husband's hormones can cause *him*.

Husbands and wives have an equal right to sex within marriage (see 1 Cor. 7:3), but they seldom share an equal desire to exercise that right. More often than not, one partner (guess which?) has a significantly stronger drive than the other. This difference in drives can create a difference in perspectives, like the couple who went in for marriage counseling and was asked about their sex life. The husband blurted out in frustration, "We almost *never* have sex—only two or three times a week!" at the same instant his wife replied, "We have sex *all the time*—at least two or three times a week!"[18]

I am convinced that a marriage fares better when a couple defers to the stronger drive in determining their frequency of lovemaking. In the vast majority of cases, that stronger drive belongs to the husband. This intense appetite for sex is the most driving force in a man's psyche. For many, it becomes an Achilles heel, and wives who deny it place a stumbling block in their husband's path.

The Bible tells us, "Greater love has no one than this, that one lay down his life for his friends" (John 15:13). Well, guess what? Your husband is not asking you to lay down *your life.* He simply wants you to lay down the newspaper, the dustpan, the craft project, the telephone, the grocery list. Basically, he just wants you to *lay down,* period—at least long enough to give *him* a little attention.[19] It won't kill you to help him out. It's the loving thing to do.

Make no mistake: God expects your husband to keep his vows and to remain faithful to you for better or worse, come what may. Ideally, his sense of honor and duty should keep him committed. But don't you want to make it as easy on him as possible? Wouldn't you like for him to count marriage to you an absolute *joy?* Then you must come to grips with the fact that sex is not just something that your *husband* asks of you. It is something *God* requires of you (1 Cor. 7:5). God expects this. He *commands* it—whether you love your husband or not, whether you're in a good mood or not, whether you are busy or tired or distracted or just want to sleep. And you should *want* to have sex with your husband, if for no other reason than to fulfill your duty before God, out of love and obedience to *Him,* as your reasonable service of worship.

It is not enough just to *know* these things; you must act on that knowledge. It is not enough to simply *believe;* you must also obey.

Therefore everyone who hears these words of [Jesus] *and acts on them,* may be compared to a wise man who built his house on the rock. And the rain fell, and the floods came, and the winds blew and slammed against that house; and yet it did not fall, for it had been founded on the rock. Everyone who hears these words of [Jesus] *and does not act on them*, will be like a foolish man who built his house on the sand. The rain fell, and the floods came, and the winds blew and slammed against that house; and it fell—and great was its fall (Matt. 7:24-27, *emphasis added*).

Flood Waters Rising

Jesus instructed us to pray, "Lead us not into temptation…" (Matt. 6:13). Yet leading their husbands into temptation is precisely what countless wives do when they marginalize their husbands' needs in this area. A wife's indifference can spell disaster. She must adjust her mindset if she hopes to preserve her marriage:

> A man's sex drive… is a powerful force. It can change a normal, intelligent, moral man into a misguided fool. This drive causes upstanding businessmen, politicians, church leaders, and others to throw away their reputations, careers and marriages for a sexual relationship. It is as if their minds turn to mush. This is not an excuse for adultery. Not every man gives into his flesh. Many men stick to their convictions about marriage, but not every man does.
>
> Some women make the mistake of living in denial about their husbands' sexual vulnerability. They naively think, "My husband would never have an affair. He wouldn't do that to me." We all hope that. Yet there are no guarantees. Avoiding denial sounds like this, "I know my husband likes sex, and I do not want him to be tempted to have an affair. What can I do to help prevent the situation?"[20]

When a man's sexual needs are not met, he "begins to look at his wife as just a roommate who doesn't pay her share of the rent but continues to harp on him about leaving the toilet seat up."[21] But a wife's neglect does more than just irritate her husband. It leaves him exposed to temptation, as outlined in the acronym HALT (Hungry, Angry, Lonely, Tired):

> If a man is working long hours, is out of sorts with the world (or his spouse), feels unappreciated, feels like a failure as a provider, or is far from home on a business trip—if he is hungry, angry, lonely, or tired—any or all of those things could weaken his resolve. If you've ever found yourself eating the entire box of cookies when you feel unhappy, you can probably understand this dynamic.[22]

One husband's confession holds true for many men: "When we're not at peace, when we aren't content, when we aren't in a good place, our radar gets turned on. We're looking. Searching. And we're sensory creatures, so it won't be long before something, or somebody, catches our attention."[23]

So we must remain on guard. Building a strong marriage is spiritual warfare, and a good sex life is one of the most powerful weapons in our arsenal.[24]

> [W]e are kidding ourselves if we don't recognize that our failure to meet the needs of our spouses places extra pressure on them and decreases their ability to resist temptation.... A husband and wife give Satan a foothold in their marriage when they do not discover how to meet each other's needs.[25]

You will never have the solid, fulfilling marriage God intends as long as the area of physical intimacy is neglected. When a wife deliberately and habitually withholds sex from her husband, whether out of disinterest, time pressures, spite, or retribution, she tears down her house with her own two hands (Prov. 14:1). You may as well dig giant holes beneath the foundation and invite the enemy to destroy your marriage from within.

Did you know that much of New Orleans was built *below sea level*? This feat was made possible by a series of pumps and levees designed to hold the waters at bay and thus protect the city. The system worked fairly well until Hurricane Katrina struck in 2005, forcing multiple breaks in this wall. Our family toured the Ninth Ward three years after the storm hit, and the desolation was still palpable. Unquestionably, it was the levee failure that caused the most devastating loss of life and property.

But you don't need a grand scale catastrophe to have a real mess on your hands.

Our next-door neighbors recently tried to divert some water on their land to create a little brook running alongside the crushed-granite nature path that meandered through their woods. The effect was charming. We could imagine the carefree days their sons would spend frolicking in dappled sunlight under a canopy of oaks and maples, hunting frogs and turtles in that quaint woodland stream, dipping their toes in its refreshing coolness. The rivulet was narrow enough that they could jump across and shallow enough that they'd barely wet their ankles if they waded right down the middle. It painted a lovely scene.

But then it rained.

Overnight, this small trickle of a stream was transformed into a gigantic gorge. Dozens of towering trees toppled into the trench as the earth washed out beneath them. Subsequent storms exacerbated the problem. It took thousands of dollars and a team of arborists, geologists, and engineers to finally get the situation under control. Even then, there was no undoing the damage. Those trees were still missing. The chasm remained. Our neighbors were wishing they'd left well enough alone and never attempted to redirect the water in the first place.

Referring to physical love, Solomon instructs husbands to "drink water from your own cistern and fresh water from your own well. Should your springs be dispersed abroad, streams of water in the streets? Let them be yours alone and not for strangers with you" (Prov. 5:15-17). God in His wisdom designed marriage to be a reservoir into which a husband can pour his sexual energy. When a wife allows that current to run strong and deep, she strengthens the embankment that channels its flow.

When she tries to keep it from pursuing its natural, God-given course, however, she risks doing irreparable damage. Countless homes have been destroyed and families shattered by wives who attempt to divert or cap or ignore this stream. Don't send your husband to sulk in the shower. Don't abandon him to his computer or cable television. Sin is crouching at his door, but with your help he can master it.

We must "be on the alert. [Our] adversary, the devil, prowls around like a roaring lion, seeking someone to devour" (1 Peter 5:8-9). We must work incessantly to preserve and protect our marriage, for we can be sure that Satan is working relentlessly to destroy it. Think of all the snares your husband must avoid every day: Billboards. Magazines. Lingerie ads. Provocatively dressed co-workers. The Internet. He daily walks through a battle zone with landmines buried at every turn. Do you want to send him out the door of your home weak and exposed, vulnerable to attack? Or completely satisfied, shielded from those fiery darts?

Spiritual Warfare

Every time you have sex with your husband, you are reinforcing the foundation of your home, testing the stability of your marriage, inspecting your relationship for unseen damage. But at the same time, you are buckling on your husband's armor, girding him up, shielding, strengthening, and protecting him. That is why tending to his sexual needs is, I think, the single most important thing a wife can do for her husband.

I know what some of you are thinking. *No way. That can't be right. The most important thing a wife does for her husband is to pray for him.*

I am in no way trying to diminish the power of prayer. I agree that prayer is vitally important for a strong, healthy marriage. But think about it this way: your husband's *mother* can pray for him. His *children* can pray for him. His pastor, his neighbors, and his co-workers can all fall on their knees before the throne of grace daily on his behalf. But *who* will have sex with him, if not you?

God promises to supply *all* our needs (Phil. 4:19). He made provision for your husband's sexual needs by giving him a wife—YOU. "He who finds a wife finds a good thing, and obtains favor from the Lord" (Prov. 18:22). Will you now make God out to be a liar, by refusing to cooperate with His design for physical unity in marriage?

Besides, sex and prayer are *not* mutually exclusive. There is no law against praying for your husband, even while you're making love to him. It's entirely possible to do both things at once. Can you think of a more fitting time, when your attention is so completely focused on this wonderful guy you married, to thank the Lord for all those things you admire most about your mate? To ask God to richly bless all his endeavors? To pray for his health, his hopes, his walk, his witness? To implore God to pour His grace upon your family? To entreat Him to mold your marriage into something that would shine brightly for His glory? Can you imagine how such a combination of physical love and spiritual warfare could completely transform your attitude? Your marriage? Your mate? Your *life*?

I know you're busy. I know your responsibilities pull you in a dozen different directions. But don't give into the tyranny of the urgent. Don't get duped into thinking that cooking meals or doing laundry is a more pressing need than lovemaking. Just slide dinner into a crock-pot and toss a load of dirty clothes in the washing machine before heading to the bedroom. You can kill several birds with one stone. That is multi-tasking at its best. What husband wouldn't appreciate a wife who can accomplish so much, and still make sex a priority?

Cultivate Love

As I sit writing this chapter, spring has blossomed in all her glory. The dogwoods and azaleas are in full bloom, a sight to behold. The sun is peeking out from behind scattered clouds after several days of rain, and everything looks fresh, verdant, and *alive*. Here in East Texas, we are blessed with a rich, sandy loam that will grow just about anything. I can literally bury my arm up to my elbow in the soft earth. Even with minimal effort, an average gardener can achieve spectacular results.

But we haven't always lived in Tyler with its fertile soil. The first part of our married life was spent in Dallas. No sandy loam there. Our house and all the houses around it were built on hard black clay. It took a considerable amount of work to even *plant* anything in that unyielding ground, let alone get it to *grow*. I remember struggling to bury over two hundred tulips one year. By the time I'd attained the required seven-inch depth, it felt like I'd dug to China—and only six of the bulbs ever bloomed!

Foundation plantings are of extreme importance even with this kind of ground, not so much to hold the dirt in place—that clay's not going *anywhere*—but to help trap water. Otherwise, the mud gradually bakes and cracks in the sun, the ground shrinks, the slab shifts, the doors and windows stick fast, and telltale fault lines creep up the walls and across the ceiling. Then you have to dig down to bedrock and jack up the foundation to keep the house from sliding into the street.

Interestingly, Doug and I found that having to toil and sweat to achieve the results we desired helped us to appreciate them all the more. Trial and error taught us which methods worked and which didn't. For starters, we learned that faithful watering makes a *huge* difference. We found which fertilizer yielded the most favorable results. And we discovered that timing is everything when it comes to pruning or trimming flowering trees and shrubs. By the time we sold that house, we had the greenest, most luxuriant lawn on the block, our impatiens were thigh-high and loaded with blooms, and our pecan tree was producing bumper crops. It took a load of effort, but it was extremely satisfying to see it pay off.

When it comes to cultivating love, some couples have an easier time than others. Like growing things in sandy loam, nurturing a fulfilling sex life seems almost effortless when a couple is blessed with good health, high salaries, loads of free time, and few worries. But such is rarely the case.

Most couples must consciously commit to making physical intimacy a priority in their marriage. This was certainly true of us when we lived in Dallas. Doug worked as many as three jobs at a time while going to school. He fought traffic for an hour or two every day, to be welcomed home by a passel of young children who required constant supervision and an exhausted wife who desperately needed a nap. Finances forced us to clip coupons, shop thrift stores, and tackle plumbing problems ourselves (a "How To" book from the library in hand). That was a busy, busy, physically demanding, emotionally draining season of our lives. Conserving enough energy for sex required some serious forethought, but we managed and are grateful we did.

You may find that, like gardening in black clay, carving out time together amid all your other responsibilities presents a daunting challenge. Let me encourage you that the benefits to your marriage are worth the extra effort. Don't wait for your circumstances to improve before you begin to nourish your relationship to your husband by making sex a priority. If you wait until things are better before you obey the injunctions of Scripture, you may wait forever. Satan will do everything in his power to ensure things *don't* improve. So consciously commit to set aside time for one another *today*, and stick with the decision.

Cultivate love. Faithfully sprinkle your sex life with prayer, and see if God doesn't bless you with a bumper crop in the end!

Chapter 11
A Tried and True Testimony

*"Concerning these things I want you to speak confidently,
so that those who have believed God
will be careful to engage in good deeds."*
Titus 3:8

I am sure that if anyone had told my mother during my adolescence that I would grow up to write a book extolling the virtues of sex,[1] she would have had a hard time believing it (in the same way she would have doubted that anybody whose closet looked like mine could ever maintain an orderly home). Back then, I would flee the room at the very mention of birds or bees or (*gasp!*) boobs. Everything I knew about sex, I learned by looking up words in the dictionary (which, as you might imagine, left huge gaps in my understanding) and by listening through the keyhole while my mother explained things to my younger sister, who was always much bolder about asking questions and not so easily embarrassed by the answers. I think Mom must have suspected she had a hidden audience during those heart-to-hearts, for she always spoke so slowly and clearly that I seldom missed a word of the conversation.

The only time I remember my *father* ever mentioning sex was when he made an offhand remark that the good Lord *could* have designed people to reproduce like paramecia (asexually), but "it would not have been *nearly so much fun.*"

I was about ten years old at the time. The comment puzzled me, and I noticed my mother blush when he said it.

This is not to imply that Dad never talked about *intercourse*. He used *that* word a lot. He would say things like, "I overheard some interesting *intercourse* down at the coffee shop this morning." Such statements sent me searching for the dictionary again in a hurry. I assume he intended the first definition (conversation), but the second meaning (sexual intercourse) was circular and vague and served only to compound my confusion.

I promised myself that once I reached adulthood, I would neither humiliate nor bewilder my children by using the word *intercourse* to refer to everyday conversations. Nevertheless, despite my best efforts, I have managed to find plenty of other ways to embarrass my kids. I have one son, in fact, who shudders to hear me use the word "visit," in much the same way as I cringed to hear my father speak of "intercourse". It came from years of creeping out of bed at night to beg for one more drink of water, only to be commanded from behind locked doors to "Go back to bed! Mom and Dad are trying to *visit!*" Having caught on early to our intended meaning, this child was mortified whenever he heard me use the word *visit* in a different context, such as "I'm running next door to visit the neighbors" or "Nana and Papa are planning to visit this weekend."

Little Pitchers Have Big Ears

Little House fans will recognize that saying—"Little pitchers have big ears"—as a favorite in the Ingalls household. It means, simply, that children hear and understand more than we give them credit for. Caroline often reminded Charles of this fact.

Whether you realize it or not, the level of sexual intimacy you share (or don't share) with your husband will have a profound effect upon your children's attitudes toward sex. When you as a wife make this aspect of your marriage a priority, your children will eventually come to recognize it. The day will come when they will figure out what is going on behind that locked door. For all the eye rolling that goes on in our household when my husband and I tell the kids, "We'll be in our bedroom. Don't disturb us unless it's an emergency," there isn't one of them who does not hope to someday enjoy the same kind of marriage that their parents share. They understand "that sex is not an optional thing for a marriage, something couples can take or leave. [They know that the] sexual bond is central to what it means to be married."[2] They understand, not because we've told them this in so many words, but because we live it out, day after day, week after week, year after year.

So consider: What message is *your* sex life sending to *your* sons and daughters? This is particularly important as our children enter their teen years. Do they consider sex a normal and happy part of married life, well worth the wait? Or are they convinced that they'd better gather the rosebuds while they may, fearing that if they wait until they're married, they'll never see any action at all?

Is Dad frustrated? Is Mom full of excuses? Do not be so naïve as to think the dynamics of your physical relationship to your husband have escaped your teenager's notice. Actions speak louder than words.

Is the idea of having sex with her own husband something your older daughter looks forward to with joyful anticipation or mortal dread? Has life at home convinced your older son that taking on the responsibility for a wife and family is well worth the benefits such a commitment bestows? You would like for your children to stay sexually pure until they marry[3], but does *your* relationship to *your* husband provide them any hope for delayed gratification? "The concept of deferred gratification only works so long as there is the future prospect of gratification," warns Debbie Maken in *Getting Serious About Getting Married*. "What's

the point of waiting for something that may never come? The
sheer hopelessness of seeing that marriage isn't [all it's
cracked up to be] becomes incentive to pursue immediate
gratification."[4]

"It is critical that your words and actions are
consistent with one another," notes Christian author Bob
Barnes. "If you say you love your husband but your actions
suggest otherwise, your children will not hear your words."[5]
But if your kids aren't hearing your words, to whose words
are they listening? If they aren't learning healthy attitudes
toward sex from you, what will shape their understanding?
Every day, the world sends our kids countless messages about
sex, the vast majority of which are dead wrong.

"For all the hype and buildup about sex-God's-way
being the most fulfilling, most of the Christians around me
weren't very convincing," remembers Eric Ludy:

> Other than my parents and a small handful of
> others, most Christian couples I observed as a young
> person didn't hold hands, kiss, smile at each other,
> speak sweetly to each other, or show any
> demonstration of a passionate love and fulfilling sex
> life. Hollywood, on the other hand, made casual, non-
> married sex look fun, romantic, exciting, and
> extremely satisfying. When it came down to the
> question of who was enjoying sex more, the evidence
> was strongly in favor of the just-do-it-right-now
> crowd."[6]

Carol Platt Liebau expounds further upon this
problem in her eye-opening book *Prude*:

> Certainly, there's little in the movies—or on
> television—that would make married sex seem
> appealing.... Given what they're seeing, one can
> hardly blame young people for looking on premarital
> sex with a friendly eye. After all, who wants to abstain

until marriage if married people rarely have sex—and when they do, it's no fun? Little on the screen suggests that married couples can and do have exciting relationships, and that sex can be even more meaningful and enjoyable in wedlock than out of it. Being exposed to these ideas might be healthy for young people, helping them to understand that committed sex is both worth waiting for and wonderful—not just the purview of the old and boring."[7]

"You can't fully and adequately understand God's gift of sex apart from God's gift of marriage," observes Tim Gardner in *Sacred Sex*.[8] Your child's best hope for fully comprehending the depth of love and commitment a great marriage requires is to grow up watching *you* pour that same level of love and commitment into your relationship to your husband. "People often develop patterns of relating as adults that are not so different from how they learned to relate as children. If you grew up in a family in which love, nurturing, and intimacy are in short supply," Dean Ornish warns in *Love & Survival*, "then you are more likely to view your current relationships with mistrust and suspicion. If your family experiences were filled with love and caring, then you are more likely to be open and trusting in your ongoing relationships."[9]

Our lives may be the only book our kids ever read about marriage and family and how both should function. We must make it count. The years we have with our children at home are a golden opportunity to build into them the godly ideals and strength of character they will need when they establish homes of their own someday—which is an undertaking they may tackle sooner than we expect.

They won't adopt views and virtues they've not seen modeled; our commitment must be steadfast and our love without hypocrisy. As George Barna notes in his book

Revolutionary Parenting, "The amount of time spent together, the variety of situations they experience, and the way in which children can grasp the context of their parents' behavior make the mother and father the ultimate living examples of what godliness looks like in real time."[10]

Extending Our Reach

Christian marriages should be the *example* to the rest of the world," admonishes Leslie Ludy in *Set-Apart Femininity*, "demonstrating that following God's ways brings abundant life, joy, peace, and supernatural victory."[11] *Abundant life*. Isn't that a fitting description of the blessing that comes from fully embracing God's purpose for passion in marriage? That kind of commitment and communion affects everything else a couple does and makes the depth of their love for one another obvious to all who know them.

Children aren't the only ones who observe their parents' interactions. Extended family, friends, neighbors, and coworkers have an eye on your marriage as well, straining to see if the love you profess is genuine, if the bond you share is as unbreakable as you'd like them to think. "Your relationship to your husband is the single most important role you will ever play," writes Debi Pearl in *Created To Be His Help Meet*. "If you fail here, then you have failed at your life's work and have missed God's perfect plan."[12]

"Marriage is a rigged institution," warns pastor Tommy Nelson. "Only the holy survive.... If you try to just get by, you will eventually find yourself in a big mess. Only the standard of Christ is big enough to see you through." If you're determined to live a selfish life, then you'd better avoid marriage altogether, for "God made it ruthlessly perfect for helping us learn to lay down our lives for Christ and our mates."[13]

Our success in marriage depends on our unwavering commitment to live by the principles God has set forth in His Word. Until we learn to cooperate with His plan, we will never experience the matrimonial bliss our hearts so deeply desire. The Bible charges older women to teach the younger women to love their husbands (Titus 2:4), but how can we do this, if we've not first mastered the art of loving our own husbands? If what we have is not working, we needn't export it. It is only by God's grace that we can develop the deep, self-sacrificing love for our husbands that will carry us through, strengthening our marriages, enriching our homes, reassuring our children, and qualifying us for service and ministry. Once a woman learns such love, "Her children rise up and call her blessed; her husband also, and he praises her, saying: 'Many daughters have done nobly, but you excel them all'" (Prov. 31:28-29 NKJV).

More to Life

Marilyn Monroe once said of her failed marriage to Joe DiMaggio, "If marriage were only bed, we could have it made."[14] Sex may be a suitable starting point for experiencing oneness within marriage, but we can't stop there. "No couple can enjoy a mutually fulfilling sexual connection if other significant issues are being ignored."[15]

Ideally, sex should set off a self-perpetuating cycle: "Having been joined by the oneness of intercourse, that union should affect every other part of our relationship," writes Tim Gardner in *Sacred Sex.*

Being unified in all areas of marriage—feeling cherished, valued, respected, and cared for—creates within us a desire to become one with our mates again through sex. Sex creates oneness, and oneness fosters a climate that naturally leads to more and better sex.[16]

Danielle Crittenden uses a beautiful analogy to describe this kind of union. She says that a man and wife who honor their marriage vows, remaining committed to one another through thick and thin, stand "a better chance of growing old together; they become bound and entwined with the other like the sturdy, thick vines of wisteria, clambering up the same wall. Over time, the two souls blur together; it becomes hard to judge where she ends and he begins." Crittenden admits this may be "a terrifying thought for a feminist, perhaps, but [it is] the essence of enduring, romantic love."[17]

Doesn't that fragrant, intertwining vine imagery paint a beautiful picture? Isn't such oneness in marriage worth all the patience and work and sacrifice and putting of the other first? Is that the sort of rapport people see when they look at *your* marriage? Does your marriage exemplify the kind of relationship you would wish for your children? If not, will you commit afresh to making your marriage the union God intends it to be? In the next section, we will examine what you can do, beyond meeting your husband's physical needs, to begin building a God-honoring, soul-satisfying marriage *today*.

PART TWO
Love Him Unconditionally

Chapter 12
The State of a Union

*"...make my joy complete by being of the same mind,
maintaining the same love,
united in spirit, intent on one purpose."*
Philippians 2:2

The year was 210 BC. The setting was the eastern coast of China, on the eve of the Battle of Julu. After crossing over the Yangtze River, the Chu rebels bedded down for the night, hoping to store up strength for their planned attack on the Qin dynasty the following day. As they slept, their commanding officer, a Chinese general by the name of Xiang Yu, took measures to ensure his soldiers would not retreat even when the fighting grew fierce: He set fire to his own fleet, sinking every last ship. He also destroyed their cooking supplies, so that if his men wished to eat, they must first force their way into their enemy's larder. His tactic worked. The Chu forces fought ferociously and won nine consecutive battles.[1] What choice did they have? If they didn't press on, if they didn't persevere, if they didn't remain fully committed to the cause, they would without question be defeated. They must do or die.

Pulling Together

As important as physical love is, it takes much more than great sex to keep a marriage together. It also takes *commitment*—something that is sorely lacking in many marriages today. There was a time when "until death do us part" meant exactly that. All or nothing. Do or die. Husbands and wives pledged to remain true one to another for better or worse, richer or poorer, in sickness and health, as long as there was life within them. Divorce was not an option. If golden anniversaries were rare, it was because a spouse's health did not hold out, not because the marriage had failed. Husbands had integrity. Wives were devoted. Both pulled together to *make* the marriage work. They kept their promises. They honored their vows. They understood marriage "is about more than signing a lease, splitting bills, sharing chores, and professing a vague sort of long-term commitment;" they knew, as Danielle Crittenden writes in her deeply wise book *What Our Mothers Didn't Tell Us,* that "it's about more, even, than happiness and contentment and compatibility. It is about life and death, blood and sacrifice, about this generation and the next, and one's connection to eternity."[2]

Sadly, this is no longer the case. Many couples these days place so little faith in wedding vows or the motives behind them that they are reluctant to exchange them at all. If and when they do marry, it is not until a legally binding pre-nuptial agreement can be drawn up, signed, and notarized. Such measures remind me of the amiable housekeeper Annie in *It's a Wonderful Life.* Dropping her contribution into the collection basket in George Bailey's living room, Annie cheerfully confides, "I been savin' this money for a divorce, if ever I get a husband." If you have no more confidence your marriage will last than *that*, why even bother?

"Marriage is no marriage at all if it is conditional or partial with the fingers crossed. There must be, on both sides, an uncalculating abandon, a mutual outpouring of love and loyalty."[3] Like the farmer who reconsiders after setting his hand to the plow (Luke 9:62), a couple who enters into marriage with a "try and see" mentality is doomed from the start. Unless we commit to marriage with a dogged determination to persevere whatever betides, we will be unable to maintain the focus and energy and effort necessary to ensure its success.

As Xiang Yu demonstrated when he sank the boats and smashed the pots, we fare better when we decide upfront that running away is not an option. The things that at first glance seem to be most limiting and confining—things like monogamy and commitment and discipline and work—are the very things that bring us the most freedom and joy in the end.[4] Dean Ornish expands upon this thought in *Love and Survival*, noting that a sense of duty can be protective: "It's not without responsibility and obligation and some constraints on people, but it's probably what makes societies tie together... [and] promotes health."[5]

This sharpened sense of responsibility and personal integrity has enabled many a marriage to weather difficult times. As Danielle Crittenden points out,

> A man stays in a marriage not simply because he loves his wife and children, but because he could not respect himself—or expect others to respect him—if he casually up and left, or had an affair, or brought harm to those who so deeply loved and trusted him. Likewise for a woman. She stays in a marriage and takes risks like leaving her job when the babies are born not because she finds changing diapers so intrinsically interesting or doing the laundry so fulfilling but because she feels it is right for her family.[6]

But what happens "if a couple is uncertain that their marriage will last—or even that it's *important* for it to last"?[7] The less confidence a couple has in the stability of their marriage, the less willing they'll be to completely pour themselves into it. Instead of investing all their strength and hope and energy into making the best marriage they possibly can, they must divert at least a portion of their resources toward making contingency plans. The fear that things might not work out can become a self-fulfilling prophecy, because it causes us to hold back, to pull away.[8] Women who seek "to protect themselves within marriage [by taking] an adversarial stance pre-maturely...precipitate trouble [and make] daily interactions extremely unpleasant."[9]

Crittenden comments on this trend in *What Our Mothers Didn't Tell Us*:

> I think it's generally true to say that women—
> no matter how individualist or ambitious they may
> be—still wish to marry men who will remain faithful
> to them, who will be able to support their families,
> who will be responsible and loving fathers, and who
> will stick by their wives into old age. To find
> husbands with such qualities, however, seems vastly
> more difficult than it did a generation ago. This is not
> only because there is less sexual incentive for a man
> to tie himself down to one woman. It's also because—
> as awkward as this may be for women to admit—
> marriage is not as good a deal for men as it used to be.
> A generation of wives whose prime concern in
> marriage is not the care of their families but the
> anxious protection of their autonomy has brought into
> being millions of relationships in which the woman is
> unwilling to do much for the man while expecting
> much in return.[10]

How can we, as wives, ever expect to *become one* with our husband when we are "withholding ourselves, or pieces of ourselves, instead of giving to our marriages wholeheartedly"?[11] Scripture teaches that "there is no fear in love...perfect love casts out fear" (1 John 4:18). If we have reservations, if we don't open up, if we refuse to become vulnerable, then we will never experience the spiritual, physical, and emotional intimacy that God intended for a husband and wife to share.

When a husband and wife pursue individualism rather than intimacy, and sacrifice unity in favor of autonomy, their relationship cannot but suffer as a result. "If good marriages seem more unattainable than ever before, it is because of our determination to remain as separate and distinct individuals within an institution that demands the opposite from us, that insists upon the merging of identity—of both husband and wife—if it is to be sustained."[12]

One of the most poignant parts of Amy Tan's *Joy Luck Club* involved a couple, Lena and Harold, who married but failed to merge. Determined to split everything fifty-fifty, they keep a running tally of expenses taped to their refrigerator. "We've had philosophical arguments," Lena explains, "over [who should pay for] things that have gray borders, like my birth control pills... or food magazines that I subscribe to but he also reads only because he's bored, not because he would have chosen them for himself." Harold expects Lena to pay for half the ice cream, despite the fact she doesn't like ice cream and never eats it, but insists she foot the entire bill for an exterminator to get rid of fleas, because the fleas belong to the cat, and the cat belongs to *her*, never mind that she received it as a birthday gift from *him*.[13] What a wretched existence!

Marriage is not about two separate lives being lived side by side. It is about one life being shared by one couple. Husband and wife become so intertwined that "they are no longer two, but one flesh" (Matt. 19:6). We should not be pulling ourselves back, but pouring ourselves out. "There is something about losing yourself to another and their losing themselves in you at the same time that defies our ability to categorize," notes Rob Bell in *Sex God*. "Healthy marriages all have this sense of mutual abandon to each other. They've both jumped, in essence, into the arms of the other.... If one holds back, if one refrains, it doesn't work."[14]

But when neither holds back, when husband and wife both invest themselves fully and completely, something truly amazing takes place: the two become one. This merging through marriage goes far beyond a sexual joining. Although physical oneness is vitally important to a healthy marriage, it can't stop there. A husband and wife are also to be of one heart and mind, "maintaining the same love, united in spirit, intent on one purpose" (Phil. 2:2). In this way, they model an even deeper and more perfect love; they reveal to a passing world an eternal truth. "When husband and wife are united in marriage, they no longer seem like something earthly, but rather like the image of God Himself."[15]

A Higher Purpose

Have you ever been to a carnival and walked through the Fun House? Remember in the Hall of Mirrors how distorted your reflection looked when viewed through a looking glass that was badly warped? Aren't you glad your head isn't really so gargantuan and your legs aren't quite that short and stubby? Imagine how disheartening it would be if *all* mirrors made us look so ridiculous. Think how helpless we would feel to improve our appearance, if we could never get an accurate view of it.

This is similar to the situation modern society faces with regard to marriage. God intended the love shared by a husband and wife to *mirror* the love that Christ has for the Church—pure, holy, selfless. He "repeatedly draws upon concrete familial relationships and uses them as a framework from which we can understand the permanency of his love for us (Matt. 7:9-11)," notes Debbie Maken in *Getting Serious about Getting Married.* "He loves us as his own dear children, as a husband loves his wife."[16]

Yet, even Christian marriages fall short of reflecting such love accurately. "As we accept the ways in which our culture has cheapened [marriage and family] relationships," Maken warns, "our understanding of God and [of His] love for us can only diminish. What good is the love of a parent who gives up children for her own convenience or a husband who leaves on a whim?"[17] The world is left to wonder if marriage—something God designed and pronounced "very good"—is really worth the effort.

These things ought not be.

From the beginning, God's perfect design for marriage has been made clear. We read in Genesis 2:18 that God declared, "It is not good for the man to be alone" and purposed to make a companion to help and complete him. "So the LORD God caused a deep sleep to fall upon the man, and he slept; then He took one of his ribs and closed up the flesh at that place. The LORD God fashioned into a woman the rib which He had taken from the man, and brought her to the man" (Gen. 2:21-22).

Writing early in the eighteenth century, a Bible scholar named Matthew Henry commented on this passage, and his thoughts have been quoted in wedding ceremonies ever since. He noted, somewhat poetically, that God had fashioned the first woman using a rib out of Adam's side: Eve was "not made out of [Adam's] head to rule over him, nor out of his feet to be trampled upon by him, but out of his side to be equal with him, under his arm to be protected, and near his heart to be beloved."[18] Isn't that a lovely observation?

What a wonderful relationship our first parents must have enjoyed there in the garden, in the very presence of God. Their lives would have been a continual feast had they persisted in this state (see Psalm 128:1-4). But to their everlasting shame, Adam and Eve chose to follow their own way instead of walking in the path God marked for them. They allowed sin to enter in, and with it came deceit and separation and power struggles. In time, the perfect one-man-one-woman-together-for-life model that God established was forsaken, and polygamy, divorce, and remarriage became commonplace.

When questioned about this fact, Jesus explained that such things had come about because of the hardness of man's heart, not because God's initial intent had changed. "Have you not read," Christ asked his examiners, "that He who created them from the beginning made them male and female, and said, 'For this reason a man shall leave his father and mother and be joined to his wife, and the two shall become one flesh'? ... What therefore God has joined together, let no man separate" (Matt. 19:4-7).

Paul expounds upon this union in the book of Ephesians, comparing the marriage relationship to the relationship the Church shares with Jesus:

> Wives, be subject to your own husbands, as to the Lord. For the husband is the head of the wife, as Christ also is the head of the church, He Himself being the Savior of the body. But as the church is subject to Christ, so also the wives ought to be to their husbands in everything.
>
> Husbands, love your wives, just as Christ also loved the church and gave Himself up for her, so that He might sanctify her, having cleansed her by the washing of water with the word, that He might present to Himself the church in all her glory, having no spot or wrinkle or any such thing; but that she would be holy and blameless. So husbands ought also to love their own wives as their own bodies. He who loves his own wife loves himself; for no one ever hated his own flesh, but nourishes and cherishes it, just as Christ also does the church, because we are members of His body.... This mystery is great; but I am speaking with reference to Christ and the church. (Eph. 5:22-32)

"Marriage is the outworking on earth of the picture of this glorious theological truth.... It can only be accomplished by allowing the Holy Spirit to daily have His way in our lives by allowing the fruit of the Holy Spirit—love, joy, peace, long-suffering, gentleness, goodness, faithfulness, meekness, and self-control," writes Nancy Campbell. It is only achieved "by having the same mind that Jesus had, who did not hold on to His own rights, but humbled Himself and became obedient to the death of the cross; by having a tender and soft heart to one another; and by giving up every selfish motive and living only for the other. This is the true picture of marriage."[19]

Candice and Steve Watters address the Ephesians passage in their book, *Start Your Family*. Explaining how their own views on marriage have been refined over the years, they write:

> Paul's letter to the Ephesians... begins: "Be imitators of God, therefore, as dearly loved children and live a life of love, just as Christ loved us and gave himself up for us as a fragrant offering and sacrifice to God" (5:1-2). This passage sets up the verses that follow, the ones that call a wife to respect her husband and submit to him in the way the church submits to Christ; a husband to love his wife as Christ "loved the church and gave himself up for her" (5:22-33); and parents to raise children in the training and instruction of the Lord (6:4).
>
> These verses have tripped people up over the years, especially in cultures sensitive to gender equality. But the foundational context established in Ephesians 5:1 and 2 makes it clear that God isn't calling families to the kind of oppressive domination and doormat submission that some imagine. Instead, couples can find in this almost two-thousand-year-old passage a model for directing their lives, marriage, and family that when applied consistently is more innovative, more effective, and more fulfilling than any other social system the world has attempted.[20]

As Christian couples, *this* is our purpose and calling: to model to the world the unconditional, sacrificial love that Jesus has for us. Perfect love is not selfish; it does not seek its own; it endures all things; it never fails (see 1 Cor. 13).

Where do we find such love? Only in Christ. By God's grace alone we remain true, we love, we honor and cherish, for better or worse, for richer or poorer, in sickness and health.

"There are so many negative things going on in our society today. Marriages are falling apart all around us," writes Matthew White in his book *Married To Jesus.* "We have an opportunity to shine a light into our world. We have an opportunity to show others how a marriage built on the life of Jesus and his relationship with his bride, the church, will not only survive but thrive."[21]

We shouldn't think for a second that such a commitment won't be tested, for it most assuredly will. Still, we can say with confidence, "Though a host encamp against me, my heart will not fear; though war arise against me, in spite of this I shall be confident" (Psalm 27:3).

The Battle is On

When Doug and I built our house six years ago, we planted two ginkgo trees on either side of our front yard. The trees looked identical the day we put them in the ground, but since that time one has flourished and the other has flopped.

The tree on the west side of our house gets plenty of sunshine. It is planted on level ground, not susceptible to erosion. Tall and straight, it has more than quadrupled in size. Its leaves are a deep green, its bark smooth, and its limbs symmetrical. Even when my husband accidentally backed into the tree with his truck and gashed the trunk, it managed to survive.

The tree in the east yard has not fared so well. It was planted on a slope, where water runs off instead of soaking in. Surrounded by larger trees, it stands in shade most of the day. Gophers keep digging tunnels through its struggling root system. It has served as "base" for far too many games of tag and shows visible signs of wear from our little ones whipping the tree back and forth as if it were a stick horse.

Consequently, the trunk is crooked and spindly. Its uppermost branches were broken off at some point, so the tree is severely stunted—barely seven feet tall, as compared to its 35-ft brother. My husband has been sorely tempted to just chop it down and plant another in its place. He nearly acted on that impulse this past spring, but like Fern Arable, I spotted him just in time with the axe in hand and begged for mercy on behalf of the runt. Doug relented, and I am now attempting to nurture the scrawny thing back to health (a little staking and strategic pruning have already worked wonders for its appearance).

It's important to note that my axe-wielding husband is not responsible for this tree's present sorry state. He is simply responding to the damage already done by its other enemies—the gophers, erosion, and overly rambunctious children. If I wanted to fault somebody for the tree's miserable appearance, I should fault myself for not tending to it more faithfully, for not vigilantly protecting it from its various assailants.

No, Doug isn't to blame, nor does he have anything against ginkgo trees in general. He has no desire to fell the heartier specimen, and although he considers this *particular* ginkgo an eyesore, he is perfectly willing to replace it with a new one. The presence of the healthy, robust ginkgo in the west yard—and the knowledge that there are countless others like it—reassures him that it *is* possible to raise one successfully.

But what if the west tree were just as sickly and stunted as the east? What if every ginkgo tree Doug had ever encountered were uniformly puny and pathetic? Wouldn't it stand to reason that he might be less willing to take a chance growing one himself? That he might decide to plant something entirely different? At least he wouldn't be pinning his hopes on something with a high failure rate. Would *you* buy a tree that had, say, less than a fifty percent chance of surviving?

I think the reason some groups are seeking to "redefine marriage" these days is that so many "traditional marriages"—at least the ones they've personally observed or experienced—seem sickly and unappealing. Although I disagree with their response, I do not consider these groups the enemy. They didn't cause the problems; they are merely reacting to them.

The damage was done by a much subtler Adversary. Like the gopher that tunneled under my ginkgo, this Enemy attacked marriage at the root, digging away at its foundation, gradually shifting our focus away from God and onto ourselves. Mary Pride asserts that Christian marriage should be God-centered (producing what God wants), rather than me-centered (obsessed with my own desires).[22] But mirroring the love of Christ and raising children for His glory no longer seems to be our primary concern. Finding happiness and personal fulfillment is our new end goal.

"We may pledge to love each other until death do us part—but we blanch at the first hint of sacrifice."[23] How many couples have I heard rationalize their divorce by saying "we're just not happy together anymore"? I've lost count. "Like the advent of refrigeration and modern plumbing," Danielle Crittenden notes, this shift in priorities may "seem progressive: Why should anyone stay in a marriage that is unhappy? Why should women compromise their ambitions to raise children? But, like the drywall and plywood substructures of modern houses, these attitudes have made our institutions much flimsier, and over time they endure less well."[24]

By making happiness our main objective, we "demote marriage from a unique public commitment—supported by law, society, and custom—to a private relationship, terminable at will, which is nobody else's business. This demotion is done in the name of choice, but," as Waite and Gallagher report in *The Case for Marriage,* it "doesn't expand anyone's choices. For what it ultimately takes away from individuals is marriage itself, the choice to enter that uniquely powerful and life-enhancing bond that is larger and more durable than the immediate, shifting feelings of two individuals."[25]

Author Leslie Ludy agrees. "Nothing will kill a marriage faster than two people who are only concerned with meeting their own needs and desires," she writes in a book entitled *Set-Apart Femininity*.[26]

Selfishness breeds misery.

"Every week in every state, couples begin divorce proceedings," observes Kathy Peel in *Desperate Households*, "Yet there's probably not a couple in the world who entered marriage thinking, *No way will this marriage work. Our goal is to make each other miserable.*"[27] More likely than not, they had good intentions of making each other happy—or at least of making *themselves* happy—when they first married.

Either way, if happiness is all they sought, it makes sense they'd be ready to throw in the towel when happiness is not forthcoming. But *should* they call it quits? Is unhappiness really a sufficient reason to divorce?

Not according to a report released by the Institute for American Values in 2002. Their studies found that two-thirds of couples who were unhappy in their marriages, but stuck it out anyway, considered themselves "happily married" just five years later. In fact, "the most unhappy marriages reported the most dramatic turnarounds. Among those who rated their marriages as *very unhappy*, almost *eight out of ten* who avoided divorce were happily married five years later."[28]

Even so, many couples don't persevere long enough to discover this fact. And that's too bad.

It's bad for their families, but it's also bad for society as a whole. Strong and stable families make for a strong and stable nation, according to Focus on the Family founder, James Dobson:

It is the great contribution marriage makes to a civilization. But in its absence, ruination is inevitable. When men have no reason to harness their energies in support of the home, then drug abuse, alcoholism, sexual intrigue, job instability, and aggressive behavior can be expected to run unchecked throughout the culture. And that is the beginning of the end."[29]

This connection was evident to Albert Barnes, as well, who wrote in his 1885 commentary, "Every community where the marriage tie has been lax and feeble, or where it has been disregarded or dishonored, has been full of pollution, and it will always be. Society is pure and virtuous, just as marriage is deemed honorable, and as its vows are adhered to and preserved."[30]

In his 1974 book, *Divorced in America,* Joseph Epstein expresses a similar sentiment:

> To the extent that divorce can be obtained with relative facility and with lack of social censure, to that extent is the ideal of permanence in marriage damaged. To the extent that divorce is used to solve other people's marital unhappiness, to that extent does living with one's own imperfect marital happiness come to seem less tolerable.[31]

The "old knowledge that happiness is overrated" has been lost, according to Peggy Noonan, former speechwriter for Ronald Reagan and George Bush:

> We have lost, somehow, a sense of mystery— about us, our purpose, our meaning, our role. Our ancestors believed in two worlds, and understood this to be the solitary, poor, nasty, brutish, and short one. We are the first generations of man that actually

expected to find happiness here on earth, and our search for it has caused such—unhappiness.[32]

And why is that?

It's because we treat happiness as if it were a destination that we must trample upon others to reach. In reality, happiness is a disposition that is naturally cultivated as we seek to live for God's glory. That, after all, is "the chief end of man... to glorify God and enjoy Him forever."[33] It's the purpose for which we were created in the first place, and we'll never be genuinely happy if we neglect it.

"As with all of God's designs, our needs do get met, but by the route of faith. First we do what God commands;" writes Mary Pride in *The Way Home*,

> ...then to our surprise we find ourselves blessed. First we deny ourselves and take up our cross, and then we find the burden light and pleasant.... Then we find our hearts set free, and the love of God shed abroad in our hearts, and our marriages blossoming and blooming.[34]

We will only find lasting happiness when we learn to love with a selfless, sacrificial love. "When [a husband and wife] are joined together in harmonious concord and love, Jesus Christ is sung."[35] May our lives and marriages be such that the melody sounds sweet to all ears that hear it.

Chapter 13
Let Him Lead

"Suppose the woman does not follow me."
Genesis 24:39

For several years in my early twenties, I sang with the Dallas Symphony Chorus. We shared the stage with the Dallas Symphony Orchestra, performing the works of Mozart, Mendelssohn, Haydn, Handel, Beethoven, Brahms, and Bizet under the direction of such world-class conductors as Robert Shaw, Victor Borge, and Eduardo Mata.

As a first soprano, I sat directly behind the tympani. I was close enough to the percussionist that I could read his music over his shoulder, could see the sweat trickle down his brow as he played. On performance nights, my adrenaline started to surge the minute the strings began to tune. By the time our last note was sung, my heart felt full to bursting. I was enraptured by the magnificence of it all.

What struck me then—and what still impresses me now—was the respect each musician had for the maestro. When it came time for his entrance, an expectant hush would descend over the entire concert hall. The conductor would stroll to center stage, bow to the audience's polite applause, step onto his platform, take a few deep breaths, and raise his baton resolutely. All eyes would be riveted to him, nerves tinged with anticipation. Then, with a flick of his wrist, he would begin to draw the most intensely beautiful music out of us, as if by magic.

Beethoven's *Ninth Symphony,* Mozart's *Requiem,* Prokofieff's *Alexander Nevky,* Bizet's *Carmen*: Many of the pieces performed during my tenure with the chorus remain personal favorites to this day. It was immensely gratifying to have had even a small part in producing such exquisite sound. Every performance required the cooperative effort of hundreds of talented musicians, each committed to following the conductor's lead unflinchingly. A symphony would simply be impossible without it.

For an orchestra to be successful, each member must be willing to defer to the musical interpretation of the conductor. Nobody considers this unfair or offensive. It is in no way demeaning. The arrangement is not meant to suggest that the instrumentalists are somehow inferior to the maestro musically, intellectually, or otherwise.

In fact, it's feasible that the members of an orchestra could be older, smarter, or more musically gifted than the one under whose direction they sit. Most musicians undoubtedly have more experience playing their individual instrument than does their conductor. But does that give them license to ignore him? A right to usurp his authority? Think what cacophony would result if they did: If the tympani disliked the tempo he'd established and refused to keep time with it. If the piccolo wanted more playtime and jumped in unbidden whenever she fancied. If the cellist grew bored and wandered offstage mid-performance. If the pianist read from a different score entirely.

It would be absolute pandemonium.

Without order, without unity, without consistent and willing subjection, all hope for accurately representing a composer's work would be lost. But what beauty results when each person plays his part and plays it well! This is true of music, and it is true of life.

Harmony in the home is a work of the Master Composer and takes the cooperative effort of every member of the family. Unless we are unflinchingly committed to following God's plan, we will never experience the melodic beauty He meant to permeate family life.

A family is comprised of wonderfully distinct individuals. Each member has been blessed by God with a unique personality. Each has different strengths, talents, and aptitudes, all of which are to be used in service to others, to the glory of God. But in a family, just as in an orchestra, *somebody* has to lead. Somebody has to make decisions regarding which projects will be undertaken, when, and for how long. Somebody has to determine the family's tempo, tone, and dynamics. Someone must conduct and coordinate the efforts of the others, sharpening their focus and honing their skills so that they will be prepared to do all that the Composer requires.

Whom has God appointed to serve in this capacity? The Bible makes it clear: It is the husband. The responsibility for directing his family lies squarely upon a man's shoulders. If he hopes for his home to ever exude a heavenly melody, he must have the respect of those under his authority; they must willingly—joyfully—follow his lead, which is precisely why the Scriptures command children to obey their parents and a wife to be subject to her husband.

The "S" Word

Feminists treat this concept of submission as if it were a dirty word. They rankle at the thought of subordinating their wishes to those of another, as if doing so somehow demeans them, as if marriage victimizes women or robs them of self-respect.

Whereas a century ago, we had Marmee telling her daughters that marriage to "a good man is the best and sweetest thing which can happen to a woman,"[1] we now have the likes of Ann Ferguson contending that "housewifery and prostitution have the same structure," and that it's "hypocritical to outlaw one and not the other."[2] Or Simone de

Beauvoir, who considers "the *existence* of [married] women... who live as parasites" to be "extremely demoralizing for the woman who aims at self-sufficiency."[3]

That's hogwash.

"The true ideal of feminism—that men and women should have the same rights and opportunities—is an obvious positive civil rights issue," writes Laura Schlessinger. "But that is not the feminism that has ever dominated. The feminist movement as such was totally co-opted by a mentality that despised femininity, motherhood, wifehood, and men in all forms except castrated."[4]

Being a helpmeet is not the same thing as being a slave. Being under authority is not the same thing as being a doormat. Far from it. Expounding upon the creation account in Genesis, Matthew Henry writes:

> Eve's being made after Adam, and out of him, puts an honor upon that sex, as the glory of the man, 1 Cor. 11:7. If man is the head, she is the crown, a crown to her husband, the crown of the visible creation. The man was dust refined, but the woman was dust double-refined, one remove further from the earth.[5]

Submission isn't a question of superiority; it's a question of structure. Without structure there is no order, no unity, and no possibility of working together toward a common goal. In contrast, "the woman who submits to her husband will share a oneness with him, a communion she never dreamed of, an emotional peace and security positively unattainable when she struggles with him for power in the home."[6]

Yet feminists feel that if they defer to any man—and especially a husband—then they are somehow selling out. Unfortunately, too much of their thinking has infiltrated the church and wrongly influenced the way Christian wives relate to their husbands. We think it's progressive to assert ourselves, to push for control, to insist on having our own way. We "follow our own plans, and... act according to the stubbornness of [our own] heart" (Jer. 18:12), little realizing that by doing so, we fight against God's purposes and destroy any possibility of representing accurately to onlookers His beautiful design for marriage.

Obedience to the biblical teaching of submission is often regarded as "an unwelcome and sometimes positively offensive duty," writes Larry Crabb in *The Marriage Builder*:

> When a man is married to a woman who incessantly complains, withholds affection, or reliably points out his social errors, the instruction to "love your wife" will seem more like an invitation to step on a nail.... If we honor our commitment [as] husbands and wives in a spirit of reluctant surrender or grudging compliance, we are not honoring our commitment at all.[7]

A wife who has a problem with submission most likely has a problem with trust and respect, as well. She needs to acknowledge the fact that God is capable of leading her *through* her husband. Just as Sarah put her faith in God, but called Abraham "lord" (1 Pet. 3:5-6), I must trust God and follow my husband. If the hearts of kings are "like channels of water in the hand of the Lord [which] He turns...wherever He wishes" (Prov. 21:1), how much more are the hearts of our husbands under His influence? Our responsibility is to treat them with honor and respect.

Show Some Respect

Men and women are clearly motivated by different things. Generally speaking, a woman wants love, and a man wants respect. I'm certainly not the first to notice that God addressed these different needs when He inspired Paul to write Ephesians 5:33: "Nevertheless, each individual among you also is to love his own wife even as himself, and the wife must see to it that she respects her husband." The King James Version uses the word "reverence."

The Amplified Bible translates it thus: "Let the wife see that she respects and reverences her husband [that she notices him, regards him, honors him, prefers him, venerates, and esteems him; and that she defers to him, praises him, and loves and admires him exceedingly]."

The grammatical construction in this passage is curious: Let the wife *see that* she does this. Let her *make certain* she does this. The implication is that this is something entirely under our control. Respect is more than just a feeling I have toward my husband. It is something I willfully purpose to show him. Just as I can choose to show love even when those warm feelings of affection are not present, I can *choose* to honor my husband, to act respectfully toward him, even when I don't think he deserves it.

"What God commands a woman to do does not hinge on the man loving his wife as Christ loved the Church," Debi Pearl observes in *Created To Be His Help Meet.* "If it did, there is not one single husband who ever lived and breathed who would be worthy of his wife's submission or reverence. Each of them, the man and the woman, has been given their own directive from God with a model or pattern to attain to. What God said stands, regardless of the man's goodness or the apparent lack thereof."[8]

"We've come to think that love should be unconditional, but respect must be earned," writes Shaunti Feldhahn in *For Women Only.* "Instead, what men need is *unconditional* respect—to be respected for who they are [i.e., our husbands] apart from how they do." She elaborates,

> Women often tend to want to control things, which, unfortunately, men tend to interpret as disrespect and distrust (which, if we're honest with ourselves, it sometimes *is*). Marriage is about putting

the other person's needs above your own… and it does tremendous things for your man to know that you are choosing to trust and honor him.[9]

One of the most perceptive books I've read on this topic is Emerson Eggerichs' *Love and Respect.* In the opening pages, Eggerichs draws a diagram of what he labels "the crazy cycle." It is a simple circle with these words written around the perimeter: "WITHOUT LOVE → SHE REACTS → WITHOUT RESPECT → HE REACTS →."[10] In other words, when a husband feels disrespected, he tends to respond unlovingly, and when a wife feels unloved, she tends to react disrespectfully. As you can imagine, once a couple gets caught in this cycle, it often spirals down and down.

Shaunti Feldhahn warns, "if [your husband is] angry at something you've said or done and you don't understand the cause, there is a good chance that he is feeling the pain or humiliation of your disrespect."[11] Men often desire respect even more deeply than they crave sex. This says a lot. We've already established how desperately most men want sex, but whereas their drive for sex may wane somewhat as they grow older and their testosterone levels begin to decline, this acute need to feel respected will persist throughout their lives. God makes provision for both these needs when he gives a man a wife. "Your man will never become all he was meant to be," warns Bob Barnes, "until you believe in him and tell him so with sincere words of encouragement."[12]

"When you honor your husband, you honor God," writes Debi Pearl. "As we serve our husbands, we serve God. But in that same way, when you dishonor your husband, you dishonor God."[13] Our obligation to our husbands is clear in Scripture: Don't deny him sexually, and show him respect. When we do both these things faithfully and willingly, we are living in obedience to Christ and acting as a balm to our husband's soul.

"You are marrying a man," Laura Schlessinger reminds us in *The Proper Care and Feeding of Husbands.* "Always treat him like one and he will always act like one[14].... Showing respect for a husband in his own home not only sends him a message that he's loved and appreciated, it sets the game plan for the next generation's marriages. How much more important could it get?"[15]

But how does this kind of respect play out? What, exactly, does it look like in real life? The apostle Paul provides a clue when he writes, "Do nothing from selfishness or empty conceit, but with humility of mind regard one another as more important than yourselves; do not merely look out for your own personal interests, but also for the interests of others...." Tommy Nelson echoes this advice in his book, *Better Love Now*: "When you respect someone, you care more about what they want than what you want. Respecting your spouse means focusing on 'you' before 'me.' How well are you doing in truly placing your spouse before yourself? That's a diagnostic for respect."[16]

Head Bashing

Soon after our first son learned to crawl, he crept into our entry hall, propped himself up in a sitting position, and began to rock in such a way as to hit the back of his head against the wall. Knock. Knock. Knock. Knock. The sound was so loud that I could hear it from the kitchen. Thinking company had come to call, I dashed to the front door. My little one giggled with delight, then banged his head again. What a fine new game he had discovered! He thought it was hilarious.

A similar thing plays out in many households. Hollywood creeps into our homes, props itself up in the middle of the living room, and makes a game out of male bashing. The head of the house is the butt of the jokes. Television sitcoms serve up boorish husbands and inept fathers as standard fare. Men are made to look ridiculous, and laugh tracks try to convince us this is all hilariously funny.

Of course, exaggerated stereotypes have been used for centuries to invoke belly laughs. The ability to laugh at oneself is an admirable trait. This is true regardless of gender. Humor can help us recognize and overcome our weaknesses by poking fun at our foibles, but trouble brews when we begin to view satire as reality. There is a huge difference between good-natured jesting and character assault. Far from innocent entertainment, much of what comes out of Hollywood today is a calculated attack on traditional family values.

When my husband witnessed our firstborn's antics in the entry hall, he wisely called an immediate halt to it. "Don't let him do that," he admonished me, "he'll damage his brain." At the time, Doug was in his first year of medical school and was taking a course in neurology. He had no desire to see his son become a clinical case study, so all head knocking in our household was thenceforth strictly forbidden.

In the same manner, wives must not give opportunity to Hollywood's stereotypes to damage our minds and attitudes. Although their influence may initially seem innocuous, those depictions of moronic husbands on television and in the movies do shape the way society thinks of and relates to men. We should not allow anything into our homes that will undermine the respect our husbands receive from wife and children.

Regrettably, this tendency to ridicule men seems to already be well-rooted and bearing bitter fruit. Playing the "my-husband-is-a-bigger-dope-than-yours-is" game seems to have become a favorite pastime for many women. Have you ever witnessed this? Disgruntled wives sit around a table over lunch and try to outdo one another with detailed accounts of all the stupid things their husbands do.

I was fairly newly wed when I first witnessed such a thing. It grieved me to hear the women rant. I felt shame for their spouses and guilt for being privy to the conversation, which centered on mostly minor offenses: some purchase the wife deemed frivolous or a bungled household repair. It wasn't even so much *what* they said, but the *way* they said it.

I felt like announcing to everyone present, "Well, *my* husband's *wonderful*, and I admire him more than any man I know." But as that would clearly not have been helpful, I kept my mouth shut.

Understand: It's not that my husband is perfect. It's not even that I *think* he is perfect. Doug makes mistakes just like the next guy. But that has never been my focus. Sometimes *I* do stupid things, too. Sometimes *I* make thoughtless comments. Yet, I would feel betrayed to think that Doug would ever get together with his buddies and gripe about *me*!

Whatever happened to, "Treat others as you yourself would like to be treated"?

A wife I'll call Joyce shares my abhorrence for this head-bashing game. She joined a women's group hoping to find "practical ways to become a better mother," but discovered, instead, that "the group was a gripe session for women to vent about their husbands' idiosyncrasies, bad attitudes, and failures in general and in specific." She writes, "I was becoming trained to complain and whine about real or imagined behavior and look for sympathy from other women."[17] She quit the group and sought counsel from a happily married Christian couple, who taught her the value of family privacy and mutual respect.

How many wives would be hurt and disappointed to hear their husbands speak of them with the same disdain and lack of respect that the wives display in their own conversations? We should try living so as to make our husband's complaints to friends unlikely. We should behave in such a way that he would choose to boast instead, "Many daughters have done well, but my wife excels them all" (see Prov. 31:29).

What goes around comes around: "Just as your man will be hurt and angry if you disrespect him in public," notes Shaunti Feldhahn, "he will think you are the most wonderful woman in the world if you publicly build him up."[18] So, no matter what his faults, you must find some good points about your husband. Magnify and meditate on *those* things. In the end, you will both benefit.

I have a cousin who, as a small girl, overheard her parents disparaging an ornery little neighbor. My aunt and uncle went on and on, enumerating the young boy's many faults (not to his face, thankfully). They found nothing nice to say about him. My cousin was moved to come to the boy's defense, but even she had a hard time thinking of any redeeming qualities. At the first lull in the conversation, she finally blurted out, "Well... at least... he can... *whistle!*"

Her parents laughed out loud and quit the tirade. My cousin's comment became a family catch phrase, and for the rest of their lives, they'd use it whenever they caught themselves being overly critical, as a reminder to look for the good in others. "Well, at least he can whistle."

This looking-on-the-bright-side is an attitude the Scriptures encourage us to cultivate: We are commanded to let our minds dwell on "whatever is true, whatever is honorable, whatever is right, whatever is pure, whatever is lovely, whatever is of good repute, [whatever is excellent and] worthy of praise" (Phil. 4:8).

One of the subscribers to Nancy Campbell's magazine, *Above Rubies*, is experiencing the benefits to focusing on positives rather than negatives. She writes:

> One day, about two years after we were married, it dawned upon me that this man I married was not all I had imagined. I started questioning what I was really doing being married to him? I could no longer see anything good—only the bad. These thoughts soon reflected in my behavior toward him....

I was encouraged to look for ONE good thing in my husband and thank God for it. Not only did I do that, but I also thanked God for that quality when we prayed aloud together, e.g., 'Thank you, God, for Chris and his patience with the children"…. I [even thanked] God in our prayers together for his strong muscles and the way he uses them to provide for us. Chris would thank me for my prayers and walk with a lighter step.

These prayers continued. My focus on one Christ-like quality grew and grew until I could no longer see the faults and thought more and more of my husband's fine qualities. In the process, Chris was greatly encouraged. Even today, the most encouraging thing that I can do for him is to pray aloud for him and specifically thank God for his Christ-like qualities.[19]

My own dear father had faults that must have been glaringly evident to those who knew him, but growing up, I was blind to them all. My mother instilled in me such a respect for him that I honestly thought he could do no wrong. He was my hero, and I miss him deeply now that he's gone.

As an adult, I marvel at Mom's wisdom—and at her ability to bite her tongue (no doubt, more of a challenge once those estrogen levels dropped off post-menopause!). The way she honored my dad was one of the most valuable gifts she ever gave me. As an adult, I came to recognize some of Daddy's shortcomings, but because of my mother's faithfulness to honor and respect him, those areas of weakness could not eclipse his many, many areas of strength.

"When you consider whether your husband is worthy of your respect," writes Bob Barnes in *What Makes a Man Feel Loved*, "consider what your standards for him are. Are you expecting him to be perfect?" Barnes continues:

When a wife holds her husband up against this perfect standard, she will notice the blemishes in her very human spouse, and these blemishes can destroy intimacy. It's one thing for young girls to have fantasies about the special man in their future and to grow up with that fairy-tale prince in mind. But a mature woman lets go of that fantasy and comes to know a real man and loves him for who he is, not who she wishes he were.[20]

Even the best men will sometimes struggle this side of heaven. Will you choose to focus on the things your husband does wrong—belittling and nagging and magnifying those faults to anyone who will listen? Or will you choose to be grateful for the many things your husband does right—encouraging and loving and honoring him? All of us are works in progress, and we can trust that God who began this work will be faithful to complete it (Phil. 1:6).

Give Him a Chance

Shortly before we married, Doug's grandmother offered to teach me how to tat. For those unfamiliar with this dying art form, tatting is a very tedious, time-consuming method of handcrafting intricate lace using fine cotton thread wound about a two-inch shuttle. This shuttle is woven in and out and around the loose end of string until a delicate web of loops and knots begins to take shape.

At least, that is how it's supposed to work. I never got the hang of it myself. Nanny refused to let me keep the shuttle in my hands long enough to figure it out. No sooner did I get the cotton threaded through my fingers than she would snatch it away. "Not like *that*! Like *this*! Now *watch*!" I was allowed three fleeting attempts before she announced that "some people just aren't cut out for this sort of thing," plucked the shuttle from my fingers, and locked it away in her secretary for good. So my first and only tatting lesson was a miserable failure.[21]

It wasn't because I lacked coordination—my fine motor skills were superb. It wasn't because I hadn't the patience for such intricate work—I'd been making fine lace for years using a crochet needle with a microscopic hook. It wasn't because my mind couldn't grasp the complicated stitches—I'd done needlework (with a pen in hand for taking notes) through all my college classes and still graduated summa cum laude with a degree in mathematics. It wasn't because I lacked interest or time or aptitude or creativity or resolve.

No, the only reason I failed at tatting is because Doug's spirited little grandma—bless her heart—couldn't stand to watch me struggle. She insisted on *showing* me how to do it again and again and again, and in the process prevented my ever *learning* how to do it myself.

I wonder how many husbands feel in their marriages the way I felt on the couch next to Nanny that night? How many men would *love* to lead their families—they're capable, ready, and willing to do so—but their wives refuse to hand over the reins? How many are never given the opportunity to prove themselves, because their wives fear they'll fail, or won't do things the way the wife thinks they should be done? How many find the power struggle that ensues so enormously frustrating that they're ready to give up on the whole relationship?

Few men enter marriage as experts in the management of a household. Whatever experience they get must be gained through on-the-job training. Do your husband a huge favor and don't breathe down his neck. Give him a chance to find his sea legs. Give him room to grow. Allow him freedom to make decisions, even decisions you think are mistakes. You may be surprised to see how often the choices you initially thought were poor ones turn out to be exceedingly wise.

Case in point: During my husband's first year of medical school, he learned that one of our elderly neighbors—we didn't know his name, but had often seen him walking his dog—was to be evicted from his apartment for failing to pay his rent. Doug came home obviously burdened about the situation. "I think we need to pay his rent *for* him," he told me. While I appreciated my husband's desire to help, I was not convinced this was a smart idea. We were borrowing money (in the form of school loans) just to pay our own rent; loaning money to a stranger when we were living on loans ourselves made absolutely no sense. "I don't want to *loan* him the money," Doug clarified, "I want to *give* it to him. I feel like that's what God would have us do." I was still skeptical, but knew better than to argue with him further. So in addition to paying our own rent that month, Doug paid two months back-rent for our neighbor so the man could keep his apartment.

The Bible states that a person who gives to the poor lends to the Lord, and the Lord will repay him (Prov. 19:17). Even so, I was surprised to get a call from our landlady a few days later. She needed somebody to answer phones for the leasing office three nights a week—would we be willing to do it? (We were.) If so, she'd transfer the calls to our apartment and would reduce our rent by half! I'm convinced she would never have thought to make us such an offer had she not seen Doug's signature on our struggling neighbor's rent check. We lived in those apartments for several more years, and Doug's kindness to that relative stranger was repaid manyfold. We wouldn't have fared nearly so well financially had I persuaded Doug to ignore God's prompting and to rely instead on common sense.

There were other times Doug made what I initially considered a wrong decision that turned out to be a right one. I was also nervous about him going into anesthesia, joining the army, and buying our land—three choices that proved providential, indeed. There was the computer he bought which I didn't think we needed (the one that enabled me to begin reviewing educational software for a weekly radio program two weeks later, thus providing free curriculum for our home school during the three years I stayed with the show); the top-of-the-line speaker system he insisted on installing in our home which I was convinced we'd never use (it came in mighty handy when we found ourselves hosting over 100 people a week in our home church a year later); and the tiny two-seater Mazda Miata he bought when we were expecting our sixth child (oh, wait….that one really *was* a mistake—a mistake he freely admitted when he traded it for a truck two months later—but at least it wasn't the pricey Porsche he'd considered!).

My point is this. You have got to trust your husband to make wise decisions and forgive him if he makes unwise ones. There is room for a wife to share her thoughts and concerns and reservations, certainly. But she must be careful to do this with an attitude of humility and respect. She shouldn't question his knowledge and argue with every decision.[22] She must learn to let him have the final say in a matter, without coercion or condescension—and with no "I told you so" if things don't work out. Your quiet confidence will encourage him to try again, even if he initially fails. "Let go of any unrealistic standards of perfection you have and love your husband for who he is, a fallible human being," advises Bob Barnes in *What Makes a Man Feel Loved*. "Focus on his skills and abilities and let him lead from his strengths. Finally, don't keep track of the poor decisions he makes. Your husband will become a more confident decision-maker and a better leader when he knows that you are in his corner no matter what the outcome."[23]

In *The Excellent Wife*, Martha Peace argues, "A wife will *never* be what the Lord wants her to be until she graciously and joyfully comes under the authority of her husband."[24] I'd go so far as to say that a husband will never be all that the Lord wants *him* to be, either, until his wife recognizes and honors his God-given authority. Her quiet, loving submission will spur him on, build him up, and enable him to achieve his full potential for spiritual leadership in the home.

So show your husband some respect. Follow his lead. Encourage him with your approving smile. Give him room to grow. Then stand back and watch what happens.

Chapter 14
Build Him Up

"Encourage one another and build each other up...."
1 Thessalonians 5:11 (NIV)

For years, Doug and I heard what a strain building a house puts on a marriage. Almost everyone we knew warned against it. We'd seen couples split before the framing was even finished. Neither of us wanted to follow suit, so we'd contented ourselves with buying pre-owned homes.

Even so, it was becoming obvious the little homemade trundle beds, which worked so well when our kids were toddlers, would not long accommodate the adult-sized bodies they were speedily acquiring. As our family size hurtled toward critical mass, we began contemplating the possibility of building out of sheer necessity. We drew up house plans ourselves, bought a couple of acres south of town, and broke ground in early 2003.

Fortunately, the building process was not the nightmare we expected. Our tastes are so similar that we had zero arguments regarding selections. I'd bring home, say, three dozen samples of green paint, pencil a star on the back of the one I liked best, then spread all 36 chips out on Doug's desk, face up, and ask him to pick a favorite. Time and again, he'd point to his preference, flip it over, and find my star.

We had an equally easy time selecting flooring, cabinetry, light fixtures, windows, countertops, plumbing, and hardware.

That's not to say 2003 wasn't a stressful year—it was. But the stress had less to do with our home-building than it did with Doug's being elected president of his anesthesia group (fifth largest in the state of Texas at the time), selected for a random audit by the IRS, and activated for a three-month tour of duty with the Army Reserves—all simultaneous to my giving birth to our ninth child!

I delivered that baby the same day the contractor began bricking our house. Doug got a four-day pass from the Army and made it home just three hours before Isaac was born. With my being in the hospital and Doug's being in sole charge of the other eight kids, we didn't make it back to our building site for a few days, by which time the entire east wing of the house had been completely bricked.

That was when we discovered our mason was using the wrong color of mortar. Instead of the bright white we'd ordered, he'd mixed up an ugly blackish-gray, which gave our house a downright spooky feel.

It looked *horrible.* I cried.

The contractor assured us he could fix the problem, so don't worry. But do you know what fixing it entailed? It meant tearing down three days worth of work—brick by brick!

The entire process made me sick to my stomach. I could scarcely bear to watch. Yet the recollection of those haphazard piles of scruffy bricks scattered about our lot remains indelibly fixed in my memory. It's the scene that springs to mind whenever I read the verse, "The wise woman builds her house, but the foolish tears it down with her own hands" (Prov. 14:1). I imagine myself pulling down all those bricks—one by one—that had been so painstakingly set into place, and I am nauseated at the thought.

I don't believe this passage necessarily refers to a physical residence, although destroying a literal house, whether intentionally or through neglect, would indeed seem irrational. I remember touring Quigley's Castle in Eureka

Springs, Arkansas, as a young girl, and hearing how one day while her husband was at work, Mrs. Quigley completely demolished the wooden shack they'd been living in and moved her entire family (including five children) into a chicken coop.

Even then, that impressed me as a strange thing to do.

But there are ways a woman can tear down her home without attacking bricks and mortar. She can tear down the people inside it with a sharp, biting tongue, with angry criticism, with coldness and neglect, with unforgiveness and resentment and ingratitude. Lord, let none of us be guilty of committing such crimes against our loved ones.

Let us rather "put on a heart of compassion, kindness, humility, gentleness and patience; bearing with one another, and forgiving each other, whoever has a complaint against anyone; just as the Lord forgave you. [Let us] put on love, which is the perfect bond of unity" (Col. 3:12-14). It isn't enough that we refrain from "tearing down." A wise woman "builds." But how? How does one go about it?

We find a clue in the Book of Proverbs. There we read, "By wisdom a house is built, and by understanding it is established; and by knowledge the rooms are filled with all precious and pleasant riches" (Prov. 24:3-4).

To be successful, a building project takes not only patience and determination, but also expertise. It takes knowledge and understanding. "In my judgment, a tragically high number of marriages fail to achieve real oneness, not because the spouses weren't trying hard, but because they were not working with the right materials," writes Larry Crabb in *The Marriage Builder*:

> The carpenter may swing a hammer with force and accuracy, but without good wood and nails, the effort is wasted. No matter what else may be right about a relationship—sincerity, honest effort, noble aspirations, warm feelings, common beliefs,

communication skills—a marriage will not and cannot reach the goal of oneness without the basics.... The building blocks required for the development of oneness in marriage are—grace, commitment, [and] acceptance.[1]

Grace. Commitment. Acceptance. We already addressed commitment in chapters 12 and 13. But what about grace and acceptance? How are those things incorporated into a healthy marriage?

Rob Bell answers our question with another question:

> What if [a] woman, [even] one with [a] husband who constantly disappoints her, what if she treated him as if he already were the man she wishes he was? What if she [loved] him exactly as he is, today, with all of his flaws? If you are him, which is more motivating: being reminded of all of your failures and shortcomings, or being loved as if you're a great man?[2]

Don't make your husband work so hard to earn your approval. Lavish it upon him. When you are especially pleased by something he has done, let him know it! Smile at him. Encourage him. Laura Schlessinger suggests that women should approach their husbands with the same gentle enthusiasm they would show a new puppy: "Instead of constantly screaming 'NO!' to every little annoyance, transgression, or difference of perspective, opinion, or style, they should compliment the heck out of the things they like and want. Betcha that way you'll get more of it!"[3]

Focus as much on his effort as the end result. By so doing, you will endear yourself to him. He will cherish you above all others. The knowledge that his wife loves and respects him will spur him to accomplish greater things than any amount of nagging could ever bring to pass.

"If you've fallen into the habit of nagging," writes Kathy Peel,

> ...there will never be a better time than now to stop because (a) nagging is a poor motivator, so you're wasting your breath; (b) it doesn't inspire people to cooperate, so you're defeating your own purpose; and (c) it can downgrade the atmosphere in your home quicker than you can say, "If I've told you once, I've told you a thousand times." In other words, nobody wins.[4]

Our husbands can easily "recognize the difference between being accepted and merely being tolerated!"[5] So instead of nagging, praise him. Admire him. Love him for who and what he is now. TODAY.

George Eliot describes "the comfort, the inexpressible comfort of feeling safe with a person; having neither to weigh thoughts nor measure words, but to pour them all out, just as they are, chaff and grain together, knowing that a faithful hand will take and sift them, keep what is worth keeping, and then, with the breath of kindness, blow the rest away."[6]

That is what grace and acceptance look like in a marriage. If you "speak blessings about [your] husband, then blessings are what [you'll] get in return."[7]

Look on the Bright Side

When setting out to describe the cultural climate of late 18th century Europe, Charles Dickens writes,

> It was the best of times, it was the worst of times, it was the age of wisdom, it was the age of foolishness, it was the epoch of belief, it was the epoch of incredulity, it was the season of Light, it was the season of Darkness, it was the spring of hope, it was the winter of despair....

Thus begins *A Tale of Two Cities*, a masterfully written novel and one of my personal favorites. Dickens continues,

> ...we had everything before us, we had nothing before us, we were all going direct to Heaven, we were all going direct the other way—in short, the period was so far like the present period, that some of its noisiest authorities insisted on its being received, for good or for evil, in the superlative degree of comparison only.[8]

In other words, certain folks insisted the cup was brimming over, others declared it was drained dry, but—note well—*they were all looking at the same half-glass of water.* The only thing that differed was the perspective and mindset of the person making the pronouncement.

And so it has always been. Some people possess a perpetually sunny disposition; others tend to wallow in despair. Undoubtedly, brain chemistry plays a role in this, but I am convinced much of it becomes ingrained through force of habit.

The Bible seems to bear this out. Christians are commanded to "rejoice always" (1 Thess. 5:16) and to "count it all joy" (James 1:2), which would indicate we *do* have some say in the matter. As Martha Washington once observed, "The greatest part of our happiness or misery depends upon our dispositions, and not upon our circumstances."[9] Our moods needn't be dictated by our milieu. When we *choose joy*, irrespective of our environs, we remain open to God's purpose and plan—whereas when we react negatively to what trials and troubles come our way, we give place to bitterness and resentment.

So what kind of person are you? Optimist or pessimist? Do you think the cup is on the verge of overflowing or on the brink of exhaustion? Half-full or half-empty? The future health of your marriage, as well as that of your mind and body, may hinge upon your answer.

"The notion that the mind can influence our health is really not new," writes Carl Charnetski. "Physicians as far back as 2nd-century Rome observed a relationship between depressed mood and later development of cancer."[10] Even earlier, the author of Proverbs noted that "a joyful heart is good medicine, but a broken spirit dries up the bones" (Prov. 17:22), and "a happy heart makes the face cheerful, but heartache crushes the spirit" (Prov. 15:3 NIV). Our thought life and our immune system are intricately and extensively related in ways that "science is only just beginning to fathom."[11] Charnetski elaborates:

> Disposition, attitude, emotional state, and certain personality traits exert enormous influence on immune health and thus on the progression of disease. Whether you are optimistic or pessimistic, how well you handle anger and negativity, how downhearted and dispirited you are... all of these predict your tendency to get sick and to what degree....
>
> If you happen to be angry, upset, or otherwise negative just minutes before you ran your hand along a stairway railing that harbors a flu virus, you are more likely to get a cold than if you were happy-go-lucky and hostility-free when you came into contact with the bug. You will also remain sicker longer and feel sicker than you otherwise would have if you had been in a better frame of mind.[12]
>
> If you are pessimistic about your lot in life, science suggests, you can create a self-fulfilling prophecy that leads to disease.... No matter how dire your lot, just being optimistic engenders success, health, and happiness. In other words, being an optimist or a pessimist doesn't merely reflect how healthy or successful you are currently; it actually predicts your future health and your success in all aspects of life—how well you do in school, how much

money you make, how stable your relationships will be. The more science investigates, the more confidently we can say that disposition determines health.[13]

Consider, if you will, the following proverbs: "All the days of the oppressed are wretched, but the cheerful heart has a continual feast. Better a little with the fear of the LORD than great wealth with turmoil. Better a meal of vegetables where there is love than a fattened calf with hatred" (Prov. 15:13-17 NIV). Have you ever asked yourself what "the oppressed" in verse 13 are being oppressed *by*? I don't think it is poverty, for the verses that follow indicate it is just as possible to be content with little as it is to be dissatisfied with abundance. I don't think it is sickness: the boil-plagued Job maintained hope even as his presumably still-healthy wife derisively urged him "to curse God and die" (see Job 2:9-10). I don't even think it is persecution: history is replete with examples of martyred Christians who died with songs of joy on their lips.

So what is it that makes "the days of the oppressed" so wretched? I believe it's their own tendency to see the cup half-empty, instead of half-full. They are oppressed by their own fears and anxieties, their own selfish desires, their own ungrateful hearts—hearts that dwell on the bad instead of focusing on the good, hearts that fear the worst instead of believing the best, hearts that covet what they've been denied instead of contenting themselves with what they've been given. Just as Adam and Eve fixated "on this one piece of fruit from this one tree when God [had] given them endless trees with infinite varieties of fruit to enjoy,"[14] so we sometimes fixate on what we don't have and completely miss out on enjoying anything else. Truly has it been said, "Happiness is not having what you want, it's wanting what you have."[15] You've seen two-year olds pout and pitch fits when they don't get their way? Sadly, some of us have never outgrown that childish behavior—and it is making us miserable.

Count Your Blessings

Did you know that men are prone to "judge themselves—and feel that others judge them—based on the happiness and respect of their wives"?[16] One of the cruelest, most selfish things a wife can do to her husband is to never be happy.[17] The Bible says that such a wife "is like rottenness in his bones" (Prov. 12:4). Why? Because, in essence, she is advertising to the world, "My husband is a failure. Life with him is miserable. He doesn't know how to satisfy me."

Please don't do this to your man.

Purpose instead to become an excellent wife, a wife who doesn't shame her husband with sour attitudes and unrighteous behaviors. The Bible calls an excellent wife "the crown of her husband" (Prov 12:4). Why a crown? A crown is an outward, public symbol of royalty or achievement. Just as laurel wreaths were placed upon the heads of victorious military leaders and accomplished athletes to distinguish them from the masses, so a godly wife distinguishes her husband; he is "known in the gates, when he sits among the elders of the land" (Prov. 31:23). She is like an ornament of refined beauty resting upon his head, accentuating his best features, drawing public attention to them.

Does this describe you?

When you look at your husband, do you see all the wonderful traits that originally attracted you to him, or do you focus on some annoying little habit that grates on your nerves and makes you wonder why you ever married the guy in the first place? Ben Franklin's advice to "keep your eyes wide open before marriage, half shut afterwards" is not far off the mark.[18] Even if he has changed considerably since the wedding, you must learn to love your husband as he is *now*, not for what you thought he was or wish he would become.

Remember Harold and Lena from *The Joy Luck Club*? When Harold first declared his feelings for her, Lena "swooned inside, caught off balance by this... revelation of love, wondering how such a remarkable person as Harold could think I was extraordinary."[19] Later, when the hard realities of marriage start to set in, Lena writes:

> Now that I'm angry at Harold, it's hard to remember what was so remarkable about him. And I know they're there, the good qualities, because I wasn't that stupid to fall in love with him, to marry him. All I can remember is how awfully lucky I felt, and consequently how worried I was that all this undeserved good fortune would someday slip away.... I worried that Harold would someday get a new prescription for his glasses and he'd put them on one morning, look me up and down, and say, "Why, gosh, you aren't the girl I thought you were, are you?"[20]

What about you? Are you still looking at your husband through eyes of love and admiration, or have you switched prescriptions? Do you count yourself blessed to even know him, or wonder why you married him in the first place? Elizabeth Barrett Browning had the right idea when she penned the lines, "How do I love thee? Let me count the ways...."[21] It would be a productive exercise for wives to compile a "*Why* do I love thee" list. Instead of dwelling on your husband's faults, real or imagined, write down what you appreciate about him, even if it's a short inventory. Just one thing is a starting point.

Once you've made your list, start reflecting these qualities back to your husband. Just as a mirror lets us know what other people see when they look at our outward appearance, a wife can provide a "reflection" for her husband of what she sees in him, on the inside. "We choose what we reflect, and what we choose has much to do with what the other person becomes," writes Margaret Compolo.

Positive reflecting will make your spouse feel good about [himself] and about you, but it will also change the way you feel. As you look for the positive and overlook the negative, you will become happier about your marriage and the person you married. This will happen even if your spouse does not change at all![22]

"A man [is] a sponge for admiration from his wife," observes Bob Barnes. "In all of the healthy marriages I have ever seen, the wife sincerely admires her husband—and she doesn't keep it a secret from him or anyone else!"[23] Barnes continues:

> We have all heard that behind every great man is a great woman. A loving, admiring, and godly woman will indeed cause a man to gain greater stature than he would on his own. A wife's encouragement can make her husband a better man....
>
> Your man wants you, his wife to be his most enthusiastic fan. He becomes stronger and more confident from your support and encouragement.
>
> Treat me as I am and that's just where I will stay. Treat me as if I were what I could be and that's what I'll become.[24]

But, some wives don't appreciate what they have until it's too late. A woman whose husband had died once wrote Laura Schlessinger to express concern that so many of her friends complained and whined about "stupid stuff in their marriages. She noted that these women didn't realize how lucky they were to have those little problems in their lives and that they should be happy to have someone to care for and worry over. In short, they lacked gratitude for what they had."[25]

We would all do well to view our lives and marriages from that widow's perspective. Perhaps then we'd be less inclined to "sweat the small stuff."[26] Elizabeth Handford has a friend who needed that sort of attitude adjustment early in her marriage. She recounts the story in her book:

> A girl I'll call Sue phoned. Her voice sounded panicky. "Libby, come quick. Everything's fallen apart!"
>
> I hurried to their home, dreading some catastrophic news. Sue and her husband had just weathered a stormy time of adjustment, and I could hardly imagine what could have gone wrong now.
>
> "Just look," she cried, pointing to two ordinary-looking, innocent shoes lying in front of the front door.
>
> "Yes?"
>
> "Tom leaves stuff where he drops it all the time. All day long I have to pick up after that man. This is the last straw! You can't even walk in the door without falling over his things!"
>
> I giggled. (A pastor's wife shouldn't, I know—after all, how many times am I equally as foolish?) "Sue, if you picked up every sock, every dirty shirt, every sticky pair of pants Tom leaves down, all day long, how much time would it take?"
>
> She wrinkled her forehead. Then it was her turn to giggle. "Maybe twenty minutes."
>
> "Is it worth your spending twenty minutes a day to have a happy home?"
>
> She threw up her hands in surrender. "O.K., I get it. No more preaching. Yeah, I'll pick up his old dirty clothes, and love him anyway."
>
> And she did! Six years and four children later, she's still picking up after Tom, *and* still enjoying her happy home.[27]

An Attitude of Gratitude

Can you relate? Do you become angry and irritated at the sight of your husband's shoes on the floor? Next time you see them lying where they don't belong, use them as a reminder to give thanks. Thank God that you *have* a husband to pick up after. Thank Him that your husband has shoes to wear, feet to put them on, strength to walk, and a job to rush off to, even if it means leaving his shoes by the door to get to work on time. Be thankful that you have eyes to notice the shoes, hands to put them away, and a mind that can follow through on the task. Be thankful you have a floor to clean, a house to de-clutter, the health and energy to do both. If you stop to think about it, you have been richly blessed, indeed—and you can thank that pair of your husband's misplaced shoes for reminding you of this fact.

"Joy begins with thankfulness," writes Debi Pearl:

> ...Quite often our attitudes hang in the balance; by making a conscious choice, we can tip our souls into dark moods of complaining, or into thankfulness and praise. It is amazing how much your mouth controls your soul. You can smile with your mouth and say, "Thank you, God; thank you, husband; thank you, children," and your spirit is directed into gratitude with joy following. Thankfulness is *how* you think; joy is the *abundance* it produces.[28]

In *Simple Secrets of a Great Marriage*, Cloud and Townsend observe: "Many people never find the wonder and joy that marriage *can* provide because they look for something it can't provide. People set themselves up for failure by expecting a good marriage to be one without [problems]."[29]

Instead of expressing gratitude—both to God and to their mates—for all that is *right* in their lives, they perseverate on the problem areas. The results? "Anxiety attacks, depression, somber moods, feelings of not being in control of your mind, unfounded fears, and bursts of anger"— all of which start in the mind and are the natural outcome when you allow your 40,000 daily thoughts to be negative in nature. When you repeatedly react in the same way, you develop deeply entrenched habits "that become so much a part of you that they may seem to be organic—a part of your physical make-up. Any cigarette smoker will tell you how powerful an addiction can be. Stinking thinking is an addiction that will grow into such a habit that it controls the body and deceives the mind."[30]

But there is hope! The solution is found in Colossians 4:2, which reads, "Devote yourselves to prayer, keeping alert in it with an attitude of thanksgiving." The praying is important, but the thankfulness is key. Telling a person who is troubled or dissatisfied to "pray about it" can be counterproductive[31]—especially if those prayers are merely used to rehash old grievances and ruminate on the wrongdoings of others. Prayer must be more than that. God desires that we use prayer as an opportunity to express gratitude, as is made obvious in Scripture:

∞ "Offer to God a sacrifice of *thanksgiving*...." (Psalm 50:14)
∞ "He who offers a sacrifice of *thanksgiving* honors Me." (Psalm 50:23)
∞ "Praise the name of God with song and magnify Him with *thanksgiving.*" (Psalm 69:30)
∞ "Enter His gates with *thanksgiving* and His courts with praise. *Give* thanks to Him, bless His name." (Psalm 100:4)
∞ "Sing to the LORD with *thanksgiving*...." (Psalm 147:7)
∞ "Be anxious for nothing, but in everything by prayer and supplication *with thanksgiving* let your requests be made known to God." (Phil. 4:6-7)

∞ "Blessing and glory and wisdom and *thanksgiving* and honor and power and might, be to our God forever and ever." (Rev. 7:12)

Unhappy marriages don't just need prayer, they need a particular kind of prayer. Thanksgiving is the "transforming ingredient."[32] We are told to give thanks *in* everything, not to give thanks *for* everything. Even when our problems seem insurmountable, we can still thank God for His faithfulness to see us through, for the lessons He is teaching us along the way, for the wisdom He provides to all who ask, for the work He has promised to complete in our hearts, and for the opportunity to glorify Him in the midst of difficult circumstances.

As we do this—as we cultivate this attitude of gratitude—we not only change the way we think, but we inevitably change the way we respond, as well. Focusing our minds on pleasant thoughts predisposes us to react in pleasant ways, as demonstrated in a behavioral study done by John Bargh, Mark Chen, and Lara Burrows. Participants were asked to rearrange a scrambled list of words to form sentences. "For some of the participants, the task was based on words such as *aggressive, rude, annoying,* and *intrude.* For others, the task was based on words such as *honor, considerate, polite,* and *sensitive.*" This technique, commonly used in social psychology, "primes" the participants "to think of politeness or rudeness as a result of constructing sentences from these words". After unscrambling the sentences, participants were sent to another lab, where they found an experimenter trying to explain the next task to an uncomprehending person ahead of them (actually another experimenter who was only *pretending* not to understand). Long story short: the folks who'd been pre-conditioned to think of courtesy waited almost twice as long before interrupting as those who'd been primed to think of rudeness.[33]

In the same way, when we make a habit of counting our blessings instead of magnifying our problems, we prime ours hearts and minds to respond with thanksgiving. Scripture tells us as a man "thinks in his heart, so is he" (Prov. 23:7 NKJV). If your heart is filled with gratitude, gratitude is what will come out. If your heart meditates continually on things that are good, good things will flow from it. In the words of Jesus, "The good man out of the good treasure of his heart brings forth what is good; and the evil man out of the evil treasure brings forth what is evil; for his mouth speaks from that which fills his heart" (Luke 6:45).

Still not sure where to start? Debi Pearl gives some great advice for adopting an attitude of gratitude and using it to transform your marriage:

> During the day, sing and play and dance as you work around the house. Your children will be delighted as you dance around the house with the broom or mop, and this lighthearted mood (visible joy is the only joy children understand) will be an encouragement to your children. The lightness in your soul will help put you in a good frame of mind for your husband when he comes home. If you have reason to be hurt or discouraged and yet you sing with thanksgiving, this is a true sacrifice of worship to God.
>
> Think of other ways and times during the day that you can establish a habit of praise and thanksgiving by showing joy. Write them down, think of yourself doing them, and then practice this new and wonderful habit *all day long.*[34]

"Gratitude is always in order," so thank your husband for everything he does for you, even when it's something expected.[35] Your sincere appreciation and happy smiles will brighten his day and nourish his soul. Your love and admiration will build him up and strengthen and encourage him. Love is like a rose—it won't grow without plenty of sunshine. In the words of Debi Pearl, "Has your lover seen your sunshine lately?"[36]

Chapter 15
Watch Him Grow

*"The righteous man will flourish like the palm tree,
He will grow like a cedar in Lebanon."*
Psalm 92:12

The thing about *growth* is that little can be done to hurry it along. We can fertilize our lawns. We can make sure our kids eat balanced meals and get regular exercise and plenty of sleep. We can give our husbands lots of encouragement and affirmation. But the growth itself is a work of God. We must never lose sight of that fact or become discouraged if desired growth doesn't take place fast enough to suit us.

Certain kinds of growth—a tree's root system, a child's brain development, a husband's deepening faith—are neither easily quantitated nor immediately evident, but are nonetheless vitally important. And like a mighty oak compared to a lowly mushroom, the strength gained through slow, steady growth often endures better over time.

Even so, it's easy to become impatient. We don't like to wait. We want results now. In an attempt to hurry things along, sometimes we wives try to take responsibility for things that God never intended us to shoulder—things like our husband's spiritual maturity. This is one of the effects of the fall.

Have you ever wondered what God meant when he told Eve, "Your desire shall be for your husband, and he shall rule over you" (Gen. 3:16)? Some commentators suggest that this verse refers to a wife's physical desire for her husband: In other words, she will have a deep longing to be sexually joined with him. As much as our husbands might wish this were true, empirical evidence doesn't seem to validate such an interpretation. A more accurate rendering might be that a woman will desire to control her husband—she'll want to tell him what to do—but that he will have the final authority in the home. While a wife's sex drive may wax and wane with her monthly hormones, her yearning to be in control never seems to fluctuate.

In support of this interpretation, the Hebrew word "desire" used in Genesis 3:16 is the same word used in Genesis 4:7 where God tells Cain, "sin is crouching at the door; and its desire is for you, but you must master it." As sin wants to rule over and dominate us, so wives wish to rule over and dominate their husbands. That has been our natural inclination since the fall, but we mustn't succumb to it.

You married a man, not a child, so don't treat him like a two-year old. God never intended you to *mother* your husband, but to *admire* him. You are to be his confidante, not his conscience. He needs your respect, not your reprimands.

Let the Holy Spirit Work

Some wives don't stop at trying to usurp their husband's authority; they want to do the Holy Spirit's job, as well. Remember the young bride from Chapter 1 who was told that the fastest way to teach her husband to die to self was to deny him sex? It is all too common for wives to manipulate their men through the use of such tactics. Whenever they are dissatisfied with his behavior, "they give their mate the silent treatment or humiliate [him] in public or cut [him] off sexually,"[1] observes Tommy Nelson.

Nelson warns wives, "Don't chasten your mate. Instead, let [him] see Christ. Paul said if your enemy's hungry, feed him. If he's thirsty, give him a drink, and in so doing you heap burning coals upon their head."[2] It is through *meeting* our husband's needs—including his need for respect and his need for sex—that we are able to influence him for good. "A good woman, deeply loving her husband, happily submissive, earnestly praying for him, eager to help him, a good woman can inspire a man to service far beyond what he could have dreamed of alone,"[3] writes Elizabeth Handford.

If your husband isn't living up to your expectations or demands, treating him badly as "punishment" will never change his heart; it will likely serve only to make him even more stiff-necked and stubborn. As Michael Pearl is fond of saying, "No man has ever crawled out from under his wife's criticism to be a better man—no matter how justified her condemnation."[4] A wife's "approval is as important as oxygen" to her husband, and surviving a wife's "lack of approval is emasculation" to a man.[5]

"Some wives save their disapproving expressions for those times when they think it is necessary to remind their husbands of how sad they are that he sits in front of the TV, plays video games, or engages in any number of carnal activities," writes Michael Pearl's wife, Debi. "They keep the pressure on—just like the Holy Spirit would do. At least, that's their justification for doing his job so 'faithfully.'"[6] But their homes would be happier and healthier if they turned that critical eye inward and focused on removing the log which is obstructing their own vision before attempting to take the splinter out of their spouse's eye (Matt. 7:3-5).

"Are you demanding more of him than you demand of yourself?" asks Elizabeth Handford, "Are you really doing all that you ought to do about your own spiritual life? Wouldn't it be better to ask God to show you your [own] failures, and let Him deal with your husband as He sees best?"[7]

Authors Henry Cloud and John Townsend agree: "The best thing you can do right now to turn your marriage in the direction of greatness is to focus on [changing] yourself, not on [changing] your spouse. Good things can happen to the relationship when you start working on yourself instead of trying to change your mate."[8] The take-home lesson from all this? We must stop trying to manipulate our spouses, stop vying for control, and for the love of peace, lay off our nagging! The book of Proverbs issues three separate warnings about embittered, complaining women:

∞ "...better to live in a corner of a roof than in a house shared with a contentious woman." (Prov. 21:9)
∞ "...better to live in a desert land than with a contentious and vexing woman." (Prov. 21:19)
∞ "...better to live in a corner of a roof than in a house shared with a contentious woman." (Prov. 25:24)

To be contentious is to be critical, nagging, demanding of one's own way. Is *this* the tone I want to set in my home? The Bible says my husband would fare better in the blistering sun and scorching heat of a desert than with a bitter, faultfinding, self-serving wife. He'd be more comfortable being exposed to the elements on the corner of the roof than being subjected to the tempest in the teapot of the house. A man should be able to find peace in his own home. He should "be able to feel relaxed, accepted, loved, and content," notes Laura Schlessinger, otherwise, "he begins to not only hate coming home, but he begins to hate his life. That sad reality is often the precipitator of stupid behaviors like drinking or taking drugs, Internet shenanigans, and inappropriate flirting or worse."[9]

When we criticize our husbands and push them "to change because we believe those changes will make us happier, we are in effect putting ourselves in the place of God."[10] Happiness, as we noted in Chapter 12, should not be our ultimate goal in the first place. Cloud and Townsend explain:

> If you are not open to growth—both as individuals and as a married couple—your marriage will fall far short of what you want it to be.... Many couples are swept up in the fantasy that happiness is the supreme goal of marriage. Now, there is certainly nothing intrinsically wrong with wanting to be happy. Happiness is a good and positive thing, and a gift from God. Psalm 68:3 says, "But may the righteous be glad and rejoice before God; may they be happy and joyful." But in reality, *happiness* is *not a good goal for life or marriage.* A much better goal is *growth*, and one of the by-products of growth is happiness.[11]

We must keep in mind that we are all still works in progress. God began the work, and He'll be faithful to complete it (see Phil. 1:6). He will finish the good work he started in you, in me, and in our husbands. We must not grow impatient or doubt His purposes.

If you disagree with some course of action your husband is considering or if you are burdened by something you perceive to be a character flaw, don't try to change him yourself, don't manipulate him, don't attempt to wrench the right to make decisions out of his hand. Pray. Pray. Pray. And pray some more. As Debi Pearl sagely advises:

> Think of the thing your husband does that irritates you the most. Now say to yourself, "I do not see the whole picture. I do not know what God is doing in my life or my husband's life. My critical attitude is a far graver sin than his bad habits. I am guilty of blaspheming the written Word of God when I do not love and obey my husband. Therefore, I am laying down my campaign against him concerning this issue. And, as far as I am concerned, it is God's

business to direct my husband and convict him. I am trusting God.[12]

You may, of course, tell God that you are worried your husband is making a mistake or that you are bothered by the way he is acting. But you must let God take it from there. Turn the matter over to Him. Leave that burden at the foot of the cross, where it belongs.

Many times when I've done this, my husband has changed his mind or altered his behavior without my saying *anything* to him directly. But just as many times, God has changed my perspective and allowed me to see and appreciate the wisdom in my husband's decisions or the advantages to his personality quirks, and to be grateful for them. We must exercise patience and leave plenty of room for the Holy Spirit to work in our husbands' hearts. Otherwise, they may never be able to hear that still, small voice of God over the din of our constant harping.

Pray for Him

Jesus tells his disciples in the gospel of Matthew, "Ask, and it will be given to you; seek, and you will find; knock, and it will be opened to you. For everyone who asks receives, and he who seeks finds, and to him who knocks it will be opened" (Matt. 7:7).

He illustrates God's eagerness to bless us by drawing this comparison: "What man is there among you who, when his son asks for a loaf, will give him a stone? Or if he asks for a fish, he will not give him a snake, will he? If you then, being evil, know how to give good gifts to your children, how much more will your Father who is in heaven give what is good to those who ask Him!" (Matt. 7:7-11).

Who can fathom the depth of God's love for us? He "is able to do far more abundantly beyond all that we ask or think" (Eph. 3:20). Who can measure "the riches of His grace" which He willingly lavishes upon us (Eph 1:7-8)?

We cannot overestimate the importance of prayer and its power to effect change in our personal lives and in the lives of our husbands. "If there is a problem in your life that you can't seem to overcome, don't waste your time complaining, analyzing, or talking about it," writes Leslie Ludy in *Set-Apart Femininity*:

> Take it to God in importunate prayer. Wrestle until the breaking of day. And remember, as Martin Luther said, "God may delay, but He always comes."[13]
>
> ...If our spiritual life is a joke, if prayer is nonexistent, and if Christ is squeezed into random corners of our day, then we are susceptible to every pestering problem the enemy could throw our way—marriage and family disintegration, relational conflicts, financial frustration, depression, sickness, discouragement, and so forth.
>
> But when our spiritual lives are thriving, when prayer is the foundation of our existence, every other area of our lives begins to thrive as a result.[14]

Prayer should characterize the life of a Christian. Scripture tells us to "pray without ceasing" (1 Thess. 5:17). We are admonished to "be anxious for nothing, but in everything by prayer and supplication with thanksgiving let your requests be made known to God" (Phil. 4:6). The Bible promises, "the effective, fervent prayer of a righteous man avails much" (James 5:16 NKJV).

If you earnestly desire your husband to be everything God created him to be, you will not waste one precious minute trying to change him yourself through feminine trickery. Instead, you will humbly acknowledge that God alone can mold and mature him, and you will relentlessly storm the gates of heaven on his behalf. You will pray, and you will keep on praying. E.M. Bounds expressed it well: "He prays not at all who does not press his plea."[15]

"On two different occasions, the disciples fished all night long and caught absolutely nothing," Leslie Ludy reminds us. "But when Jesus came and stood in their midst, they merely had to let down their net once and such an abundance was caught that they didn't even have room in their boat to contain it all (Luke 5:4-11 and John 21:3-6)."[16]

> When prayer is missing from our lives, we spend countless time and energy trying to make our lives work, constantly failing and beating our heads against the wall in frustration. But as it says in Psalm 1, when we meditate upon our Lord day and night, we become like a tree that brings forth much fruit—and everything that we do *just works*. Our time is multiplied. Our effectiveness is multiplied. Our energy is multiplied. Life becomes fruitful instead of frustrating.[17]

Ideally, in addition to praying *for* your husband, you should also pray *with* him. Did you know that spouses who pray together regularly have less than a *one-percent divorce rate*?[18] Yet experts estimate that *less than five percent* of Christian couples pray together on a daily basis![19]

Can you think of a better way to draw spiritually close to your husband, than to approach the throne of grace daily at his side? Yes, I know life gets busy. I know it's easy to forget. That's why Doug and I advise couples to connect their joint prayer life to something they are already motivated to do regularly, anyway. For us, that something is making love. Other couples we know make a habit of praying together before having breakfast each day or after finishing dinner or as they're going to bed. Whatever time you choose, establish the habit now, and you will reap the benefits for the remainder of your lives.

If you are among the 95% of couples who do not pray together with any regularity, be careful that in your enthusiasm to change matters, you do not send your husband the message that you think he's a poor spiritual leader because he hasn't already made praying with you a daily habit. If you broach the topic, do so in a non-accusing way. "Honey, I read that couples who pray together have less than a one-percent divorce rate. Do you think that's something *we* should do?" If he rejects the idea, then answer cheerfully, "Okay, Sweetie, whatever you think," and commit the matter to (private) prayer. God is fully capable of warming your husband to the idea without your attempting to guilt-trip him.

If, however, you are among that five percent of couples who do pray together, consider yourself blessed. Also, be sure to pray *for* your husband as you are praying *with* him. It will bless him to hear you petitioning God to bless his life, his job, his health, his home, his witness, his personal goals.

A word of caution: Make certain you do not use your joint prayer time as an opportunity to "preach" to your husband. Do not pray in his hearing for God to convict him of (some particular) sin. Don't pray that God will forgive him for being such a jerk. Don't use prayer as a thinly veiled disguise for accusations or attacks on his character. When you're talking to God, you should be talking to God, not to your spouse. If your husband suspects joint prayer time to be just another opportunity for his wife to chasten and correct him, he will never be very excited about participating.

So, in the words of Ruth Bell Graham, "Tell your mate the positive, and tell God the negative."[20] Simple yet profound, that is a rule of thumb we all should adopt. Instead of using joint prayer time as a soapbox, address these emotionally charged matters in your personal, private prayer life. If they are mentioned at all during your prayers together, it should only be in the most general terms. Pray: "Lord, help me to see my husband's perspective on this matter and to joyfully submit to his decision." Not: "God, show my husband how unreasonable he is being." If you cannot guard your words, you had better wait until you are alone on your knees before pouring your full heart out to God.

Interestingly, I've often found that the more convinced I am that *my husband* is in the wrong, the more likely God is to reveal that the real problem lies with *me*. It's like the little old man who was concerned his wife was losing her hearing. He waited until she was busy at the sink washing dishes, then snuck up behind her and said quietly, "Honey, I'm talking to you. Do you hear me?" Sure enough, there was no response—she just kept right on washing dishes. *I knew it,* the man thought, *She didn't hear a word I said.* He decided to try it a little louder, so he said more firmly, "Honey, I'm talking to you. Do you hear me?" Still, there was no response. *Her hearing is even worse than I suspected,* the man thought to himself. He tried once more, this time shouting, "HONEY! I'M TALKING TO YOU! FOR THE THIRD TIME, DO YOU HEAR ME?" At this point, his wife turned around with a hand on her hip and answered, "Yes, Dear. I'm listening. For the third time, what is it?"

Obviously, the wife's ears were fine. It was her husband who needed a hearing aid. In the same way, sometimes my husband is right where he should be, and I'm the one in need of an attitude adjustment. Have you ever found yourself in that predicament? That's why you must make a point, while you are praying for your husband, to pray for yourself, as well. Pray that God will open *your* eyes to problem areas and change *your* wrong attitudes. Pray that He will cultivate in you a grateful heart, a respectful demeanor, a gentle and quiet spirit. These things will go a long way toward softening your husband's heart and strengthening your marriage. With such regular nourishment, you and your husband and the love you share will be sure to bloom and grow and flourish.

Chapter 16
Celebrate the Differences

"If the whole body were an eye,
where would the hearing be?"
1 Corinthians 12:17

I am married to a man who loves to shop. Doug can leave home completely unaware of any pressing need, but let him browse long enough, and he'll eventually find something we cannot possibly live without.

Take our new bathroom scales, for instance. Does it matter that the scales we already owned still worked perfectly well? Not in the least. Those old scales merely measured our *weight*. They were embarrassingly archaic.

What makes the new scales remarkable is that they also measure *body fat percentage*. So what choice did Doug have but to buy them on the spot?

For months after making this purchase, he would drag the scales out anytime we had company and subject our unsuspecting guests to surprise weight checks. Seriously! Not everyone shared my husband's enthusiasm for new technology or his eagerness to compare vital statistics; nevertheless, most of our guests would dutifully follow the doctor's orders, removing their socks and shoes and stepping on the scales in turn.

By the time this book was ready to print, Doug had upgraded our bathroom scales yet again.

The *new* new scales are even more high-tech than the *old* new scales. Not only do they measure weight and body fat, but they simultaneously analyze your torso and each separate limb for bone mass, water percentage, and muscle composition, then assign a metabolic age based on those readings. The scales told Doug that *he* has the body of a thirty-something, so of course he brought them home. I wish he hadn't—I was happier not knowing that *my body* belongs in a nursing home!

Different Strokes for Different Folks

My husband is what social theorists call an *early adopter*—a person who invests in brand-new technology the minute it hits the market.[1] He doesn't wait for the kinks to get worked out or the price to drop. If it's for sale, he buys. Early adopters drive the market. They are constantly upgrading, and their spending habits help fund further technological advances. The life of an early adopter is in constant flux.

The fact that Doug falls into this early adopter category was something I did not fully understand or appreciate before we wed. The telltale signs were easily overlooked in those heady days of young love, but impossible to ignore once we were married. It took years for me to reconcile with this quirky aspect of my husband's personality—and I still struggle with it at times.

That's because I'm what sociologists call a *laggard*.[2] I don't believe in paying full price for *anything*. I can wait decades for the cost to drop, especially when it comes to new technology. The old stuff works well enough for me. Our grandparents didn't even have that, and they managed, didn't they? "Use it up, wear it out, make it do, or do without"[3] — that's always been *my* motto.

I learned frugality from my parents. My dad was a do-it-yourself extraordinaire and my mom an avid garage sale hunter. When I was little and just learning to read, my mother and I had the following conversation:

"What does C-A-T spell?"

"*Cat!*"

"What does D-O-G spell?"

"*Dog!*"

"What does S-T-O-P spell?"

This one had me stumped, so Mom gave a not-too-subtle hint: "You know. We see S-T-O-P signs when we're riding in the car? And whenever we do, we *stop*?"

"*Now* I remember," I brightened. "*Garage Sale!*"

When my daddy heard this, he laughed. "That's right, Jennifer. Your mother considers the words *Stop* and *Garage Sale* synonymous!" Pretty soon, I did too. You might say bargain hunting is in my blood.

Different is Okay

"Differentness" is one of the first causes of conflict in a marriage. Spouses may have different opinions concerning what time they go to bed or when they get up, where or how they'll spend holidays, "how clean to keep the house, which foods they like to eat, where to squeeze the toothpaste tube," whether the loose end of the toilet paper roll should hang toward or away from the wall, and whether to paint the bedroom blue or beige.[4]

Please try to remember: Just because your husband thinks and acts differently than you doesn't automatically mean he's in the wrong. A divergent opinion or dissimilar approach to doing a task does not constitute "a breach of sanity or a display of contempt.... Instead of immediately correcting a husband, [a wife should] first see if there is something [she] could learn... then see if the job gets done (that was the goal, wasn't it?), and then offer a compliment."[5]

The key to overcoming "differentness conflicts" is *forbearance*. "Differentness is certainly not a sin, but sometimes husbands or wives do respond sinfully," warns Martha Peace. "We do not like to be told what to do, [so] when there is conflict, it may be because we are selfish. The conflict then results in angry outbursts, pouting, manipulating, nagging, or resentment."[6]

For as long as I can remember, I've liked to have things my own way. I may not always get to, but I can certainly try and usually do. The problem is, my husband likes to have things *his* own way, too—and sometimes our individual ways don't mesh very well.

So what's to be done?

Ideally, a husband and wife should bear with one another in love, patiently "showing tolerance for one another [and] being diligent to preserve the unity of the Spirit in the bond of peace" (Eph. 4:2-3). They should "put on a heart of compassion, kindness, humility, gentleness and patience" (Col. 3:12), each yielding the right to follow their own selfish way and choosing instead to go God's way together.[7] However, sometimes our husbands are unwilling to budge, even an inch. What then? Do we reach an impasse? Do we split up? Cite irreconcilable differences?

God forbid.

It is still possible for a couple to move in a unified direction—even when the husband is resolute—but it requires that the wife adapt herself to doing things *his way*.[8] Does that seem unfair? Why should *she* be the one that has to change, you ask?

For two reasons: First, because that was God's original design: "Man was not created for the woman's sake, but woman for the man's sake" (1 Cor. 11:9). And second, because this book is directed to wives, not to husbands. You will never have control over how your husband acts; you only have control over how you respond.

Are you familiar with the Prayer of Serenity? "Lord, grant me the serenity to accept the things I cannot change, the courage to change the things I can, and wisdom to know the difference."[9] That's a great thought for us wives to keep in mind when it comes to living in peace with our husbands. When it comes to issues of personal preference, we should remind ourselves that these things will matter very little in eternity. In fact, they may not even matter much next *week*.

It is an "immature love [which] seeks sameness and similarity. That's why partners are often first attracted to each other by similar interests, likes, dislikes, and preferences. But as the relationship develops," authors Cloud and Townsend explain, "mature love should supplant immature love. Instead of being threatened by your differences, you grow to enjoy them. Your life and perspective are enhanced and stretched by your partner's varying views and experiences."[10]

When Doug and I first married, his "early adoption" tendency was a major source of contention. What bothered me most was not the new stuff he brought home, but the old (read: *good as new*) stuff he tossed out immediately thereafter. No matter how much I begged and pleaded, I could seldom persuade him to keep anything he'd mentally marked to go. He eventually agreed to send more stuff to Goodwill and less to the dump, but long, long after we stopped fighting about sex and finances, we still argued over which things should be donated to charity and which should be squirreled away, "in case we need them later."

Although I knew my husband's personality and spending habits were things I would never be able to change, I was still firmly convinced that our family would be better off if Doug could only be a little more like *me*. Then one day I had an epiphany. I realized that if it weren't for people like my husband donating their barely-used stuff to Goodwill, people like me would never find anything worth buying when we shopped there...which I still do! Regularly![11]

As for the notion that the Flanders household would be better off with a tightfisted head, I'm pretty sure now that it wouldn't—not for a long stretch. Nevertheless, God has been busily at work, bringing balance to both our hearts.

I've heard it said that a man will pay $2 for a $1 item he needs because it's convenient, and a woman will pay $1 for a $2 item she doesn't need because it's on sale. That was definitely true of *us* a few years back, but we've gradually come to meet in the middle. Doug has now learned to ask for quantity discounts (a family our size almost always qualifies for group rates), and I've learned to avoid those 90%-off sales the day after Christmas.

We're Different By Design

Our modern society likes to pretend there are no differences between the sexes. As Wendy Shalit explains in *A Return to Modesty*, there are members of academia who vehemently deny the existence of even *physical differences* between male and female. Anyone who points to breasts or genitals as proof of such alleged distinctions is branded an "essentialist"—a slur just two steps removed from "heretic" or "ignoramus".[12]

Even those who concede physiological differences between the sexes will often backpedal when it comes to psychological differences. They insist behavioral dissimilarities are the byproduct of social conditioning, sexist upbringing, or cultural expectations. Buying into this philosophy requires we ignore all empirical evidence to the contrary. Whenever such differences emerge, we do our utmost to minimize them—"we give our little boys Ritalin to reduce their drive and our little girls Prozac to reduce their sensitivity."[13]

Yet, "from the beginning," Scripture tells us, "God made them male and female" (Mark 10:6). He made us different by design. When Adam saw Eve, he exclaimed, "This is now bone of my bones and flesh of my flesh" (Gen. 2:23). The word *bone* denotes strength, and the word *flesh* denotes weakness—so Adam was "essentially saying, 'Where

I am weak, she is strong, and where she is weak, I am strong.'"[14]

"The single male [has] aggressive tendencies [that] are largely unbridled and potentially destructive," writes James Dobson in *Straight Talk to Men and Their Wives*:

> By contrast, a woman is naturally more motivated to achieve long-term stability. Her maternal inclinations (they *do* exist and are evident in every culture throughout the world) influence her to desire a home and a steady source of income. She wants *security* for herself and her children.
>
> Suddenly, we see the beauty of the divine plan. When a man falls in love with a woman, dedicating himself to care for her and protect and support her, he suddenly becomes the mainstay of social order. Instead of using his energies to pursue his own lusts and desires, he sweats to build a home and save for the future and seek the best job available. His selfish impulses are inhibited. His sexual passions are channeled. He discovers a sense of pride—yes, masculine pride—because he is needed by his wife and children. Everyone benefits from the relationship.[15]

God made men and women to be complementary in their differences. He made each to need the other. We should not seek to eradicate these design differences, but rather to celebrate them, to accentuate them. The old understanding of sexual differences "recognized the unique and often mysterious traits we instinctively think of as masculine and feminine," writes Danielle Crittenden in *What Our Mothers Didn't Tell Us*,

> ...traits that have persisted despite all the ideological sandblasting of the past three decades. They are too subtle and elusive to be inscribed in law. They

confound both poets and social scientists. But they are differences that complement each other—that ignite passion and sexual attraction, give love its depth and emotional sustenance, and ultimately form women into mothers and wives and [mold] men into fathers and husbands.[16]

God instilled in men a deep desire to lead and protect and provide. He designed women with an enormous capacity to nourish and nurture and love. It is a beautiful thing to see a husband and wife embracing God's purpose and design individually and as a married couple. Rousseau correctly perceived that "when the differences between the sexes are appreciated, each sex needs the other, [but] when women pretend to be men, men tend to need them less".[17] When differences in design are downplayed, something important is lost.

Still, there must be a balance. A husband is to lead, but must do so with integrity and compassion. He is to provide, but should not allow work to displace wife and family in his affections.

A wife must likewise exercise care, lest her role as mother and nurturer to her children causes her to forget her duties as helper and lover to her husband. "In many families today, children have become idols and an object of worship," observes Tommy Nelson in *Better Love Now.*

> Everything the family does revolves around the children—their schedules, their interests, their desires…. In these families, it's easy for moms to become more emotionally connected to their children than they are to their husbands. They spend more time with the kids and talk more with their kids— especially their daughters—than they do their husbands. If moms are not careful, their relationships with their children can begin to supplant the

emotionally unsatisfying relationship they have with their husbands.[18]

Laura Schlessinger warns, "It is of life-and-death (to the marriage) importance that a wife and mother not make her husband feel as though the children are sufficient for her fulfillment."[19]

The tendency of a mother to become absorbed in the lives of her children to the neglect of her husband is an age-old problem. It is "a very natural and forgivable mistake...but one that had better be remedied before you [and your spouse] take to different ways; for children should draw you nearer than ever, not separate you, as if they were all yours and [your husband] had nothing to do but support them."[20]

This was the sage advice given by mother to daughter, when Marmee saw that Meg's devotion to her children was causing a rift in her relationship to her husband. The shift in Meg's priorities was evidenced in her behavior:

> If [her husband] came gaily in at night, eager to embrace his family, he was quenched by a "Hush! They are just asleep after worrying all day." If he proposed a little amusement at home, "No, it would disturb the babies." If he hinted at a lecture or concert, he was answered with a reproachful look and a decided "Leave my children for pleasure—never!" His sleep was broken by infant wails and visions of a phantom figure pacing noiselessly to and fro in the watches of the night; his meals were interrupted by the frequent flight of the presiding genius, who deserted him half helped if a muffled chirp sounded from the nest above.[21]

This passage from Louisa May Alcott's *Little Women* leapt off the page at me when I first read the book as an adult. Reading the quote again now causes me to wonder: In the twenty-plus years I've spent nursing infants, training toddlers, soothing sick ones, teaching teens, how often have I sent my husband the message that he takes second place to everybody else in my immediate world? Are such questions as convicting to you as they are to me? No man enjoys being marginalized—especially not by the loved ones for whom he labors so long and so hard to provide. A husband should not be made to feel that he is merely being tolerated the way a temperamental cat tolerates the hand that feeds her, as an irritating but necessary nuisance. His wife's every action should rather reassure him that he is honored and appreciated and loved. He must know beyond the shadow of a doubt that his life's companion cherishes every minute she spends in his presence.

So invest in your friendship with your husband. Feed it continually. You will reap rich rewards in the long run, for children will eventually grow up and leave home. The mother who has spent eighteen years wrapped completely up in her child to the neglect of her spouse will have much greater difficulty letting go when it comes time for her fledgling to fly.

Together is Better

Ever since Ruth Hulburt Hamilton's "Song for a Fifth Child" was first published, snippets of the poem have graced the walls of innumerable nurseries, neatly embroidered in cross-stitch on cotton muslin. The poem ends,

> Oh, cleaning and scrubbing will wait till tomorrow,
> But children grow up, as I've learned to my sorrow,
> So quiet down cobwebs. Dust go to sleep.
> I'm rocking my baby. Babies don't keep.[22]

It's a sweet sentiment and a true one. But the same thing might be said of husbands. Husbands don't stay young forever either, you know. We have no guarantee that our spouse will even *survive* until the nest is empty, much less that he'll still be around to appreciate the extra time we can then spare for him. How much better to give him our attention now, while we still have opportunity.

"The truth is that a godly marriage is built on simple things and is destroyed by simple things," observes Tommy Nelson:

> When a marriage goes south, it's because one or both spouses misplaced their priorities. They began to think something else was more important than their spouse. Over time their friends, their children, their jobs, their hobbies—something—began to take the most special place in their heart. And their spouse was pushed aside.[23]

The quality of time a couple spends together is important, without question, but the quantity of time they spend together is likewise essential. "Marriages last not just because the people within them love each other but because the time they have spent together, the events they have mutually experienced, the memories they share, and the depth of their intimacy and comfort with each other make marriage to anyone else seem impossible."[25]

"Traditional wisdom suggests a regular date night as key to a happy marriage," writes Mary Ostyn in *A Sane Woman's Guide to Raising a Large Family*:

> Date nights are wonderful and restorative. Some couples even manage to coordinate an overnight getaway once or twice a year. But for most of us, times away only comprise tiny slices of life. It is vital to find ways to connect that don't always involve arranging sitters and packing bags for weekend getaways. Don't get me wrong—getaways are lovely. But what you do with the many ordinary days in between is much more important.[26] Let's face it, if your life is so frantically busy that you can't fit in

something small like squeezing your hubby's rear as you run past him on the way to baseball practice or putting the paper down to look [him] in the eyes for two minutes while [he] talks to you, well, then, your whole life needs a little reworking.[26]

I recently read a book by Bob Barnes entitled *What Makes a Man Feel Loved.* I had long suspected that the things a man considers loving might not be the selfsame things a woman interprets as loving—God made the sexes different in this respect, too—so I was grateful to read a man's perspective on the subject. Barnes writes:

> Think back to those early courting days. Do you have memories of tennis, golf, hiking, camping, sporting events, and Lakers basketball? Now that you have been married a few years and have a child or two, have you stopped doing those things? Or maybe your husband still enjoys those activities, but you are happier reading books, listening to good music, watching a good romance movie on television, or spending an evening at the theater. Or maybe you're the athlete and your husband prefers more sedentary activities. Do you remember how you and your husband use to love doing everything together? Is that still true? Or are you wondering what went wrong along the way?
>
> Think about those couples you know who seem to have a strong marriage. They almost certainly exhibit an ability to enjoy each other's interests.... Such compromise and sharing of our time keeps us growing together, something that separate vacations and long-term or frequent solo outings would not allow. In fact, such separateness can be very dangerous to a marriage relationship.[27]

"When you do things separately, you have a tendency to grow apart, each experiencing your most enjoyable moments of fun and relaxation without the other" warns Willard Harley in *His Needs, Her Needs*. "Couples with separate recreational interests miss a golden opportunity. They often [create their fondest memories] in the company of someone else. It stands to reason that the person with whom you share the most enjoyable moments will give you the greatest dividends."[28]

There is too much separation in marriages today. The husband has his career. The wife has hers. He has his hobbies. She has hers. They have separate cars, separate closets, separate bathrooms, separate email addresses, separate savings accounts, and separate cell phone numbers. Even at church, they go to separate Sunday school classes and are involved in separate ministries. It seems that everything is segregated. They have different interests, different friends, different goals and aspirations, different lives.

Any one of these things by itself might not be a big deal; but taken cumulatively, such segregation strikes a huge blow to the cohesiveness of our marriages. Where's the intertwining? Where's the blending? Where's the sharing? When you pitch in the myriad, separate activities in which each of the children is involved, the family becomes just so many individuals residing under one roof.

Wives who "complain that they are not getting what they want from their husbands should stop and look…at what they put their time and energy into at the expense of him and their marriage."[29] Sometimes, we become so wrapped up in our other roles and outside responsibilities that there is no time left for our primary relationships. We never stop to consider, "Why am I even doing these things, anyway?" Kathy Peel writes in *Desperate Households*:

> We move through life in such a distracted
> way that we do not even take the time and rest to

wonder if any of the things we think, say, or do are *worth* thinking, saying, or doing.[30] ...If we fail to keep clear priorities in mind, it's highly likely that the atmosphere in our homes will turn out very different than we dreamed it would be. Different in ways that everyone will regret.[31]

As wives and mothers, we really must be *pro*active as to how we invest our time and energy and "avoid any obligations that would impinge on couple or family time without first talking [it over with our husband]."[32]

When Shaunti Feldhahn was doing research for her book, *For Women Only*, one of the married men she interviewed told her:

> Most married men don't want to abandon their wife to do guy things. They want to do "guy things" with their wife. They want her to be their playmate. It's no different from when they were dating. For a guy, a big part of the thrill was doing fun things together.
>
> The woman who is having fun with her husband is incredibly attractive. If you see a woman out playing golf with her husband, I guarantee that all the other guys are jealous. Getting out and having fun together falls off in marriage because of various responsibilities, but men still want to *play* with their wives.[33]

Perhaps this is why Elizabeth Handford suggests we should look for ways "to make your husband feel he is the most important human being in your life.... You ought to enjoy and share your husband's interests.... [S]ome things he likes you can share with real enthusiasm."[34] Does your husband want you to take a walk with him? Go fishing? Ride bikes? Watch a movie? Try to accommodate him as often as you can.

"Don't get miffed if you end up going to the basketball game with him more than he goes to the symphony with you," advise Cloud and Townsend: Love doesn't seek its own way (1 Cor. 13:5). One secret of a great marriage is that partners *give* more than they *receive*, and they don't make demands for fairness. "Love gives up keeping score in order to build connection and compassion."[35] When Doug brought home two tickets to the Tyler Area Tough Man Competition (a surprise for *Mother's Day!*), I accompanied him to the fights. Not because I'm a big boxing fan—far from it—but because I enjoy my husband's company and wanted to spend time with him (besides, he agreed to let me bring along my crochet to work on ringside).

I've found that showing interest in the things that interest my husband broadens my base of experience, feeds my love for learning, and stretches me into a more well-rounded person. I knew almost nothing about classic cars or cardiac catheterizations or Kung Fu movies before I got married.... Okay, so I still don't know *much*! But it's more than I knew before Doug explained the finer nuances of those topics over the years. At least now I can differentiate a Mercedes from a Toyota (provided I get a close enough view of the emblem on back); I have a rudimentary understanding of atherosclerosis; and I can appreciate the different fighting styles of Bruce Lee, Chuck Norris, and Jackie Chan.

Doug and I see more action films than chick flicks. We eat more steak than sushi. We go on more grocery shopping dates than weekend getaways. But do you know what? That's okay by me, as long as we're together.

Because together is better, different or no.

I encourage you to embrace your husband's differences. Be glad for them. What a dull, boring world this would be if we were all exactly alike. The fact that God made you and your husband different is not something to mourn or resist. It's something to celebrate!

Chapter 17
Foster Friendship

"A friend loves at all times...."
Proverbs 17:17

I have a friend whose husband used to do something that really irritated her. As soon as he got home from work each day, he'd walk silently past his wife and head straight to the backyard where he'd spend half an hour petting and rubbing and loving on his dog, a little dachshund named Weasel. He would hold Weasel's head in his hands, scratch her behind the ears, and pour his heart out to her, as if she were his only friend in the world. Weasel would wag her tail incessantly, fixing her full attention on her master, alternately licking his hands and face in turn. Not until the man had unburdened his soul to this four-legged companion would he go back inside the house and nod hello to his wife.

My friend eventually confronted her husband about his behavior. "You talk more to that dog than you do to me!" she complained.

"Well," her husband shrugged, "if you acted even half as excited to see me every night as Weasel does, then I'd talk to *you*, instead!"

I don't know whether my friend ever mended her ways and began giving her husband a more enthusiastic welcome home, but I hope for both their sakes she did.[1] Either way, she certainly wasn't the first wife to ever be frustrated by the fact that her husband doesn't talk to her. The "strong silent type" may be an icon at the movies, but he's often an irritation at home. Most women hope for a man who'll communicate.

Communication 101

Communication is an area where we typically notice *big* differences between the sexes. Beginning as early as eight weeks in utero, the female brain develops differently from the male brain, sprouting "visibly more connections in the communication centers that process emotion". This may help explain why, generally speaking, girls are much more verbal than boys. On average, "men use about seven thousand words per day. Women use about twenty thousand."[2]

While most men come in from work each evening having nearly exhausted their daily allotment of words, their wives may still have another 13,000 ready to unleash. Maybe the reason some husbands don't talk to their wives is that their wives never give them the chance: They are trying so franticly to use up those leftover stores that their poor husbands can't squeeze a word in edgewise.

"The truth is that wives generally overwhelm their husbands with communication," observes Laura Schlessinger. "Much of what motivates that communication might better be dealt with through personal circumspection, triaged for significance, selected for true communication (connecting) value, whittled down to its essence, timed better, and expressed more appropriately."[3]

I suspect my own husband would say *amen* to that. Whenever I go into too much detail while telling Doug a story, his eyes start to glaze over. He'll sometimes even make a little rolling motion with his index finger, to let me know that I need to wrap things up. I've learned to follow the Spaniard's example from *The Princess Bride*, who tells his companion, "Lemme 'splain. No, will take too long. Lemme sum up."[4]

According to the Greek philosopher Epictetus, God gave us two ears and only one mouth so that we can listen twice as much as we speak. Maybe that's true. If you'd like for your husband to talk to you more, try talking less yourself and letting *him* choose the topic of conversation. You might even learn something new.

Just last week, Doug and I got stuck in traffic next to a motorcycle rally. I would have been happy to read the book I'd brought along while we waited for traffic to clear, but Doug was in the mood to admire motorcycles and kept commenting on them as they drove by. So I tucked my book into the seat pocket and joined him in gawking at the bikers as they paraded past. I'd never paid much attention to motorcycles before, but that didn't matter. My husband knew enough to keep the conversation going, and by the time the policeman waved us through the intersection, he had taught me how to recognize a Harley Davidson by its distinctive V-twin engine. Now, how many of you can do *that?*

"Communication," writes Tommy Nelson, "is one of the foundations of any friendship. You talk to people whom you like, and you like people whom you talk to. Communication is fertilizer for friendship. If you don't communicate well, you'll forget why you thought this person was so fascinating and loveable [in the first place]."[5]

Unfortunately, *that* is precisely where many couples live. They *don't* converse well, if at all, and their friendship suffers accordingly. Perhaps the husband really doesn't find his wife fascinating or loveable anymore—at least, that's how she interprets his apparent lack of interest. Truth be told, she's not so thrilled with him anymore, either. Here is a woman who is desperate: desperate for conversation, desperate to hear the sound of a human voice. The silence she is living with seems deafening. She is sick of being ignored, sick of her husband's nose being stuck in a book, sick of his attention being glued to a television or computer screen 24-7. She's tired of his acting increasingly annoyed at her slightest interruption. She longs to have him *talk* to her—to have a *normal* conversation—and she'd be *happy* to let him pick the topic. But how is she to draw him out? How can she ever pull him out of this shell? It seems so hopeless. She despairs of ever finding fulfillment in the pathetic, one-sided marriage she finds herself trapped in.

Other couples have plenty to say to one another, but virtually every verbal exchange is filled with anger and contempt. There is no warmth, no peace to be found in their homes, just tension and turmoil and strife. Any love they once felt in their hearts has been poisoned by the venom now spewing from their mouths.

If either of these scenarios describes your marriage, I want you to know that there *is* hope. There *is* a way for your deepest longings to be satisfied, a way which does *not* involve divorcing your present husband and snagging a new one. Don't throw in the towel just yet—you'll inevitably trade one set of problems for another.[6] Instead, realize that the solution you so desperately desire will never be found in worldly wisdom. The answer to these problems is found solely in God. He can melt a heart of ice; He can soften a heart of stone. Both become clay in His hands[7] as He molds and remakes them. God alone can change your husband's heart, but first He wants to work on yours.

You've Got a Friend

I can recall the conversation clearly, although the details leading up to it have grown fuzzy in my memory. I must have been about nine at the time—a tall, gangly redhead with freckles and buckteeth who wore corrective shoes and attended speech therapy—a misunderstood miserable misfit. Leastwise, I felt miserably misunderstood on the afternoon in question.

"Nobody *likes* me!" I sobbed to my mother. "I don't have *any* friends!"

My angel mother did her utmost to comfort me as I sat crying inconsolably at the kitchen table, my face buried in my hands. As a mom now myself, I know it must have broken her heart to see me in such anguish. There were tears in her eyes and a lump in her throat as she offered, "Well, what about Suzy? She's your friend."

"No—she's not," I told her between sniffles. "Suzy never—even plays with me—at recess—anymore."

My mother listed several of my other classmates: What about Becky? Shelly? Lori? Pam?[8]

No. No. No. I answered in turn. *She* says I'm a dork. *She* broke my crayons. *She* made fun of my headgear.[9] *She* told everyone I wet my pants at her slumber party.[10]

Something had to be done—that much was obvious. I couldn't spend my entire childhood friendless. An outcast. A loner. Mother was undoubtedly as annoyed as I that my former friends were so fickle. I saw a look of determination and quiet resolve come over her face as she said, "Don't worry, Jennifer. We'll find you a friend."

Taking me by the hand, Mother led me door-to-door throughout the neighborhood until she finally found a girl my age who was willing to play with me. The crisis was contained, but only for the time being. My loneliness was eased temporarily, but it would be back. An afternoon playmate is not the same thing as a best friend—and a best friend is what I craved.

A best friend, in my childish imagination, was a bosom-buddy, a soul-mate who spent every waking minute in your presence, came to your defense when others picked on you, shared—and kept—your most precious secrets, and loved you despite all your shortcomings.

Although I was eventually blessed with a couple of close friends in high school, none of them ever met up to that imaginary ideal. In the end, they all disappointed me, as I most assuredly disappointed them, and my profound loneliness returned—a loneliness for which, in retrospect, I am extremely grateful, because it ultimately drove me into the arms of a Friend who sticks closer than a brother (Prov. 18:24). It was that heartache, that void, which taught me to take solace in God. Long before I ever met my husband, who truly is my dearest and best friend on this Earth, I discovered in Jesus a Friend who never disappoints, and I began looking to Him to satisfy my heart's deepest longings.

I believe this fact, this knowledge that Christ is all-sufficient, is what makes my marriage a happy one. Likewise, I think that what makes unhappy marriages unhappy, more than anything else, is that spouses expect one another to satisfy longings only Jesus can satisfy, to fill a void only He can fill.

The love of a husband was never intended to *replace* the love of Christ, but only to *reflect* it. It is Christ's love alone that ultimately sustains us. No husband is able to reflect Christ's love perfectly or completely, though by God's grace, some do a better job of modeling it than others. Perhaps your husband's heart has been so warped or broken by sin that the image of God's love is badly distorted or altogether shattered. That does not negate the fact that God's love itself is real and powerful, perfect and complete, fully capable of transforming your life. Just as the squatness of my reflection in that fun house mirror does not diminish my actual height, the ugliness of your husband's treatment of you in no way changes the awesome beauty of God's love.

The sooner you realize this, the better. For once you experience that perfect, unending love, you no longer feel compelled to manipulate your husband into meeting needs he is incapable of meeting. Instead, you find full satisfaction in Christ. And that satisfaction frees you to minister to your husband like you've never done before. To love *him* with the love of Christ. To become God's hands and feet as He addresses your husband's needs through you.

It is God's grace that makes the virtuous wife virtuous. It is His love that inspires her to do her husband "good and not evil all the days of her life" (Prov. 31:12). It is His strength that enables her to serve her husband faithfully, as a helpmeet and a friend. Too many women focus too much attention on "what their marriage and their man can do for them, and not what they can do for their men. And when there is so little emphasis on the giving, the nitpicking and pettiness chews up and spits out what could have been a good marriage" otherwise.[11]

It Don't Come Easy

My sons took a woodworking class this summer, taught by a master craftsman who takes painstaking pride in making fine, handcrafted rocking chairs that he sells through a local specialty shop. The boys were excited about sitting under this man's tutelage and could hardly wait to begin practicing dovetail joints and mortar-and-tenon construction.

Imagine their surprise, then, when the first full day of class was devoted to learning how to properly care for their tools. It took eight hours and an impressive amount of effort just to sharpen all the chisels.

Honing a fine cutting edge is wearisome work. Watching my sons toil and sweat over this project—and seeing one of them nearly cut his finger off in the process—gave me an entirely new appreciation for that Scripture verse which says, "Iron sharpens iron, so one man sharpens another" (Prov. 27:17).

Prior to this summer, I never gave much consideration to how tedious and potentially uncomfortable a thing like "being sharpened" could be.

Yet God works with infinite patience at "sharpening" us, and He clearly uses our friends to help hone our character. Will you fight against the process when it gets uncomfortable, or submit yourself to the skill of the Master Craftsman, knowing that He must prepare you before He can use you?

Doug and I know a couple, Tim and Laura Coody, who realized soon after they were married that their personalities tend to rub each other the wrong way. Tim describes the early days of their marriage in his book, *Meaningless Words & Broken Covenants*: "It became clear that we only had three things in common—we were both Christians, both stubborn (she likes the word "determined"), and we both preferred brown rice to white."[12]

Whenever they were under stress, Laura wanted peace and quiet to think things through, while Tim wanted to talk and talk and talk, until whatever problem they were facing was resolved. This difference grated on both of them like coarse sandpaper. At one time, the irritation was almost more than they could bear, but as they look back now, they see how God used their differences to refine them, to shape them, to polish them. Tim explains:

> Laura and I chose the cross of staying together over the freedom from each other that our flesh craved. In the process, a little flesh died every day, while our spirits were being invigorated. I don't say this to brag or cause you embarrassment if your marriage has failed. If that's the case, my heart goes out to you. Instead, I say it to confront the lie that real peace is available in escaping one's cross. Running from your cross will only create distance between you and Jesus. "If anyone would come after me, he must deny himself and take up his cross daily and follow me" (Luke 9:23)."[13]

You should not be afraid to embrace the cross of a difficult marriage, if it is in a difficult marriage you find yourself. God can use even (dare I say especially?) a cantankerous mate to sharpen and shape you into an instrument to be used for His glory, if only you'll yield yourself completely and allow Him to work.[14]

Guard Against Annoyances

In the book *Why a Shepherd?* Bodie Thoene recounts the summer she spent tending sheep in the mountains above Central California under the supervision of a Basque widow named Maria who taught Thoene and her friends many valuable lessons about sheep and about life:

> Who could have imagined that the greatest enemies of a sheep are actually the smallest creatures on the mountain? But it's true. Flies, ticks, mosquitoes—insects of all kinds—swarmed around our sheep like a cloud of worries. It was our job to protect them from the anxiety of those maddening distractions and discouragements....
>
> As if the buzzing of flies was not enough to drive the sheep mad, some larvae were ingested through their food supply and then hatched in their digestive system, robbing the sheep of nutrients. No matter how well fed a sheep was, if it was troubled by flies or infested with parasites, it grew thin and weak, unable to eat, and never achieved the full potential of its growth.[15]

As I read Thoene's account, I marveled. I'd always imagined a shepherd's main job was to stand watch for wolves and lions; I'd never considered the much smaller pests that must also be dealt with. A shepherd's providing protection from large predators is unquestionably necessary to the survival of the sheep, but is obviously insufficient, by itself, to ensure the flock's comfort, contentment, and general health.

Similarly, safeguarding against adultery, infidelity, and homicide is not enough in itself to nurture a healthy marriage. More often than not, it is the countless little things, the small but accumulating annoyances, which ultimately destroy the happiness of a home. We cannot allow this.

We must do three things to guard our marriages against the menacing swarm of minor offenses that threatens to unmake us: we must try not to take offense, try not to give offense, and seek to soothe rather than irritate.

First, we should *be careful not to take offense*. If men can sometimes be insensitive—and we all know they can—women can be annoyingly hypersensitive. Don't let this describe you. Toughen up a bit, and don't make your husband walk on eggshells. Just as mature sheep are less susceptible to insect bites than tender lambs, you will fare much better if you do not allow yourself to be easily offended. This, after all, is the nature of mature love: it "is not provoked, does not take into account a wrong suffered... bears all things, believes all things, hopes all things, endures all things" (1 Cor. 13:5, 7).

Second, we must *be careful not to give offense*. If you know your husband is annoyed by certain behaviors, then *don't act that way*. Give "no occasion for reproach" (1 Tim. 5:14). My husband cannot stand for anybody to touch his head while he is eating. If his own hands are greasy, he assumes everyone else's are, too, and it freaks him out to imagine that grease being transferred to his facial skin. So rather than kiss his cheek or massage his neck as I might otherwise be inclined to do over a romantic candlelit dinner, I've learned to keep my hands to myself and smile sweetly at him from across the table. Given his particular phobia, that's the loving thing to do.

Third, we must seek to soothe rather than irritate. The shepherd doesn't stop at shooing insects away. Just as in the presence of our enemies, the Lord anoints our heads with oil (Ps. 23:5), so a good shepherd applies salve to the sheep's faces to relieve the itch of current bites and to protect against future irritation. It's not enough for a wife to discontinue negative habits that irritate or annoy—she must replace them with positive habits that encourage and edify.

We should think of the things our husbands most appreciate and enjoy, then do those things regularly. For my husband, this means stuff like making his breakfast, folding his laundry, and soaking in the tub with him before bed. For my friend whose husband talks to his dog, it may mean greeting him at the door with a kiss when he comes in from work, or bringing him an iced tea while he plays with the dachshund on the patio. For your husband, the list will be different.

Whatever we do, we should do faithfully and cheerfully. It takes only three weeks of repeating an action daily for it to become a habit, so put these items on your to-do list and be consistent. Before long, they will become second nature. Sometimes, I even add things like "Make Doug's Oatmeal" and "Kiss Husband Goodbye" to my daily chore chart. This prevents my feeling that such things keep me from accomplishing my goals, for these things are themselves the goals now. They're on the list, too, and once they are done for the day, I get the satisfaction of checking them off!

Do you desire a closer friendship with your spouse? Conventional wisdom tells us that *to have a friend, you must be a friend.*[16] The fastest way to a friendlier marriage is to focus more on pleasing your mate than on having him please you.

Chapter 18
Control Your Tongue

"He who guards his mouth and his tongue,
guards his soul from troubles."
Proverbs 21:23

Arguments in marriage are like dirty dishes in the sink—they're best dealt with immediately. At least, that's how we've come to see it.

Doug and I learned early that putting off washing dishes does not make the chore any easier. On the contrary, if you leave dishes long enough (which I'm ashamed to admit we did during those honeymoon weeks), milk will sour, mold will grow, and a cloud of midges will hover menacingly above your sink. It's truly disgusting. Even if you put dishes to soak in hot water to loosen the baked-on grime, you had better return before the water becomes tepid and the suds disappear, or you'll be back to dealing with a cold, slimy mess.

Having learned this lesson the hard way, I now see to dirty dishes in a more timely fashion. I take care not to make a bigger mess than is necessary. As much as is possible, I wash up as I go when preparing meals, so that it's a simple matter of loading cups and plates into the dishwasher after we eat. And I also make a point to never leave dishes in the sink overnight.

I have found that abiding by these simple rules—don't make unnecessary messes, wash up as you go, empty the sink before bedtime—makes the kitchen a vastly more pleasant place to work. But these same principles adapt readily to marriage in general and to conflict resolution in particular: Avoid unnecessary arguments. Address areas of conflict as they arise. And don't go to bed angry. The rules are simple. They're Biblical. And abiding by them makes our home an exceedingly more peaceful place to live.

Avoid Unnecessary Arguments

The Bible makes it clear that the best kind of argument is one that's avoided. Read for yourself:

∞ "The beginning of strife is like letting out water, so abandon a quarrel before it breaks out." (Prov. 17:4)

∞ "When there are many words, transgression is unavoidable, but he who restrains his lips is wise." (Prov. 10:19)

∞ "He who guards his mouth and his tongue, guards his soul from troubles." (Prov. 21:23)

∞ "A man's discretion makes him slow to anger... it is his glory to overlook a transgression." (Prov. 19:11)

∞ "Keeping away from strife is an honor for a man, but any fool will quarrel." (Prov. 20:3)

∞ "But everyone must be quick to hear, slow to speak and slow to anger." (James 1:19)

∞ "He who is slow to anger has great understanding, but he who is quick-tempered exalts folly." (Prov. 14:29)

∞ "Let no unwholesome word proceed from your mouth, but only such a word as is good for edification according to the need of the moment, so it will give grace to those who hear." (Eph. 4:29)

∞ "He who restrains his words has knowledge, and he who has a cool spirit is a man of understanding." (Prov. 17:27)

Laura Schlessinger advises wives to keep their "lips buttoned over things that *do not really matter*." Whenever she feels herself getting upset over something insignificant, Schlessinger asks herself "Is this the hill you wish to die on?" The phrase, which she learned from a retired Marine master sergeant, always makes her "priorities instantly fall into place" and reduces her tension concerning whatever she was worked up about.[1] But sometimes we find ourselves in the midst of conflict, despite our best efforts to avoid it. What then?

Address Areas of Conflict as They Arise

It is imperative that couples deal with disputes in a timely fashion, preferably as soon as they come up. Even if you decide in the heat of an argument that you need to cool off before continuing a discussion, do not put it off too long, lest you give wounds an opportunity to fester and find yourself in a bigger mess than you started with. Pray rather that God will give you the wisdom and love and patience you need to resolve the problem now.

As you pray, examine your own heart, asking God to reveal to you how *your* words, *your* actions, *your* responses contributed to the argument. Then go immediately to your husband—without pointing fingers, without making excuses, without rattling off a long list of grievances—and humbly apologize for your own wrong behavior toward him. Then ask his forgiveness.

When your husband talks to you, listen—and I mean *listen.* Do your best to hear and understand what he is saying. Resist the urge to contemplate your "defense" while he is speaking.[2]

We are "prone to excusing our lack of love for others by reminding ourselves how poorly others love us," writes Larry Crabb in *Men & Women: Enjoying the Difference*, but we "need to see that God... commands us to respond with unstained love."³ Spouses are called to love one another unconditionally. Even though your husband "may be a source of real suffering for you, Scripture is clear that you are to get rid of all bitterness, rage, and anger."⁴

∞ "But now you also, put them all aside: anger, wrath, malice, slander, and abusive speech from your mouth. Do not lie to one another." (Col. 3:8-9)

∞ "See to it that no one comes short of the grace of God; that no root of bitterness springing up causes trouble, and by it many be defiled." (Heb. 12:15)

∞ "Let all bitterness and wrath and anger and clamor and slander be put away from you, along with all malice. Be kind to one another, tender-hearted, forgiving each other, just as God in Christ also has forgiven you." (Eph. 4:31-32)

∞ "Cease from anger and forsake wrath; do not fret; it leads only to evildoing." (Psalm 37:8)

∞ "Now the deeds of the flesh are evident, which [include] outbursts of anger, disputes, dissensions.... But the fruit of the Spirit is love, joy, peace, patience, kindness, goodness, faithfulness, gentleness, self-control; against such things there is no law." (Gal. 5:19-23)

Don't Go to Bed Angry

The Bible states in no uncertain terms that we must "not let the sun go down on [our] anger" (Eph. 4:26). Solomon recommends that if we have a dispute with a neighbor, we "give no sleep to [our] eyes, nor slumber to [our] eyelids" until we've humbled ourselves and seen the matter resolved. Jesus himself emphasizes the importance of speedily reconciling with an offended brother, even if it means interrupting the presentation of one's offering upon the altar (Matt. 5:23-24). He urges us to settle differences quickly, before legal action can be brought against us (Matt. 5:25-26).

Why is it so important that we deal with conflicts swiftly and completely? We must do it so that we "do not give the devil an opportunity" (Eph. 4:27).

What exactly does that mean, "do not give the devil an opportunity"? Don't give him an opportunity to do what? I believe it means we should not allow Satan to sow seeds of discord and division, to water them with pride and dissatisfaction, until the root of bitterness burrows deep into our soul and yields a bumper crop of hatred and contempt that will destroy our life and marriage. Don't give the devil an opportunity to do *that.* Better yet, we should seek out and crush all seeds of resentment as soon as they blow our way—don't give sleep to your eyelids until they are completely obliterated—so they'll have no chance to even germinate.

You might think that refusing sleep until marital harmony is restored would rob a couple of too much rest, but the opposite is actually true. When a husband and wife make it their habit to resolve differences before turning in for the night, they are able to extend and experience forgiveness. After truly letting go of offenses, they rest with a clear conscience, unbothered by the day's affairs, at peace with God and man.

This is something couples who do not abide by this principle may never experience. Can you imagine? Tossing and turning night after night, never free of stress, guilt, resentment, anger, and bitterness? That is not a life I would choose.

"Friction between husband and wife is a terrible consumer of energy," writes Elizabeth Handford:

> It drains the body of drive, wastes the resources of the mind, dissipates the usefulness of emotion, and consumes enormous amounts of time. Talk about wasted resources! Surely conflict in the home is one of the greatest of wastes![5]

Unresolved conflicts rob us of joy for today and of strength for tomorrow.

When we refuse to give place to lingering resentments, however, we are freed to think creatively and work purposefully, secure in the knowledge that our spouse loves us, trusts our decisions, and is committed to working cheerfully alongside us rather than angrily against us. When we are not distracted by unfinished arguments and half-hashed excuses, we can give ourselves wholeheartedly to the task at hand instead of frittering away our time fighting—or yielding to—nagging doubts and fears.[6]

Guarding Our Mouths

"Some marriages don't handle conflict as well" writes Tommy Nelson. "They fight dirty. They cast away the peace of their home. Each person feels like they have to win" at all costs, and they are destroying their marriages in the process.[7] Their tempers desperately need to be reigned in and their tongues brought under control.

"There ought to be things you will never say to your spouse and a tone of voice in which you would never speak."[8] Couples would do well to discuss and agree upon such guidelines in advance, before a fight breaks out.

Doug and I arrived at such an agreement after a particularly malignant argument we had about twenty years ago while on vacation.[9] The entire exchange—which lasted over an hour—never rose above a whisper, since neither of us wished to disturb our two children who were sleeping in the room with us at the time. I probably came closer to leaving my husband that night than ever before or since, but by the staying grace of God, I thought better of that plan. Instead, I used the cover of darkness to take notes on the diatribe. As if taking dictation, I wrote down everything Doug said, just as fast as it poured out of his mouth. I wrote in shorthand to keep up and worked quietly enough so as not to arouse suspicion.

The next afternoon, once he'd calmed down and we were driving toward home with our two babies napping in their car seats behind us, I pulled out my notes and tearfully read back to Doug his words from the night before. He was grieved. He apologized sincerely. He assured me he hadn't meant any of the hurtful things he'd said—indeed, he barely even remembered saying them. I explained to him that when you truly love someone, there are things you never allow yourself to say, no matter how angry you are at the time.[10] He agreed, we compiled a mental list of such statements, and he never said any such thing to me ever again.

"Often we combat our evil thoughts most effectively if we absolutely refuse to allow them to be expressed in words," writes Dietrich Bonhoeffer. "It must be a decisive rule of every Christian fellowship that each individual is prohibited from saying much that occurs to him."[11] As important as what we do say in conversation is what we don't say. We have a clear Biblical mandate for measuring our words and holding our tongues:

- ∞ "If anyone thinks himself to be religious, and yet does not bridle his tongue but deceives his own heart, this man's religion is worthless." (James 1:26)
- ∞ "Hatred stirs up strife, but love covers all transgressions." (Prov. 10:12)
- ∞ "Do you see a man who is hasty in his words? There is more hope for a fool than for him." (Prov. 29:20)
- ∞ "An angry man stirs up strife, and a hot-tempered man abounds in transgression." (Prov. 29:22)
- ∞ "There is one who speaks rashly like the thrusts of a sword, but the tongue of the wise brings healing." (Prov. 12:18)
- ∞ "Death and life are in the power of the tongue, and those who love it will eat its fruit." (Prov. 18:21)

∞ "The one who desires life, to love and see good days, must keep his tongue from evil and his lips from speaking deceit." (1 Pet. 3:10-11)

∞ "So also the tongue is a small part of the body, and yet it boasts of great things. See how great a forest is set aflame by such a small fire! And the tongue is a fire, the very world of iniquity; the tongue is set among our members as that which defiles the entire body, and sets on fire the course of our life, and is set on fire by hell.... [N]o one can tame the tongue; it is a restless evil and full of deadly poison. With it we bless our Lord and Father, and with it we curse men, who have been made in the likeness of God; from the same mouth come both blessing and cursing. My brethren, these things ought not to be this way." (James 3:5-10)

"Discouraging words cripple, but encouraging words inspire."[12] Surely our marriages should be characterized by blessings rather than cursings, by words of encouragement rather than crippling criticisms. "Truly satisfying relationships," writes Tim Coody, "are built on the foundation of trustworthy, meaningful words."[13] This should be the goal toward which husbands and wives strive in all their communications.

For a wife who feels the need to open lines of communication with her husband, or to address—as I did—the areas in which communication is breaking down, Kevin Leman suggests taking the following steps:

1. Get [your husband] alone behind a closed door.
2. Touch him as you're talking to him. Because your guy is so touch oriented—and he especially likes to be touched by the love of his life—he's much more liable to pay attention to you. And the little-boy part of him

will be saying, *Well, she's touching my arm, so she still likes me even if she doesn't like what I did.*

3. Soften his defenses by looking him straight in the eye and saying something like, "Hey, honey, I could be dead wrong/out in left field on this, but when..." Admitting up-front that you could be very wrong will make your guy relax, instead of feeling edgy or competitive...."[14]

Taming Our Tempers

Any time two distinct people with two distinct personalities spend any amount of time together, there is a potential for disagreement. If either or both are inclined toward selfishness or frustrated by unmet expectations, the possibility for disputes only escalates.

Gary Smalley illustrates a person's propensity to lose his temper this way: Each of us carries what Smalley calls an "anger cup" in our hearts, an imaginary cup that contains all the unresolved anger we are harboring there. Some folks "have anger cups that are 90 percent empty. They can experience irritations and unfulfilled expectations without causing an overflow." But other people have anger cups that are already filled to the brim. "It may be filled with a lifetime of anger, or maybe just a day's worth. Dropping even the tiniest amount of irritation into the cup will cause the anger to overflow and spill onto whoever created the irritation. The most insignificant event—somebody cuts them off on the freeway, or ignores or rejects a single expectation—can set off the person with a full cup of anger."[15]

My husband had a professor in medical school who would describe the behavior of a patient who dramatically overreacts to minor annoyances by saying, "That's a two stimulus and a ten response!" Whenever this doctor observes a volatile temperament, he knows that there's "eight" of something unknown fueling the patient's excessive reaction.

In a normal person, the intensity of a response will match the intensity of a stimulus. Think of the tiny rubber mallet a physician uses to check your reflexes: If he gives a little tap, he gets a little twitch. If he gives a bigger tap, he gets a bigger twitch. But when a small rap on the knee sends a patient through the roof, you can be sure that something strange is going on. That's a two stimulus, ten response.

Parents of young children understand exactly what I'm talking about. Sometimes it seems that no amount of cheering will make a baby happy. He's tired and he's cranky, and everything you do just seems to make him madder. But put him down for a nap, and he'll wake up two hours later just as happy as a lark. The thing that was making him irritable was lack of sleep.

As I've already intimated, I saw a lot of "ten" responses to "two" stimuli when Doug and I first married. I can't tell you the number of holes he punched in the walls of our first apartment over what seemed like minor annoyances, or the number of china plates he shattered by hurling them across the dining room when I said something at mealtime that he didn't like.

I can't tell you how many, because I honestly don't know. Doug talks now as if such outbursts were a daily occurrence, but I only remember three holes for sure—two in the drywall, which I patched myself with sheetrock mud, and one in a wood door, which left a scar on Doug's knuckles and broke him of that habit—and although all but one of our antique blue Asiatic Pheasant dishes were eventually broken, most were casualties of accidents involving our little ones. I only remember Doug breaking two plates intentionally—the first was full of spaghetti when he sent it flying through the air, which left an orange stain on our carpet that even Windex wouldn't remove.

The thing that was making my husband angry wasn't *really* the fact that I'd failed to answer the phone on the first ring or overcooked the pasta or missed a spot while vacuuming, although it may have appeared to innocent bystanders that those were the sort of insignificant things that set my husband off. No, the *real* provocation—the "eight" of something else—was the fact that I was refusing him sex so much of the time in those early years of marriage. Would I be in the mood, or wouldn't I? It was a toss-up. The uncertainty was driving Doug insane and coloring our every interaction—even those that ostensibly had nothing to do with sex. Once I made this cause-and-effect connection and began faithfully fulfilling my conjugal duties, my husband turned into a great big teddy bear, and the peace in our home was restored.

Now for those of you who are thinking, *That's no excuse! It certainly doesn't justify his breaking china dishes or putting his fist through the wall*—you are absolutely right. Doug's angry outbursts were sin, no two ways about it. He was behaving wrongly, whether his physical needs were being met or not.

Nevertheless, I did not wish to cast away the peace of my home in my own stubborn refusal to cast off pride. It was not my intention to make life unbearable for my husband. I want to do him good, not evil. I want to be a blessing to him, not a thorn in his side. Sure, I could have waited for him to change *first*. I could have concluded that he needed to get his act together, that he needed to die to himself—and that by denying his deep need for sex and respect, I could somehow force that to happen. But I don't think such an approach would have worked any better on Doug than it does on most husbands. I am his *wife*—not his conscience, not the Holy Spirit—and I must relate to him as a wife should.

Gardeners will sometimes force bulbs to bloom indoors, out of season, but the blossoms won't come until you pull the bulbs out of the fridge and give them warmth, water, and plenty of sunshine. This seems a reasonable method for dealing with spouses, as well. If you want to see your husband grow and bloom, then let him feel the warmth of your loving embrace, the water of your supportive, encouraging, respectful words, the sunshine of your admiring smile. This will achieve much more desirable results than will cutting him off physically and keeping him in the cold. If any man matures in *that* sort of marriage, it will be in spite of his wife's treatment, not because of it.

Don't Simmer and Stew

In men, anger tends to boil over or explode. In women, it tends to simmer into bitterness and resentment. Either reaction can have a devastating effect on a marriage.

Violent outbursts destroy trust. Like villagers living on the edge of a volcano, it is impossible to ever completely relax if you live with a spouse who has a volatile temper. Every moment is spent wondering when he might blow again.

But seething tempers can be just as damaging as explosive ones. Simmering resentment silently poisons everything with which it comes in contact, like contaminated ground water. As pollutants reach critical levels, the water affected by them becomes useless. It is *worse* than useless, in fact, since poisoned water can actually do more harm than no water at all.

If you live with a spouse who simmers, attempt to draw him out gently. Ask him if you've done something to upset him, and if so, would he please tell you what it is so you can make any needed adjustments in the way you relate to him. If you already know what's upsetting him, skip this step and get to work. Adapt yourself to him. Ask his forgiveness if you have wronged him. Pray that God will give you wisdom and grace to avoid unnecessary conflicts in the future.

If you live with a spouse who explodes, tread lightly. Don't get into a battle of words with him. Remember that "a soft [gentle] answer turns away wrath" (Prov. 15:1). The virtuous woman "opens her mouth with wisdom, and on her tongue is the law of kindness" (Prov. 31:26 NKJV). Beyond guarding your mouth, you must examine your heart. Are you doing anything, intentionally or not, that is provoking him?[16] Are you denying him physically or acting disrespectful toward him? It may be difficult to *feel* respect for a spouse who is continuously enraged against you, but you are still required to *demonstrate* respect. Besides, if you ever assume an attitude of judgmental pride, you will have fallen straight into Satan's snare. Your pride is an even greater affront to God than your husband's anger.[17] So pray. Pray for your husband, but pray also for yourself. Pray that your husband will be convicted of his wrong behavior, but also that God would be glorified through your response to it.

Doug soon realized how disruptive his violent temper was to the peace of our home, how destructive it was to the people inside. One day, as he sat staring at the patches in our walls and at the scars on his knuckles, God opened his eyes. More than anything else, my husband wanted his life to have a positive impact on those around him, especially on his wife and children (we only had two at the time). Yet his actions were having exactly the opposite effect. The negative influence of his anger threatened to outweigh everything good he had done. Rather than being better off for having known him, it seemed that our spirits were being broken because of him.

That very day, Doug repented of his sin: A genuine, one-hundred-eighty-degree-turning-away-and-forsaking-it kind of repentance. A confessing-to-wife-and-children-and-parents-and-pastors-and-anyone-who-would-listen sort of repentance. A humble, I-begged-the-Lord-to-change-me-and-was-never-the-same-again type of repentance.

I can assure you this miracle did not result from any lectures on my part that Doug "should learn to control his temper"—I wasn't even at home when the Holy Spirit convicted him. The change was not prompted by any disapproving, self-righteous scowls from me. It was not effected by feminine manipulation. From first to last, beginning to end, my husband's transformation was (and is) the work of God—the same God who was (and is) patiently and simultaneously working on the yielded heart of his wife—the very God who promises to continue and complete the good work He begins in your heart, as well (Phil. 1:6).

Remember those blue Asiatic Pheasant dishes that Doug shattered against the wall of our apartment so long ago? I saved them. Fifteen years later, when we built our house, I used the fragments to make a broken china mosaic frame for a mirror that hangs in our guest room upstairs. It's simple, yet lovely. My husband enjoys showing it off and telling people the history behind it. Some of our guests look at the mirror in disbelief—Doug seems so laid back now, they have a hard time imagining that he ever hurled those plates in the first place—but others look at the mirror with hope. They understand that the God we serve is a God who frees us from the power of sin. The mirror frame is a metaphor. It symbolizes the beauty that God can create from our broken lives, if only we'll turn the fragments over to Him.

Chapter 19
Forgive and Forget

*"Be kind to one another, tender-hearted,
forgiving each other,
just as God in Christ also has forgiven you."*
Ephesians 4:32

In marriage, as in life, it pays to maintain a sense of humor.

Consider the time that, unbeknownst to me, Doug used his cell phone to video one of our babies, fresh from his bath and all dressed for bed. Little Isaac looked so sweet and rosy toddling around the bathroom in those footed pajamas that Doug couldn't resist passing the clip around the hospital the following day. Surgeons, nurses, scrub techs, housekeeping staff—almost everyone he knows had seen the footage before he bothered showing it to me. When he finally did, I was mortified. He had obviously paid no attention to camera angles and had unwittingly captured me in the background. If you looked closely, you could see me clearly over the baby's bobbing shoulder—*sitting on the toilet with my pants around my ankles!*

It's at times like that you must laugh or cry. Of what use would it be for me to get angry over this? Doug swears he hadn't even noticed the background image. "Although," he mused playfully, "that *would* explain all the sniggering in the O.R. today!"

I'm just grateful he didn't post the clip on YouTube.

We needn't "dismiss the seriousness of any event," says Dr. Carl Charnetski, but we *should* "step outside of [ourselves], if only momentarily, and laugh at how ludicrous it is."[1] I am not suggesting you make light of your husband's concerns or joke around next time he tries to discuss a problem with you. But we should be willing to laugh at ourselves, and show grace to our mates when they make honest mistakes.

But what if it's not a mistake? What about the times our husbands say something unkind, knowing full well how much it will hurt us? What about when they do things they oughtn't? What about when they sin? Do we just forgive them anyway? And let them get away with it? Without any punishment, even?

Enough Is Enough!

In her book, *Martha to the Max,* Debi Stack sums up my sentiments, exactly: "If a Martha [remember Mary's hard-working sister?] ever devised a recovery program, it wouldn't dillydally through twelve long steps. Hers would get to the point—and fast: Step 1: Admit your problem. Step 2: Snap out of it."[2] Stack concedes that it is "easier expected of others than applied to ourselves," nevertheless, this *is* the way many of us think.

It must have been the way Peter thought, too, for he once asked Jesus, "Lord, how often shall my brother sin against me and I forgive him?" (Matt. 18:21). We can usually manage to forgive somebody a first offense, but we expect them to learn their lesson after that. Our attitude seems to be: *First time you do me wrong and I forgive you, shame on you. Second time you do me wrong and I forgive you, shame on me.* If that isn't what we're thinking, it is sure how we're acting, as if forgiving somebody more than once—especially for the same offense—is personally degrading or makes us weak.

So Peter probably thought he was being generous when he suggested, "[Shall I forgive him] up to seven times?" That really *would* be going the extra mile, now, wouldn't it? Jesus surprised him by answering, "I do not say to you, up to seven times, but up to seventy times seven'" (Matt. 18:22). In other words, just keep on forgiving, and don't bother to keep count.

Such longsuffering is characteristic of love: Love "doesn't take into account a wrong suffered" (1 Cor. 13:6). This is the kind of love that God bestows upon us. "When we fail, and often we do—God keeps no record of it," observes Norm Wright. "Because of the work of Jesus on the cross, you are accepted as blameless. [So] perhaps one of your most important callings in marriage is to follow the model of Christ by being a living benediction to your partner. Help keep your mate from stumbling, and when he or she does fall, don't keep track of it."[3]

There is no place in marriage for scorekeeping, but there's lots of room for forgiveness, and it's essential that we dispense it both freely and fully.

Notice that Jesus does not address how Peter *feels*. He only commands him to *forgive*. That's an imperative we can choose to obey, whether we feel like it or not.

Tommy Nelson talks about this fact in his book, *Better Love Now:*

> You don't have to feel like forgiving, but you do have to forgive. You do have to be quiet and not slander. You have to be kind. You have to respond according to the divine standard that God has given.
>
> I know it's a lot easier to write and read about forgiveness than it is to actually forgive. But it's the command of the King. If you are harboring unforgiveness and disrespect in your heart toward your spouse, you are absolutely disobeying Jesus

Christ. You need to repent and do what Jesus has told you to do.

Do it for yourself, for your spouse, and for the glory of God.[4]

A Pattern of Forgiveness

God makes it abundantly clear in His word that forgiveness is a pattern He wants us to follow. He sets the standard Himself by neither dealing with us "according to our sins, nor reward[ing] us according to our iniquities. For as high as the heavens are above the earth, so great is His loving kindness toward those who fear Him. As far as the east is from the west, so far has He removed our transgressions from us" (Ps 103:10-12). Even as He hung dying upon the cross, Jesus looked upon those who had put Him there and pleaded, "Father, forgive them; for they do not know what they are doing." Christ is our example, and we are to emulate Him. He expects us to love those who wrong us and pray for those who hurt us (Matt 5:44); He expects us to forgive freely:

- ∞ "Whenever you stand praying, forgive, if you have anything against anyone, so that your Father who is in heaven will also forgive you your transgressions. [But if you do not forgive, neither will your Father who is in heaven forgive your transgressions.]" (Mark 11:25)
- ∞ "If your brother sins, rebuke him; and if he repents, forgive him. And if he sins against you seven times a day, and returns to you seven times, saying, 'I repent,' forgive him." (Luke 17:3)
- ∞ "...you should rather forgive and comfort him, otherwise such a one might be overwhelmed by excessive sorrow. Wherefore I urge you to reaffirm your love for him." (2 Cor. 2:7-8)
- ∞ "So, as those who have been chosen of God, holy and beloved, put on a heart of compassion, kindness,

humility, gentleness and patience; bearing with one another, and forgiving each other, whoever has a complaint against anyone; just as the Lord forgave you, so also should you." (Col. 3:12-13)

"We are to forbear one another in love, and this involves something different from putting up with our mates with a resigned sigh (Eph. 4:32); we are to evidence the spiritual fruit of love, patience, and kindness (Gal. 5:22)."[5]

"It doesn't take very long for me to see that a couple's lack of forgiveness is traumatizing their relationship" writes Tommy Nelson:

> Sometimes, there is a serious breach of trust through adultery, misuse of money, abuse, or the like. When a couple like this wants to work it out, I say to the offender, "You *must* change." But to the one whose trust has been violated I say, "You *must* forgive." They cannot *almost* forgive. They cannot hold it in until the next violation and then drag it back out and use it to beat their spouse over the head. I've seen more than one couple say they want to reconcile and then fall apart because they cannot forgive."[6]

Why is it so imperative that we forgive, anyway? What makes forgiveness so important? I believe God commands us to forgive as much for our own sakes as for the sakes of those who offend us. Nelson explains:

> If you are an unforgiving person, two things begin to happen in your life.
> Unforgiving people inevitably become *bitter*. I can honestly say that I have never met a healthy, happy unforgiving person. At first we think it will be fun to play the part of God in judging another person.... All that energy and anger rushes out, and our hearts justify our feelings and actions: "My spouse

263

deserves to see and feel how much they have hurt me and how I really feel."

The problem is…you and I are not the judge and jury for our spouses. It's not our place to convict them and find them guilty. That's God's job.

The second thing that happens to unforgiving people is that they become *self-righteous*. The only way you can harbor anger and bitterness is if you think that you aren't that bad. You know, it wasn't that big of a deal for God to pay for your sins and get you into glory. But your spouse? God is going to have to work hard to pull that one off.[7]

If you think that attitude sounds arrogant, you are absolutely right. There's a good reason that some people cannot find it in their hearts to forgive: Their hearts are so chock-full of pride that forgiveness has been completely crowded out. Evicted. Kicked to the curb and forgotten.

You can talk about hurt feelings and deep sorrow and violated trust all you want, but those are not the things that keep us from forgiving. They may be valid concerns—they may result in rifts that God alone can mend—but they are not obstacles to our obedience. His grace is able to heal a wounded heart so that forgiveness can still flow from it.

But when forgiveness is not forthcoming, when it is viewed as an impossibility, when the offending party is thought not to deserve it, then be certain something more sinister than grief or pain or mistrust is hard at work. If you dig deeply enough, you'll find that the real reason—the only reason—that we refuse to forgive is because our hearts have been overtaken by pride and self-righteousness and ingratitude. Until these vices are rooted out and dealt a deathblow, we will never be able to fully forgive.

Oft times, our husband's faults and offenses seem glaring to us, while we remain completely blind to our own. Elisabeth Elliot puts things in perspective: "Remember, ladies, you are married to a sinner, and so is he."[8] When conflicts arise, we should be quick to accept responsibility, slow to cast blame, and as willing to ask for forgiveness as we are to extend it. We must confess wrong behavior without pointing fingers or seeking to justify our actions. "Explanations are requests not for *forgiveness*, but for *understanding*," writes Larry Crabb:

> When we regard our wrong actions as understandable, we feel only a little guilty. But meaningful repentance and enduring change require more than casual confession of guilt.... [Such change happens] only when we expose our excuses for selfishness and regard those excuses as entirely illegitimate.[9]

Don't Beat the Other Slaves

Jesus told his disciples a very poignant story about a king who wanted to settle accounts with his servants. In the process, a man was brought before him who owed the king ten thousand talents, the equivalent of millions of dollars. The poor servant had no way of repaying such an tremendous sum, so the king ordered that he and his wife and children be sold as slaves, their possessions auctioned off, and the proceeds applied to the debt.

The king's words struck terror in the poor man's heart, and he fell to his face in the dust, crying out to the king for mercy. "Please, sir, I beg you! Don't take my wife! Don't take my little ones! Just give me more time! I'll pay it back! I promise! I only need time! I beg you! Have mercy!"

Of course, the king knew that even if the lowly servant were given all the time in the world, he had no hope of ever repaying such a colossal debt. Yet the man's earnest tears tugged at the king's heart so that he took pity on the wretched creature and forgave his debt entirely.

265

Shaking with relief, the servant left the king's presence and started toward home. On his way, he stopped to see a fellow slave who owed him several denarii, that is, several days' wages. "I've got to have that money you owe me!" he told the man angrily, grabbing him by the throat and shoving him against a wall. "So pay up now!"

The man fell down before him and pleaded, "Please be patient! I'll pay it back! Just give me a little more time!"

"I've waited long enough," his creditor said coldly, then threw the man into prison until his debt could be paid in full.

Sensing the injustice of the situation, the prisoner's friends appealed to the king on his behalf. When he heard their account, the king was enraged and immediately summoned the man whose debt he'd forgiven. "What are you thinking, you miserable wretch? Did I not pity your groveling soul? Did I not show compassion by forgiving your enormous debt? How then can you so harden your heart against your fellow slaves? How can you spare no mercy for them? You yourself were rescued from the debtor's dungeon, yet you would condemn another there in your place? You contemptible rogue!"

And the angry king ordered the ungrateful servant to be sent to the torture chamber, until every last penny of his debt should be paid. "So," Jesus said, "shall my Heavenly Father do to you if you refuse to forgive those who wrong you" (Matt. 18:23-35).

Forgiving from the Heart

Before we can freely extend forgiveness to others, we must more fully appreciate the magnitude of God's forgiveness for us. Reflect on this with me:

∞ "For He rescued us from the domain of darkness, and transferred us to the kingdom of His beloved Son, in

whom we have redemption, the forgiveness of sins."
(Col. 1:13-14)

∞ "You are a God of forgiveness, gracious and
compassionate, slow to anger and abounding in loving
kindness...." (Neh. 9:17)

∞ "In Him we have redemption through His blood, the
forgiveness of our trespasses, according to the riches
of His grace which He lavished on us." (Eph. 1:7-8)

∞ "For You, Lord, are good, and ready to forgive, and
abundant in loving kindness to all who call upon
You." (Psalm 86:5)

∞ "If we confess our sins, He is faithful and righteous to
forgive us our sins and to cleanse us from all
unrighteousness. If we say that we have not sinned,
we make Him a liar and His word is not in us." (1
John 1:9-10)

C.S. Lewis put it well: "If on consideration, one can
find no faults on one's own side, then cry for mercy: for this
must be a most dangerous delusion."[10] It is necessary that we
be cognizant of the dear price at which our forgiveness before
God was purchased, for it is such forgiveness that God
desires that we reflect to those around us—forgiveness fully
and freely bestowed, forgiveness both perfect and complete.
How are we to do such a thing? Debi Stack explains:

A mirror has no image of its own. We have no
perfection of our own. Instead of fabricating a fake,
outward perfection—an endless, impossible, and
exhausting task—you and I can reflect God's
authentic perfection. The real thing! How do we do
this? By thinking and acting in accordance with His
character.

1. *God is perfect truth.* We reflect that not by
operating from lies, but by thinking on, acting in, and
speaking truth.

2. God is perfect love. We reflect that not by withholding affection when we're displeased, but by loving ourselves and others unconditionally.

3. God is perfect mercy. We reflect that not by being judgmental and bitter, but by extending extravagant compassion.

4. God is perfect grace. We reflect that not by rationing pity, but by showing reckless benevolence.

5. God is perfect peace. We reflect that not by clenching control, but by surrendering to His sovereignty.

Are you thinking, *But if I let go of control, everything will fall apart! If I forgive someone who's not repentant,* [he'll] *never change!* The point is: We're not God. (Surprise!)[11]

A wife's refusal to forgive her husband turns too easily into demands meant to control him, observes Bob Barnes in *What Makes a Man Feel Loved.* "She holds him captive by not giving him the freedom to fail. Maybe she won't let him forget a mistake he made or a hurt he inflicted—despite the command to forgive as we have been forgiven by our heavenly Father."[12]

In his many years of counseling, Larry Crabb has observed a variety of retaliatory behaviors that "offended and unforgiving" clients often impose upon their spouses. Among them are:

- ∞ Reminders of the offense
- ∞ Cold Shoulder
- ∞ Angry pouting
- ∞ Cooled affection
- ∞ Withheld sex or dutiful participation
- ∞ Elimination of routine kindnesses
- ∞ Stubborn uncooperativeness
- ∞ Superior smiles

∞ Clipped and abrupt conversation
∞ Veiled or open threats to end the marriage
∞ Humiliation in front of others

and a host of others whose number is limited only by the creative imagination of a vengeful mind....[13]

But "forgiveness requires more than an agreement to end a checklist of retaliatory activities," writes Crabb. "The forgiving partner must be committed to requiring *no consequences at all* for the offense. There must be (1) a decision to forgive, followed by (2) a renewed commitment to minister, which then must (3) bear the fruit of extending kindness to the offending mate."[14]

This is not to say that a husband will *bear* no consequences of his sin, but that his wife will not be the one to *decide* and *inflict* those consequences. She will not be punitive toward him. If a husband gambles away their life savings, his wife's forgiveness does not mean he won't end up in bankruptcy court. If he contracts HIV through an illicit affair, his wife's forgiveness does not mean he won't die of AIDS. If he drinks and drives, he still loses his license, but she can chauffeur him to work. If he robs a bank, he still goes to jail, but she can visit him on the weekends. Just as God's forgiveness does not erase every consequence of our sin, a wife's forgiveness does not give her husband a free pass. Yet it does free *her*—it frees her from the bitter resentment and vindictive malice that would otherwise enslave her.

Words of Wisdom

We know that "all have sinned and fall short of the glory of God" (Rom. 3:23), but there is a difference between philosophically acknowledging your husband's inherent sin nature, and experientially coming face to face with a particular offense which affects you. This is where the rubber meets the road, where forgiveness becomes more than a theoretical platitude.

I first grappled with this distinction back in 1986, the year I finished college. Doug and I had met two weeks before graduation and become fast friends. We held so many things in common—values, goals, beliefs, even mannerisms—that my own mother told me she would fear we were siblings had I been adopted as Doug was. We were soon making plans for the future, determined that our life together should be built on trust and transparency. Against the advice of all his friends, Doug was completely candid with me about his past failings, and I am eternally grateful for his honesty. Although the events he described had occurred in the distant past, his confession was difficult for me to bear; it consumed my thoughts by day and tormented my dreams by night. Careworn and weary, I finally wrote to Elizabeth Elliot for counsel. With her permission, I close this chapter with her response, dated September 30, 1986.

Dear Jennifer:

How my heart went out to you last night as I read your letter, just received. I understand perfectly how you felt.... Even God, who forgives the sin and casts it into the depths of the sea, does not undo the effect of that sin, nor can you.... The tears, the nightmares, the unbidden imaginary pictures that torment you—how well I empathize with all of that, and pray for your comfort and healing.

First let me say that Doug is to be commended for not allowing himself to deceive you. He must have been in an agony over the decision to tell you, knowing at least a little bit how much it would hurt.

Second, you suffer not alone, but actually and redemptively with Christ (see Col. 1:24, Phil. 1:29, 1 Pet. 4:12, 13, and many other passages). This aspect of suffering is a real life-changer. Study it for the rest of your life.

Third, you suffer quite literally because of another's sin, which is exactly what Christ did. Because He paid the price for yours, you too must be willing to pay the price for Doug's—the price of sorrow, heartbreak, the sense of irremediable loss.... Forgiveness means absolute relinquishment of all that. It is a laying down of your life. Your dream of the "perfect" man has to go—it is this man God has given you, another sinner (there isn't anything else to marry!)—it is this gift you receive in thanksgiving, acknowledging the fact that in this fallen, broken world, there is no place where the heart may be perfectly at rest and wholly filled except at the Spring of Living Water. Drink there, dear Jennifer, and be at peace.

Doug's admission will always be a reminder to you that he needs your sacrificial, self giving love. When you sin against him, as you certainly will, any wife does, you will then know, when you have to ask his forgiveness, that you are two human beings in need of the Amazing Grace that saves WRETCHES!! You are, as Peter wrote, "heirs together of the grace of life."

So forgive him freely, utterly, joyfully—for that is how Christ has forgiven you (Eph. 4:32). Bring all those awful thoughts and imaginations under the Lordship of Christ (2 Cor. 10), and receive this man as your God-given husband, promising to honor, which means, among other things, never to bring up again that which has been put under the Blood.

I know a young woman who steadfastly refused to forgive her husband.... She has, in spite of Christian profession, destroyed her marriage, destroyed her own life, and blighted the lives of others. Don't refuse the grace of God for your own deep needs, nor refuse to Doug the grace He will give you to forgive him.[15]

Lovingly,
Elizabeth Elliot

I'm not sure what I had expected Elizabeth Elliot to say to me, but—twenty years and eleven children later—I finally wrote back to thank her for what she did say, and to let her know that I had happily taken her advice.

I sincerely hope that you will take it, too.

Chapter 20
Stay the Course

"...forgetting what lies behind
and reaching forward to what lies ahead,
I press on toward the goal for the prize
of the upward call of God in Christ Jesus."
Philippians 3:13-14

I will never forget my first talent show. The entire fifth grade class was abuzz with excitement, for we had been invited to join the sixth graders in demonstrating our unique skills and abilities before the entire school. What a privilege! What an opportunity! How thrilling it would be to take center stage!

I had a nice singing voice even then, so my parents, teachers, and friends all encouraged me to sing a solo for the program. But in my mind, singing was too common, too boring. I didn't even consider singing a talent. *Anyone* could sing. Almost everyone *would* sing. I wanted to do something unique, something unexpected, something exotic.

So rather than stick with singing, which was something I was good at and felt comfortable doing, I chose to do something I had absolutely no talent for and looked like a bull in a china closet even attempting: *Gymnastics.*

I had actually taken gymnastics a semester or two, long enough to be in the Spring Recital. I was the girl performing the routine on the sidelines. My coach singled me out to be a "line leader" so that the rest of the class could watch me— *me!*—and thereby stay together. Although it would be several years before I realized it, this was in reality a shameless ploy for getting the tall clumsy redhead out of the lineup, so her awkward performance wouldn't mar the effect of an entire class of pixies cartwheeling, somersaulting, and pirouetting in perfect unison.

Needless to say, my tumbling routine at the talent show was a miserable failure. I fell into a row of folding chairs and made a terrible racket. The emcee closed the curtains on me early, before I could break something. Inwardly, I chafed. If only I'd had more time, better lighting, a fancier costume, stronger muscles, a better coach... then I could have been the star of the show.

But God had given me neither the talent nor the body for gymnastics. What He *had* given me was a gift for music and a beautiful voice. If I had been smart, I would have taken *that* and run with it.

Bloom Where You're Planted

Many wives waste a lot of precious time wishing their circumstances were different, wishing their husband was different. If only my husband were more loving, more patient, more understanding, more driven, more successful, a stronger spiritual leader.... *then* I could be happy, *then* I could be a good wife, *then* I would obey God, *then* I would be the perfect Proverbs 31 lady.

If you find yourself in a difficult marriage, do whatever *you* can do to make it better. "Why doesn't [my] husband have to do his part first?" you may ask. Why? Elizabeth Handford answers, "Because you are the one burdened for a Christian home. Having a home where Christ is the head is cheap enough at whatever price you have to pay! Think how long the rewards of a good Christian home will last. Then ask yourself if it is worth the trifling mortifications of obedience. Of course it is! All valuable things cost something. Certainly you will have to pay a price."[1]

If you find yourself weary of trying, drained of hope, devoid of the desire to even try to make things work, take courage! "[God's] grace is sufficient for you, for [His] strength is made perfect in weakness" (2 Cor. 12:9 NKJV). "Divorce is not the answer," writes Tim Coody:

> ...Prayer, fasting, and a desperate cry to God for the desire to keep the covenant we no longer want to keep, to love the person we no longer want to love, that is the answer. Rather than run we begin to fight, not against our mate but against the forces trying to destroy our marriage. Our self-centeredness would be a good place to have the first battle....[2]

It's time to wake up and smell the coffee: God didn't give you some other husband. God didn't give you some other marriage. He gave you the one you have—and He expects you to run with it. He wants you to bloom where you're planted. Don't waste valuable time longing for your husband to be something he's not. Love him for who he is right now, not who you thought he was when you married him, not who you wish he would become. Dedicate yourself to supporting and encouraging him in any way you can.

God chose you specially. He equipped you with unique talents, gifts, and abilities that perfectly complement your husband. You should be using those gifts to serve, to minister, to encourage, to help him in every way possible. "[T]here have been great men of God used in spite of the woman they married," writes Elizabeth Handford, "but how many men have been encouraged and strengthened by the hands of a good woman and inspired to do great service for the Lord far beyond what they could have done alone.... A good woman who marries a good man can multiply his service to God a thousandfold. And that's a privilege beyond all speaking!"[3]

A wife should give her all to assist her husband in achieving whatever God has put in his heart to do. 'Tis a high purpose and a noble calling to be a man's helpmeet. History is replete with examples of men whose wives understood this truth. We have a bookcase in our home library filled with the biographies of such men—men like John Adams, Jonathan Edwards, Jim Elliot, and Charles Spurgeon, to name a few. Each had a wife who shared his vision and who did everything she could to help him reach his goals.

In *Let Me Be a Woman,* a book she wrote as a gift for her daughter who was on the threshold of marriage at the time, Elizabeth Elliot explains the benefits of living what she calls a "poured-out life":

> Here, I think, lies the answer to the barrenness of a single life, or of a life that might otherwise be selfish or lonely. It is the answer, I have found, to depression as well. You yourself will be given light in exchange for pouring yourself out, you yourself will get guidance, the satisfaction of your longings, and strength when you pour yourself out; when you make the satisfaction of somebody else's desire your own concern.[4]

Give It Your All

A couple of years ago, our family took a tour of the East Coast. We traveled in excess of 2500 miles, and my husband brought along the unabridged audio version of Thomas Friedman's 593-page book *The World Is Flat* for us to listen to on the road. The book was fascinating, but the part I liked best was his section on the United Parcel Service. I was surprised to learn that UPS does a lot more than just deliver packages.

For instance, did you know that when your Toshiba laptop breaks down and you send it back to the company for repairs, it is actually UPS that fixes and returns it?[5] Or that when you order a Papa John's pizza, it is UPS employees driving Papa John's supply trucks, daily delivering fresh ingredients to every store in the chain, who make your pizza possible?[6] UPS also manages warehouses full of Nike shoes and Jockey underwear, so if you order either online, the order will be automatically routed to UPS, and the person pulling, inspecting, packaging, and delivering your merchandise will be UPS-employed.[7]

The descriptions of the increasingly diverse business services UPS now provides continue for ten full pages of Friedman's book. As I listened to him go on and on about all the wonderful things UPS does to help other businesses run more efficiently, I was amazed. Or perhaps a better word would be *inspired*. I admired this company's adaptability. I marveled at its dedication. It seemed to me that no job was too humble for UPS to take on. *That is the kind of wife I want to be*, I thought again and again as I listened. *I want to make it my goal to help my husband reach his goals. I want to do everything he asks me to do to the best of my abilities.*

Indeed, that is the example set for wives in Proverbs 31. It is the example I strive to emulate. If my husband needs me to put away his clothes, I fold them uniformly and place them neatly in his drawer so he can rotate them from front to back. If he wants me to teach our toddler to tie his shoes, I do so with patience and enthusiasm. If he tells me to pare down our grocery bill, I clip coupons, comparison shop, and stock up when stuff is on sale. If he asks me to build a family website, I make it as informative and fun and user-friendly as I possibly can.[8] Whatever the task—making travel arrangements for a family vacation, replacing the button that fell off his shirt, sending his mother a birthday card, plunging a stopped-up toilet, fertilizing the lawn, organizing his office's Christmas party, teaching our fifteen-year old to drive—whether it's hard or easy, whether it's big or small, whether I know how to do it or not, if it's important to him, it's important to me, and I try to do it punctually and well. "The homeliest tasks get beautified if loving hands do them."[9] Loving service is what being a helpmeet is all about.

"Two are better than one," we read in the book of Ecclesiastes,

> ...because they have a good return for their labor. For if either of them falls, the one will lift up his companion. But woe to the one who falls when there is not another to lift him up. Furthermore, if two lie down together they keep warm, but how can one be warm alone? And if one can overpower him who is alone, two can resist him. A cord of three strands is not quickly torn apart (Eccl. 4:9-12).

This is what made Ancient Rome such a formidable foe: Her soldiers fought as a unit, not as individuals. The British were physically bigger and stronger, but fought every man for himself and were miserably defeated. A husband and wife can likewise be an impressive force if they remain "united in spirit, intent on one purpose" (Phil. 2:2). They "have a good return for their labor," because "advantage accrues from their efforts being conjoined. They afford one another help, protection, and society."[10]

The Talmud rightly asserts, "A man without a companion is like a left hand without the right."[11] What man could hope for a more worthy companion than a loving and dedicated wife? Reformation theologian Desiderius Erasmus elaborates:

> The affection of a wife... is shattered by no change of fortune.... In times of prosperity, happiness is doubled; in adversity there will be someone to console and assist you, to show her devotion, to wish your misfortune hers. Do you think there is any pleasure to be compared with so close a union? If you are at home, she is there to dispel the tedium of solitude; if abroad, she can speed you on your way with a kiss, miss you when you are away, receive you gladly on your return. She is the sweetest companion

of your youth, the welcome comfort of your old age. By nature any association is pleasant for man, seeing that nature begot him for kindness and friendship. Then how can this fail to be the most pleasant of all, in which there is nothing that is not shared?"[12]

Be Faithful in Little

Don't get discouraged if you aren't there yet. Even small changes can be steps in the right direction. Sometimes "it's actually the little things that count the most," writes George Barna in *Revolutionary Parenting*. He was talking about child training, but the same truth applies to marriage building: "Rather than looking for the big bang that will revolutionize our world, true revolution will come from a series of significant micro-level changes. The little contributions add up to make a big difference."[13]

Helen Keller echoes this sentiment when she confesses, "I long to accomplish a great and noble task, but it is my chief duty to accomplish humble tasks as though they were great and noble. The world is moved along, not only by the mighty shoves of its heroes, but also by the aggregate of the tiny pushes of each honest worker."[14]

This is why it is crucial that we be faithful in little, that we do not despise "the day of small things" (Zech. 4:10). For God has chosen the foolish things of this world to confound the wise, and He uses the weak to confound the strong (see 1 Cor. 1:27). It is how He has worked throughout human history. God relies upon "the dedication of a remnant of people whose hearts [are] sold out to His purposes" and He uses them to transform society. "If you (and each Christian family) take small steps forward—as evidenced through the spiritual transformation in our [own homes and families]— then we will live to see a spiritual awakening unlike anything we have witnessed during our lifetime."[15]

But each of us must do our part. "Successful people do what unsuccessful people aren't willing to do."[16] Are you willing to do whatever it takes to have a successful marriage and a peaceful home? Then follow Charles Spurgeon's advice:

> One good deed is worth more than a thousand brilliant theories. Let us not wait for large opportunities, or for a different kind of work, but just do the things we "find to do" day-by-day. We have no other time in which to live. The past is gone; the future has not arrived; we never shall have any time but time present. Then do not wait until your experience has ripened into maturity before you attempt to serve God. Endeavour now to bring forth fruit. Serve God now, but be careful as to the way in which you perform what you find to do—"*do it with thy might.*" Do it *promptly*; do not fritter away your life in thinking of what you intend to do to-morrow as if that could recompense for the idleness of to-day. No man ever served God by doing things to-morrow. If we honour Christ and are blessed, it is by the things which we do *to-day.* Whatever you do for Christ throw your whole soul into it. Do not give Christ a little slurred labour, done as a matter of course now and then; but when you do serve Him, do it with heart, and soul, and strength.[17]

We shouldn't expect God to do His part until we first fulfill our own. We must dip in the River Jordan before our health will be restored (2 Kings 5:14). We must fill the pots with water before it can be turned into wine (John 2:7-9). "Waiting around for God to act on the things you can't do when He has given you some things you *can* do is a little like asking Him to lower your cholesterol while continuing to eat fat-laden foods," notes Kathy Peel in *Desperate Households.*

"He expects us to live wisely and change the things we can while at the same time praying about the things we can't."[18]

"Marriages don't stand still," Tommy Nelson reminds us, "they either get better or they get worse. Think back over the last weeks and months. In which direction is your marriage heading?"[19] Make sure that even the smallest decisions you make today will nudge your marriage in the direction it needs to go.

Fix Your Eyes on the Prize

For years, my husband talked of running a marathon. Every January, he would go into training. He'd run three times a week, slowly increasing his distance, but every year it was the same: he'd build up to ten miles, then quit. He'd quit not because he was tired or because he was injured or because he had changed his mind about this particular goal. No. He'd give up training, because the longer distances were just so time-consuming, and he felt bad about being separated from his family for those long hours when his schooling and work required him to be away so much of the day already.

Still, the dream wouldn't die. When he began training again in 2001 for perhaps the dozenth time, I suggested he might stick with it longer if the rest of us just joined him. That way, he wouldn't need to choose between working toward his goal and spending time with us—we'd all be together anyway.

Doug was gung ho for the idea. Never mind that I could scarcely trot ten yards without getting winded; my husband, eternal optimist that he is, insisted my past 14 years of childbearing counted as "surreptitious training" and put me in prime cardiovascular condition. He encouraged me to start out by running only between every other lamppost, and it took me an entire month to build up to a mile. The older kids ran or skated or rode their bikes ahead of us, and we all took turns pushing the babies in a jogging stroller.

Slowly, slowly, we made progress. We stayed faithful. We stuck with it. After six months of training, we packed up our *PowerBars* and headed to Austin for the Motorola Marathon. I don't imagine what Doug and I were doing could properly be called *running*—it was more of a 20-mile jog plus a 6-mile cool down—but we nevertheless managed to cross the finish line, hand-in-hand, *before* they stopped the clock!

I can assure you that those last few miles were by far the hardest. Our legs were shaky, our stomachs were empty, and our resolve was weakening by the minute. Had we spotted a taxi in that home stretch, we'd have been sorely tempted to hail it, but I'm glad now we didn't. Instead, we just kept putting one foot in front of the other until we completed the course. Now for the rest of our lives we can say we finished a marathon—and nobody can take that away from us.

Marriage is not a hundred-yard dash. Marriage is not a relay. Marriage is a marathon if ever there were one. You may feel weary at times. You may encounter hurdles. You will definitely need to refuel at those water stations. But if you keep pressing forward and don't give up, I can promise you'll be glad you did. It will be worth all the toil and sweat and trouble once you reach that finish line.

Wendy Shalit tells a very touching story about just such endurance in her book *Girls Gone Mild.* She writes:

> I once traveled by car with some elderly friends going to a family event, and it was a very humbling experience. The wife was suffering from Alzheimer's, and every twenty seconds she would ask somewhat fearfully, "Where are we going?" After ten minutes of this, I am not proud to admit that I felt my own sanity slipping, and that I needed to get out of the car. (I didn't.) Yet her husband would always respond gently and cheerfully, as if for the first time: "We're going to a bris!"

Years later, I heard from my grandparents about this couple, and how the husband gallantly continued to care for his wife during her mental degeneration. By the time she died, she no longer recognized her husband of fifty years. But she did tell him, offhand, something very beautiful: "You know, I don't know who you are, but you're the best," she had said.

Most of us, I think, are looking for that kind of love. It's the love that brings out the best in us and in others; it's the ennobling love that persists even when the brain cells are long gone.[20]

Will you rededicate yourself afresh to demonstrating such love and faithfulness to your husband? To love, to honor, and to cherish him until death do you part? To stick it out through thick and thin, for better or worse, for richer or poorer, in sickness and health, as long as you both shall live?

It is significant, I think, that the first miracle Jesus performed publicly was turning water into wine at a marriage feast in Cana. Do you remember what was said by the headwaiter when he tasted the results? He marveled to the bridegroom, "Most hosts serve the good wine first, then substitute wine of poorer quality once the guests have drunk their fill. But not you! No, you have saved the very best for last!" (see John 2:9-10).

Precious sister, is your heart empty? Are you used up? Does your marriage taste like a piece of gum with all the flavor chewed out?[21]

Then turn it over to Jesus now. Do exactly as He bids. He is still in the business of performing miracles, and He can so transform your marriage that you will marvel, *Wow! He saved the very best for last!*

Afterword
The Hope of Glory

"God willed to make known what is
the riches of the glory of this mystery...
which is Christ in you, the hope of glory."
Colossians 1:27

Self-sacrificing love is both the secret of a happy marriage and the heart of the gospel. It is also the hardest thing we will ever be called to do. It is the hardest thing we'll do, because it goes against our very nature, which is why—to make it work—Christ must give us a new nature.

Although I have included a lot of practical advice in this book, I must also give you a warning. It is only through the indwelling of the Holy Spirit that you'll ever be able to show true self-sacrificing love to your husband. Without Him to guide us, our efforts fall flat.

The Bible says, "greater love has no one than this, that one lay down his life for his friends" (John 15:13). It is such a love that God calls us to have for our husbands. It is such a love that Christ has for *us.* If you already know Jesus personally, I urge you to cling to Him. If you do not, I encourage you to turn your life over to Him without delay.

Do you want your marriage to reflect the selfless, sacrificial love of Jesus? Do you want your interactions with your children to model the tender, patient care of our Heavenly Father? Do you want your life to be filled with the fruit of the Holy Spirit—His love, joy, peace, patience, kindness, goodness, faithfulness, gentleness and self-control? Then you must yield your life to His control. Not a hokey-pokey-put-a-little-in-take-a-little-back-out sort of yielding[1], but a full-fledged surrender, once and for all, a laying of everything on the altar and leaving it there, for Christ to do with as He will.

Satan would like for us to give our full attention to the various obstacles and bumps we encounter on life's road instead of focusing on our destination. If he can get us, like Peter, to look at the waves that threaten to engulf us, instead of looking to Jesus, then we will become completely overwhelmed. But the Bible promises that those who call upon Jesus' name shall be saved: "If you confess with your mouth Jesus as Lord, and believe in your heart that God raised Him from the dead, you will be saved; for with the heart a person believes, resulting in righteousness, and with the mouth he confesses, resulting in salvation" (Rom. 10:9-10). This is all our hope and peace. "Christ in you, the hope of glory" (Col. 1:27).

I pray earnestly that "the Lord who began His divine miracles at the wedding of Cana [will] bless you in your new life and bless your house and transform things that create division into means of blessing, and fill your hearts with spiritual [self-sacrificing] love."[2] May Jesus Christ reign supreme in your heart and home, for it is only through knowing, loving, and serving Him that you will ever be truly able to love your husband or love yourself.

Acknowledgements
My Heartfelt Thanks

"We give thanks to God always for all of you,
making mention of you in our prayers;
constantly bearing in mind your work of faith
and labor of love and steadfastness of hope
in our Lord Jesus Christ."
1 Thessalonians 1:2-3

I'd like to thank our friends at Family Fellowship Bible Church, whose faithful prayer support enabled me to finish this book in a more timely fashion than I'd otherwise have done. Next time, I won't wait so long to enlist your help! Thanks to Gina Beggs, Jenny Bernhard, Molly Bodenhamer, Rhonda Brazell, Tammy Cannon, Margie Oney, Debra Taylor, and Gloria Williams for routinely checking on my progress and holding me accountable. Special thanks to Janet Baber for agreeing to read my manuscript while laid up with a broken neck. You're a real trooper!

I deeply appreciate Mimi Youngblood's wading through my wordier first draft, Sherry Haire's unflagging enthusiasm, Dana Bertino's proofreading the book before its second printing, and Teresa Praytor's and Vicenta Hartnauer's recurrent invitations to speak to the moms from our local home school group on this and related topics. Thanks also to the ladies who attended those talks and who gave me such a warm reception. I am grateful for the encouragement, feedback, and friendship each of you has extended toward me over the years.

I am beholden to my in-laws, Paul and Doris Flanders, for raising my husband in a stable Christian home and for cultivating in him a strong work ethic and a sense of integrity from his earliest years. He would not be the man he is today apart from your training.

I am profoundly grateful to my own parents, Bill and Cherree Cowan, for my upbringing and for the many sacrifices they made on my behalf. As a child, I naively assumed all parents honored their wedding vows and stuck together—not until I left for college did I realize what a rare and special blessing it is to hail from an unbroken home. I am especially thankful, Mom, for the example you've always modeled for me of what a godly wife and loving mother looks like.

I should also thank my little sister, Kimberly Hancock, for asking Mom all those questions when we were kids. Your unabashed queries made my eavesdropping a much more enlightening experience.

I need to thank my oldest son, Jonathan, and his beautiful bride, Matti, whose marriage three years ago provided the impetus I needed to put these thoughts on paper. We are indebted to Matti for cooking for us two nights a week while I edited this book. Your culinary expertise has been a blessing to our entire family. Special thanks are due grandsons Aiden and Sawyer for spreading so much sunshine whenever you come to visit and for playing so contentedly while your mommy works in the kitchen.

I owe heartfelt thanks to my other children, as well: Bethany, I appreciate your serving as a sounding board for many of the ideas presented in these pages. David, I'm grateful to you for helping me tweak my cover design, for smoothing my transition to Mac, and for doing so much of our grocery shopping last year. Thanks to Samuel, Benjamin, and Joseph for so often entertaining your baby brother, and for picking up slack on household chores—especially laundry—which would otherwise have been neglected in my press to get this book ready to print. Rebekah and Rachel, I especially appreciate your cheerful dispositions, as well as all your help in the kitchen. Isaac, Daniel, and Gabriel, your innumerable hugs and kisses always came when I most needed to take a break. I love each one of you inexpressibly much!

I am eternally grateful for my husband of twenty-two years, Doug Flanders. Not a day goes by that I do not thank and praise our Heavenly Father for bringing us together. Life with you has been more wonderful than even an idealist like me could've hoped or imagined, and I count it a privilege to be your wife and helpmeet. Thank you for the unfailing support you've given this book project and for your superb proofreading skills. As iron sharpens iron, you undeniably sharpen me!

Most of all, my heart overflows with gratitude to God for drawing our attention to the less-traveled path so many years ago, for leading us down that little grassy trail, and for lavishing His blessings upon us all along the way.

Soli Deo Gloria,
Jennifer Flanders
January 9, 2010

End Notes

Introduction—Where Did We Go Wrong?

1. Scott Stanley, in the introduction to Tim Alan Gardner's *Sacred Sex,* p. xii.
2. Gardner, T. *Sacred Sex*, p. 3.

Chapter 1—Sex: What's In It For Me?

1. Deveny, K. "We're Not In the Mood." *Newsweek*, 06/03/03, p.40.
2. Mitchell, K. and M. Sugar. "Annie's Mailbox," 7/22/06.
3. Mitchell, K. and M. Sugar."Annie's Mailbox," 5/11/06.
4. Dobson, J. *What Wives Wish Their Husbands Knew About Women*, p.28.
5. Clarke, A. *Adam Clarke's Commentary*, 1 Cor. 7:4.

Chapter 2—The Pleasure of His Company

1. Gardner, T. *Sacred Sex*, p. 70.
2. *Ibid*, p. 17.
3. Maken, D. *Getting Serious About Getting Married*, pp. 102-3, 111.
4. Peace, M. *The Excellent Wife*, pp. 120-121.
5. Torode, S. and B. *Open Embrace*, p. 23.
6. If you are a parent and do not yet have a pick-proof lock on your bedroom door, don't let another day go by without procuring one. Take a quick trip down to your local hardware store and invest in a brass flip-lock. This simple device looks like a hinge, mounts easily and unobtrusively to the door frame, works perfectly, and only costs a couple bucks. That's a small price to pay for privacy and peace of mind.
7. Boteach, S. *Kosher Sex: A Recipe for Passion and Intimacy*, p. 37, as quoted by Tim Alan Gardner in *Sacred Sex*, p. 50.
8. Feldhahn, S. *For Women Only*, p. 91-92.
9. "How sex makes you look and feel better." *Saga Magazine*.
10. Brizendine, L. *The Female Brain*, p. 72 (*emphasis added*).
11. *Ibid.*
12. *Ibid*, p. 71.
13. Ornish, D. *Love & Survival*, p. 140.
14. Feldhahn, S. *For Women Only*, p. 93.
15. Jamieson, Fausset, and Brown. *A Commentary on the Old and New Testaments*, Deut. 24:5.
16. Henry, M. *Matthew Henry's Commentary*, p. 823.
17. *Ibid*, (*emphasis added*).

Chapter 3—Health Insurance

1. Robinson, et.al. "Oxytocin mediates stress-induced analgesia in adult mice."
2. Copeland, P. "The Health Benefits of Sex."
3. Charnetski, C. *Feeling Good is Good for You*, pp. 7-8.
4. Evans & Couch. "Orgasm and Migraine".
5. Farnham, A. "Is Sex Necessary?"
6. Shapiro, 1983
7. Farnham, A. "Is Sex Necessary?"
8. Charnetski, C. *Feeling Good Is Good For You*, pp. 7-8.
9. *Ibid*, pp. 12-13.
10. *Ibid,* chaps. 4, 5, 7, 8.
11. *Ibid*, pp 113-114. There were 112 participants in this study. All were college-aged, but only one was married. Interestingly, IgA levels actually *dropped* in students who had sex *more* than three times per week—perhaps in consequence of increased promiscuity (my guess, not theirs). It would be telling to study how "very frequent sex" affected the immunity of monogamous, married couples.
12. Leitzmann, et. al. "Ejaculation Frequency and Subsequent Risk..."
13. Naitoh, *et al*. "Diagnosis and Treatment of Prostate Cancer."
14. American Cancer Society. "Cancer Facts & Figures: 2007," p. 6.
15. Cassoni, *et al*. "Evidence of oxytocin/oxytocin receptor interplay in human prostate gland and carcinomas."
16. Farnham, "Is Sex Necessary?" (*emphasis mine*)
17. Campbell, N. *Be Fruitful and Multiply*, p. 107.
18. *Ibid*, p. 108.
19. Cassoni, *et al*. "Oxytocin and Oxytocin Receptors in Cancer Cells and Proliferation."
20. "Breast Cancer." *Wikipedia: The Free Encyclopedia.*
21. Medical Patent News. "Nastech Pharmaceutical awarded new breast cancer patent."
22. Lê, M., *et al*. "Characteristics of Reproductive Life and Risk of Breast Cancer in a Case-Control Study of Young Nulliparous Women."
23. Barrett and Mingo. *Doctors Killed George Washington*, p. 84.
24. Feldman, *et al*. "Low Dehydroepiandrosterone Sulfate and Heart Disease in Middle-Aged Men," as referenced in "The Health Benefits of Sexual Expression." *Planned Parenthood White Paper.*
25. Fogari, *et al*. "Sexual Activity and Plasma Testosterone Levels in Hypertensive Males," as referenced in "The Health Benefits of Sexual Expression." *Planned Parenthood White Paper.*
26. Farnham, A. "Is Sex Necessary?"
27. Shaw, G. "The New Low for High Blood Pressure."

28. "Hypertension/High Blood Pressure Guide: Symptoms and Types."
29. Baker, *et al.* "The influence of marital adjustment on 3-year left ventricular mass and ambulatory blood pressure in mild hypertension."
30. Tobe, *et al.* "Impact of Job and Marital Strain on Ambulatory Blood Pressure."
31. "Oxytocin." *Wikipedia.*
32. Grewen, *et al.* "Effects of Partner Support on Resting Oxytocin, Cortisol, Norepinephrine, and Blood Pressure Before and After Warm Partner Contact."
33. Knox and Uvnas-Moberg. "Social isolation and cardiovascular disease: an atherosclerotic pathway?"
34. Copeland and Link. "The Health Benefits of Sex."
35. Farnham, A. "Is Sex Necessary?"
36. Billings, *et al.* "Oxytocin null mice ingest enhanced amounts of sweet solutions during light and dark cycles and during repeated shaker stress."
37. Kovacs, *et al.* "Oxytocin and addiction: a review."
38. Charnetski, C. *Feeling Good is Good for You*, p. 107.
39. Farnham, A. "Is Sex Necessary?"
40. Thomas, J. "Frequent Sex May Help You Look Younger."
41. Carmichael, K. "Osteoporosis—Prevention and Intervention."
42. Cutler, W. *Love Cycles: The Science of Intimacy*, as referenced in "The Health Benefits of Sexual Expression." *Planned Parenthood White Paper.*
43. Tur-Kaspa, *et al.* "How Often Should Infertile Men Have Intercourse to Achieve Conception?" as referenced in "The Health Benefits of Sexual Expression." *Planned Parenthood White Paper.*
44. Brody, S. "Alexithymia Is Inversely Associated with Women's Frequency of Vaginal Intercourse."
45. Bartz, J. and E. Hollander. "Is Oxytocin the Key to Understanding?"
46. Ornish, D. *Love & Survival.* pp. 26-27.
47. Farnham, A. "Is Sex Necessary?"
48. *Ibid.*

Chapter 4—Peace of Mind
1. Spafford, H. "It Is Well with My Soul."
2. Charnetski, C. *Feeling Good Is Good For You*, p. 80.
3. *Ibid*, p. 64.
4. *Ibid*, pp. 75-79.
5. Uvnas-Moberg, as referenced by M. Robinson, "The Big O isn't Orgasm."
6. Brizendine, L. *The Female Brain*, p. 132.

7. Schlessinger, L. *The Proper Care and Feeding of Husbands,* p. 23.
8. *Ibid*, p. 21.
9. Cohen, E. "CDC: Antidepressants most prescribed drugs in U.S."
10. Kirch, I. "Antidepressants Proven to Work Only Slightly Better Than Placebo," as referenced by Dan Ariely, *Predictably Irrational,* p. 178. This study showed that 75% of the effect of the six leading antidepressants can be duplicated by placebo.
11. Maines, R. *The Technology of Orgasm,* as referenced in "Female Hysteria," *Wikipedia.*
12. Briggs, L. "The Race of Hysteria," as referenced in "Female Hysteria," *Wikipedia.*
13. Charnetski, C. *Feeling Good Is Good For You*, p. 66.
14. *Ibid*, p. 67.
15. Brizendine, L. *The Female Brain*, p. 132.
16. Brody, S. "Blood pressure reactivity to stress is better for people who recently had penile-vaginal intercourse."
17. Farnham, A. "Is Sex Necessary?"
18. The *Orange County Register*, March 15, 2003, as referenced by L. Schlessinger, *The Proper Care and Feeding of Husbands*, p. xii.
19. Amy Gardner, writing in Tim Gardner's *Sacred Sex*, p. 122. My own husband would argue that even a full-body cast would not dampen some men's sex drive.
20. Brizendine, L. *The Female Brain*, p. 72.
21. *Ibid*, p. 77.
22. Gardner, Tim. *Sacred Sex*, pp. 52-53.
23. Brizendine, L. *The Female Brain*, p. 68.
24. *Ibid.*
25. Schlegel, K. "Be Still My Soul."

Chapter 5—Sweet Dreams
1. Bell, R. *Sex God,* p. 94.
2. Schlessinger, L. *The Proper Care and Feeding of Husbands,* p. 24.
3. *Ibid,* p. 26.
4. Gardner, Tim. *Sacred Sex*, p 117 .
5. Bouchez, C. "Using Your Immune System to Stay Well."
6. Peel, K. *Desperate Households*, p. 117.
7. Weeks, D. *Superyoung*, p. 27.
8. Peel, K. *Desperate Households*, p. 117.
9. Weeks, D. *Superyoung*, p. 27.
10. Roche, N. "Exactly How Does a Lack of Sleep Affect the Body?"
11. Honoré, C. *In Praise of Slow*, p. 7.
12. Trader, L. "Prescription Sleeping Pills: Who Really Gets a Good Night Sleep without Some Sort of Sleep Aid?"

13. Mulhauser, G. "Experts Warn About Growing Use of Prescription Sleeping Pills."
14. Saisan, J. "Sleeping Pills, Sleeping Aids and Medications."
15. *Ibid.*
16. "Prescription Sleeping Pill Use Tied to Cancer."
17. Trader, L. "Prescription Sleeping Pills."
18. Casura, L. "The Cortisol Connection."
19. Juan, S. "What are the scientific reasons for having sex?"
20. Copeland, P. and A. Link, "The Health Benefits of Sex."

Chapter 6—A Happy Home
1. Peel, K. *Desperate Households*, p. 171.
2. Brahma Sutra, as cited by Susan Sardone in "Love Quotations."
3. Feldhahn, S. and J. *For Men Only*, p. 144.
4. Alcott, L. *Little Women.* p. 225.
5. Leman, K. *7 Things He'll Never Tell You,* pp. 114-115.
6. Brinzendine, L. *The Female Brain*, p. 72.
7. Agren (2002), as quoted by Robinson, M. and G. Wilson. "The Big O isn't Orgasm."
8. Robinson, M. and G. Wilson. "The Big O isn't Orgasm."
9. Grant, T. *Being a Woman*, p. 46.
10. Stack, D. *Martha to the Max*, p. 144.

Chapter 7—The Fountain of Youth
1. In the classic tale *The Picture of Dorian Gray* by Oscar Wilde, the protagonist's portrait ages, while his body remains forever young.
2. Weeks, D. *Superyoung*, p.83
3. Seckel, B. *Save Your Face: The Truth About Facial Aging.*
4. Byron, S. "When Aging Hits Home."
5. Gardner, T. *Sacred Sex*, p. 155
6. *Ibid.*
7. Weeks, D. *Superyoung*, pp. 72-73.
8. According to *DeKadt Facial Skin Care Anti-Aging Market Study.*
9. Gardner, T. *Sacred Sex*, p. 155.
10. Seckel, B. *Save Your Face: The Truth About Facial Aging.*
11. Crittenden, D. *What Our Mothers Didn't Tell Us*, p. 152.
12. Weeks, D. *Superyoung*, pp. 72-73.
13. Ludy, L. *Set-Apart Femininity*, p. 17.
14. RoC® 10 Years Back.
15. According to Johnson & Johnson website.
16. "How sex makes you look and feel better." *Saga Magazine.*
17. Weeks, D. *Superyoung*, p. 74.
18. Thomas, J. "Frequent Sex May Help You Look Younger".

19. Charnetski, C. *Feeling Good Is Good For You*, p. 112.
20. Thomas, J. "Frequent Sex May Help You Look Younger".
21. *Ibid.*
22. "How sex makes you look and feel better..." Saga Magazine.
23. "Are There Cosmetic Benefits to Having Sex?"
24. *Ibid.*
25. "Sexercise Yourself into Shape." *BBC News.*
26. Weeks, D. *Superyoung*, p. 75.
27. "Human growth hormone (HGH) and anti-aging."
28. *Ibid.*
29. Copeland, P. and A. Link, "The Health Benefits of Sex".
30. "Are There Cosmetic Benefits to Having Sex?" *CareFair.com: Skin is In.*
31. Pearl, D. *Created To Be His Help Meet,* p. 27.
32. *Ibid,* p. 34.
33. From *The Sound of Music,* a 1965 musical film directed by R. Wise.
34. Charnetski, C. *Feeling Good Is Good For You*, p. 56.
35. Gladwell, M. *Blink*, pp. 207-208.
36. *Ibid,* pp. 206-207.
37. *Ibid,* p. 208.
38. Feldhahn, S. *For Women Only*, p. 101.
39. Rawlings, M. *The Yearling*, p. 113-114.
40. *Ibid,* p. 110.
41. Feldhahn, S. *For Women Only,* p. 50.
42. Leman, K. *7 Things He'll Never Tell You*, p. 107.
43. *Ibid,* p. 119.
44. Feldhahn, S. and J. *For Men Only*, p. 123.
45. Feldhahn, S. *For Women Only,* pp. 73-74. Internal quote: Jack Welch, *Jack: Straight for the Gut* (New York: Warner Books, 2001).
46. Michael Farris, *A Sacred Foundation*, pp.103-104. Internal quote: Dr. Arthur Szabo, quoted in *Bible Illustrator* on CD Rom (Hiawatha, IA: Parsons Technology, 1999).

Chapter 8—Good Clean Fun
1. "Romance Writers of America's 2005 Market Research Study," p. 2.
2. Pride, M. *The Way Home*, pp. 29-31.
3. Cal Thomas, *The Things That Matter Most*, pp. 81-82.
4. Gardner, T. *Sacred Sex*, p. 134.
5. Pride, M. *The Way Home*, pp. 29-31.
6. This quote is commonly attributed to Martin Luther.
7. Ludy, E. and L. *Meet Mr. Smith*, p. 45.
8. *Ibid,* pp.178-179.

9. Cloud, H. and J. Townsend, *Simple Secrets of a Great Marriage,* p. 130
10. Pressfield, S. *The War of Art*, p. 64.
11. Charnetski, C. *Feeling Good Is Good For You*, p. 55.
12. Pressfield, S. *The War of Art*, intro.
13. Leman, K. *7 Things He'll Never Tell You*, pp. 111-112.
14. Schlessinger, L. *The Proper Care and Feeding of Husbands*, p. 121.
15. Schlessinger, L. *The Proper Care & Feeding of Marriage*, p. 24.
16. Nelson, T. *Better Love Now*, pp. 188-189.
17. Gardner, T. *Sacred Sex*, p. 94.
18. Shalit, W. *A Return to Modesty*, p. 171.
19. Liebau, C. *Prude*, p. 189.
20. Maimonides, *Mishneh Torah, Hilchot Ishut*, (The Laws of Marriage), chapter 14, as quoted in Wendy Shalit's *A Return to Modesty*, p. 114.
21. Feldhahn, S. and J. *For Men Only*, p. 126-7.
22. Honoré, C. *In Praise of Slow*, p. 169.
23. Margolis, J. *O: The Intimate History of the Orgasm*, p. 3.
24. Mary Pride puts it succinctly: "Becoming 'one flesh' is only *one* of the purposes for which God ordained sex.... [T]he *other* purpose, the one which gets swept under the evangelical rug, is fruitfulness. For fruitfulness it is absolutely necessary that coupling be marital, heterosexual, and genital-to-genital..." (*The Way Home,* p. 28).

    Pride differentiates *coupling* from *touching*: "Fondling is one thing, and the sex act is another. The Song of Songs describes a couple rejoicing in each other's bodies, snuggling, kissing, and fondling each other" (*Ibid*).

    Nevertheless, if a couple is ever going to produce a baby, intimacy and foreplay must eventually culminate in sexual union as God designed.
25. John Senior, as quoted by Sam and Bethany Torode in *Open Embrace*, p. 34.

Chapter 9—Baby Showers

1. Doug Phillips, in the forward to Nancy Campbell's *Be Fruitful and Multiply*, p. 7.
2. Nancy Campbell writes, "The fact of the matter is this: It is not a matter of our deciding how many children we should have, or should not have, but having a vision of God's plan for marriage and family—a vision to bring forth a godly seed for God's glory.... It is interesting to note that, in so many instances in the Word of God, God gave the vision for family before children ever arrived on the scene. God wants us to have a vision for family, not just when we start a family, but also even before we are married. We should plant a vision for

family in our children as they are growing up. We should train our sons to be fathers and therefore the providers, the protectors, and the priests of their homes. We should train and give our daughters a vision for motherhood, preparing them to be the nurturers, the nourishers, and the nest builders of future families." (*Be Fruitful and Multiply,* p. 193).

3. Pride, M. *The Way Home*, pp. 39-40.
4. Watters, S. and C. *Start Your Family*, p. 92.
5. Torode, S. and B. *Open Embrace*, pp. 32-33.
6. Watters, S. and C. *Start Your Family*, p. 88, citing an on-line article entitled "Fertility: Less Time Than You Think."
7. Torode, S. and B. *Open Embrace*, p. 54.
8. Pride, M. *The Way Home*, pp. 79-80.
9. Lamer, "Unfocused families." *WORLD Magazine*, p. 27.
10. Watters, S. and C. *Start Your Family*, p. 21.
11. Campbell, *Be Fruitful and Multiply*, p. 51.
12. Crittenden, D. *What Our Mothers Didn't Tell Us*, p. 97.
13. *Ibid*, pp. 74.
14. Torode, S. and B. *Open Embrace*, pp. xiv-xv.
15. *Ibid*, pp. 24-25.
16. Watters, S. and C. *Start Your Family*, p. 46.
17. Campbell, *Be Fruitful and Multiply*, p. 50.
18. *Ibid*, pp. 47-48.
19. *Physician's Drug Handbook: 11th Edition.* (2005). pp. 518-20.
20. *Physician's Desk Reference.* (2007). "Ortho Tri-Cyclen warnings & adverse effects."
21. Sam and Bethany Torode report, "In 1976, the American College of Obstetricians and Gynecologist redefined pregnancy as beginning at the successful implantation of a fertilized egg. (see Randy Alcorn's *Does the Birth Control Pill Cause Abortion?*) Under this definition, abortifacient drugs that prevent implantation are labeled as contraceptives." So-called "emergency contraception" is no more than a double dose of regular birth control pills taken within 72 hours of having sex, which acts to thin the uterine lining almost instantly to prevent fertilized egg from implanting. So here again, it does not prevent fertilization; it terminates pregnancy. Understandably, abortion rights advocates object to defining life as starting at fertilization, since doing so would "in effect, outlaw birth control measures such as the Pill, which can rely on blocking the development of a fertilized egg.... By thinning the uterine lining considerably, the Pill [even when taken as prescribed] renders the endometrium hostile to implantation, making it difficult for a fertilized egg to survive.... The minimal endometrial thickness

required to maintain a pregnancy ranges from 5 to 13 mm, whereas the average endometrial thickness in women on the Pill is only 1.1 mm." *Open Embrace*, pp. 78-79. (cf. Randy Alcorn, "Using the Birth Control Pill Is Ethically Unacceptable" in John F Kilner, editor. *The Reproduction Revolution: A Christian Appraisal of Sexuality, Reproductive Technologies, and the Family* Grand Rapids: Eerdmans, 2000, pp 17-91).

22. Sam and Bethany Torode note, "As long as the contraceptive mentality prevails, abortion will follow. One of the most practical steps we can take to combat abortion is to renounce contraception in our homes."(*Open Embrace*, p. 71).

23. The Children of Israel were not content to just ignore these brave men. They wanted to *silence* them—permanently. Numbers 14:10 tells us "all the congregation said to stone them with stones." But God miraculously protected them. Numbers 14:36-39 tells us that, of that generation, Joshua and Caleb alone were allowed to enter and take possession of Canaan forty years later. The other ten spies died of a plague soon after their initial foray into the Promised Land.

24. Please understand that I am speaking metaphorically; I am not saying that those who die childless don't go to heaven, but only that life here on earth is made inexpressibly sweet by having children. Note also that, although *raising* kids can definitely help keep her humble, giving birth to a bunch of them does not make a woman more spiritual. (No, not even if she delivers at home, with no epidural!)

25. Trapp, M. *The Story of the Trapp Family Singers*, p.120.
26. *Ibid*, pp. 156-7.
27. Watters, S. and C. *Start Your Family*, p. 82.
28. *Joseph Hall* (1574-1656) as quoted by Craig Houghton, *Family UNplanning*, pp. 59-60.
29. Barna, G. *Revolutionary Parenting*, p. 132.
30. Campbell, N. *Be Fruitful and Multiply*, p. 107-108.
31. Robinson, "The Big O".....
32. Pride, M. *The Way Home*, p. 79.
33. Feldhahn, S. and J. *For Men Only*, p. 126-7.
34. Kaplan, *et al.* "Human Parental Investment and Fertility."
35. Shivanandan, M. *Crossing the Threshold of Love,* p. 274. (as quoted by Sam and Bethany Torode, *Open Embrace,* pp. 22-23).
36. Hiedemann, Suhomlinova, and O'Rand (1998), as quoted by Sam and Bethany Torode in *Open Embrace*.
37. Veith, G.E. "Population Implosion," as quoted by Debbie Maken in *Getting Serious about Getting Married*, pp. 100-101.
38. Graham, S. "Germans Get Incentives for Having Babies."

39. Maken, D. *Getting Serious about Getting Married*, pp. 100-101. Again citing Gene Edward Veith's *World Magazine* article "Population Implosion," Maken writes: "Fewer taxpayers in one generation also results in a heavier burden to support retirees in welfare system countries. Due to the negative birth rate in Japan, the legislature there has considered not offering any retirement benefits to older retirement age singles because never-married singles failed to produce children to support and balance the social security scheme in place. We would be shortsighted to think that that kind of measure would not take place in America where the social security system is dependent on each generation's producing enough children to support the generation retiring.... In the Western world, where we could have multiple Christian babies in freedom and raise them safely, we casually dismiss our diminished fertility, while countries like Yemen are producing 7.2 children per woman."
40. Watters, S. and C. *Start Your Family*, p. 98.

Chapter 10—A Firm Foundation
1. Handford, E. *Me? Obey Him?* p. 91.
2. Leman, K. *7 Things He'll Never Tell You... But You Need to Know*, pp. 116-117.
3. Dr. Barbara Bartlik, clinical professor of psychiatry at Weill Medical College of Cornell University in NYC, as quoted by Jennifer Thomas in "Frequent Sex May Help You Look Younger."
4. Nelson, T. *Better Love Now*, p. 166.
5. Nelson, T. *Better Love Now*, p. 176-177.
6. Clarke, Adam. *Commentary and Critical Notes*, 1 Cor. 7:5.
7. Peace, M. *The Excellent Wife,* pp. 120-121.
8. Farris, V. *A Mom Just Like You*, pp. 186-187.
9. Leman, K. *7 Things He'll Never Tell You*, p. 93, 108.
10. *Ibid*, back cover.
11. Farris, M. and R. Elam. *A Sacred Foundation*, p. 99.
12. Brizendine, L. *The Female Brain,* p. 91.
13. *Ibid*, p. 176.
14. Dobson. J. *What Wives Wish Their Husbands Knew About Women*, p. 118.
15. Brizendine, L. *The Female Brain,* p. 91.
16. Schlessinger, L. *The Proper Care and Feeding of Husbands*, p. 133.
17. *Ibid*, p. 135.
18. I think this was actually a scene from the Woody Allen film, *Annie Hall,* which I've never seen.
19. Yes, I realize proper grammar dictates *"lie"* down, but I'm using a word play here.

20. Farris, M. *A Sacred Foundation*, pp. 107-108.
21. Schlessinger, L. *The Proper Care and Feeding of Husbands*, p. 129.
22. Feldhahn, S. *For Women Only*, p 133.
23. Bell, R. *Sex God*, p. 73.
24. Farris, M. *A Sacred Foundation*, pp. 107.
25. *Ibid*, pp. 19-20.

Chapter 11—A Tried and True Testimony

1. When a friend of Jeff Feldhahn learned Jeff was writing a chapter on sex for his book *For Men Only*, he chuckled and said, "If you can get the average husband sex even a dozen more times a year, men will build statues to you in city parks across the county." Recalling this incident in the book, Feldhahn quips, "So the following is my stab at immortality." (*For Men Only*, p. 138) While I don't aspire to have any park statues erected in my honor, I *am* hoping the husbands of wives who read my book—as well as the wives themselves—will be glad they did.
2. Bell, R. *Sex God,* p. 135.
3. According to the author of "Report to the Nation: Smart & Good High Schools", Dr. Thomas Lickona, "To exercise sexual wisdom in today's sexual culture... young people need three things: (1) internally held convictions of conscience about why it makes sense to save sexual intimacy for a truly committed relationship—a vision of what they're 'waiting for'" (2) the strengths of character—such as good judgment, self-control, genuine respect for self and others, modesty, and the courage to resist sexual pressures—needed to live out this choice; and (3) support systems for living a chaste lifestyle, including, ideally, support from their families, faith communities, schools, and at least one friend who has made the decision to wait." (from a personal interview with Dr. Lickona, as quoted by Carol Platt Liebau in *Prude*, p 219).
4. Maken, *Getting Serious About Getting Married,* p. 129-130.
5. Barnes, B. *What Makes a Man Feel Loved*, p 187.
6. Ludy, E. and L. *Meet Mr. Smith*, p. 177.
7. Liebau, C. *Prude*, p. 101.
8. Gardner, T. *Sacred Sex,* p. 20.
9. Ornish, D. *Love & Survival*, p 37.
10. Barna, G. *Revolutionary Parenting*, p. 136.
11. Ludy, L. *Set-Apart Femininity*, p. 176.
12. Pearl, D. *Created To Be His Help Meet*, p. 151.
13. Nelson, T. *Better Love Now*, p. 188.
14. Marilyn Monroe, as quoted by Tim Gardner in *Sacred Sex,* p. 87.
15. Gardner, T. *Sacred Sex,* p. 90.

16. *Ibid*, p. 51.
17. Crittenden, D. *What Our Mothers Didn't Tell Us*, p. 187-188.

Chapter 12—The State of a Union
1. Ariely, D. *Predictably Irrational*, pp. 139-140.
2. Crittenden, D. *What Our Mothers Didn't Tell Us*, p. 111.
3. Trueblood, E. and P. *The Recovery of Family Life*, p. 45 (as quoted by Steve and Candace Watters in *Start Your Family*, p. 111).
4. Ornish, D. *Love and Survival,* p. 80.
5. Dr. L. Berkman, as quoted by D. Ornish in *Love and Survival*, p. 196.
6. Crittenden, D. *What Our Mothers Didn't Tell Us*, p. 104.
7. *Ibid.*
8. Waite, L. and M. Gallagher, *The Case for Marriage*, p. 180.
9. Shalit, W. *Girls Gone Mild*, p. 246.
10. Crittenden, D. *What Our Mothers Didn't Tell Us*, p. 93.
11. *Ibid*, p. 111.
12. *Ibid,*, pp. 91-92.
13. Tan, A. *The Joy Luck Club*, pp. 160-161.
14. Bell, R. *Sex God*, p. 118.
15. John Chrysostom, as quoted by Sam and Bethany Torode in *Aflame: Ancient Wisdom on Marriage*, p. 27.
16. Maken, D. *Getting Serious About Getting Married, p. 124.*
17. *Ibid.*
18. Henry, M. *Matthew Henry's Commentary* on Gen 2:21-25, p. 20.
19. Campbell, N. *Be Fruitful and Multiply*, pp. 14-15.
20. Watters, S. and C. *Start Your Family*, pp. 108-109.
21. White, M. *Married To Jesus,* p. 128.
22. Pride, M. *The Way Home*, p. 20.
23. Crittenden, D. *What Our Mothers Didn't Tell Us*, p. 184.
24. *Ibid*, pp. 184-185.
25. Waite, L. and M. Gallagher. *The Case for Marriage*, pp. 11-12.
26. Ludy, L. *Set-Apart Femininity*, pp. 182-183.
27. Peel, K. *Desperate Households*, p. 60.
28. Linda Waite, et al. "Does Divorce Make People Happy?" p. 5, *emphasis added.*
29. Dobson, J. *Straight Talk to Men and Their Wives*, p. 157.
30. Barnes, A. *Notes on the New Testament*, 1 Cor. 7:2.
31. J. Epstein, as quoted by W. Shalit in *A Return to Modesty*, pp. 227-228.
32. Peggy Noonan, as quoted by C. Thomas, *The Things That Matter Most*, p. 102-103.
33. Williamson, G. *The Shorter Catechism,* p. 1.

34. Pride, M. *The Way Home*, p. 20.
35. Ignatius of Antioch, as quoted by Sam and Bethany Torode, *Aflame: Ancient Wisdom on Marriage*, p. 45.

Chapter 13—Let Him Lead
1. Alcott, L. *Little Women*, p. 80 (as quoted by W. Shalit in *A Return to Modesty*, p 215).
2. Shalit, W. *A Return to Modesty*, p. 142.
3. Simone de Beauvoir, as quoted by W. Shalit, *A Return to Modesty*, p. 142, *emphasis added.*
4. Schlessinger, L. *The Proper Care and Feeding of Marriage,* pp. 35-36.
5. Henry, M. *Matthew Henry's Commentary* on Gen 2:21-25, p. 19.
6. Handford, E. *Me? Obey Him?* p. 90.
7. Crabb, L. *The Marriage Builder*, p. 112.
8. Pearl, D. *Created to Be His Help Meet*, p. 54.
9. Feldhahn, S. *For Women Only*, p 26.
10. Eggerichs, E. *Love and Respect*, p. 5.
11. Feldhahn, S. *For Women Only*, p 25.
12. Barnes, B. *What Makes a Man Feel Loved*, p 72.
13. Pearl, D. *Created to Be His Help Meet*, p. 22.
14. Schlessinger, L. *The Proper Care and Feeding of Husbands*, p. 161.
15. *Ibid*, p. 159.
16. Nelson, T. *Better Love Now*, p. 129.
17. Schlessinger, L. *The Proper Care and Feeding of Husbands,* p. 51.
18. Feldhahn, S. *For Women Only*, p 45.
19. Janice Wills, as quoted by Nancy Campbell in "Husbands Need Encouragement." *Above Rubies,* #69, p. 5.
20. Barnes, B. *What Makes a Man Feel Loved*, pp. 153-154.
21. "Learn to tat" remains a personal goal, but has for the time being been relegated to the list of "empty nest" projects I plan to tackle once all our kids leave home. It's right between "Take Salsa Lessons" and "Study Glass-Blowing."
22. Feldhahn, S. *For Women Only*, p. 29.
23. Barnes, B. *What Makes a Man Feel Loved*, p. 162.
24. Peace, M. *The Excellent Wife,* p. 186.

Chapter 14—Build Him Up
1. Crabb, L. *The Marriage Builder,* pp. 101-102.
2. Bell, R. *Sex God,* p. 121.
3. Schlessinger, L. *The Proper Care and Feeding of Husbands*, p. 41.
4. Peel, K. *Desperate Households*, p. 81.
5. Barnes, B. *What Makes a Man Feel Loved*, p. 182.

6. George Eliot, as quoted by Bob Barnes in *What Makes a Man Feel Loved*, p 191.
7. Schlessinger, L. *The Proper Care and Feeding of Husbands*, p. 74.
8. Dickens, C. *A Tale of Two Cities,* p. 1.
9. Martha Washington, as quoted by Kathy Peel, *Desperate Households,* p. 231.
10. Charnetski, C. *Feeling Good is Good for You*, p. 3-4.
11. *Ibid.*
12. *Ibid*, pp. 32-33.
13. *Ibid*, p. 35.
14. Bell, R. *Sex God*, p. 74.
15. Author unknown: http://www.jocund.com/happiness.html.
16. Feldhahn, S. *For Women Only*, p. 65.
17. Schlessinger, S. *The Proper Care and Feeding of Husbands,* p. 64.
18. Benjamin Franklin, as quoted by Kathy Peel, *Desperate Households,* p. 58.
19. Tan, A. *The Joy Luck Club,* pp. 155.
20. *Ibid.*
21. Browning, E. B. *Sonnets from the Portuguese,* #43.
22. Margaret Campolo, as quoted by Bob Barnes in *What Makes a Man Feel Loved*, p. 114.
23. Barnes, B. *What Makes a Man Feel Loved*, p. 91.
24. *Ibid*, p. 92.
25. Schlessinger, L. *The Proper Care and Feeding of Husbands*, p. 12.
26. *Don't Sweat the Small Stuff* is the title of a book by Richard Carlson, subtitled: *and it's all small stuff.*
27. Handford, E. *Me? Obey Him?* p. 69-70.
28. Pearl, D. *Created to Be His Help Meet*, p. 37.
29. Cloud, Henry and John Townsend, *Simple Secrets of a Great Marriage,* p. 146.
30. Pearl, D. *Created to Be His Help Meet*, p. 73.
31. Baker, D. *Thank You Therapy*, p. 15.
32. *Ibid*, p. 24.
33. Ariely, D. *Predictably Irrational*, p. 170.
34. Pearl, D. *Created to Be His Help Meet*, p. 34.
35. Peel, K. *Desperate Households*, p. 88.
36. Pearl, D. *Created to Be His Help Meet*, p. 27.

Chapter 15—Watch Him Grow
1. Nelson, T. *Better Love Now,* p. 46.
2. *Ibid.*
3. Handford, E. *Me? Obey Him?* p. 58.
4. Pearl, *Created to Be His Help Meet*, p. 30.

5. Schlessinger, L. *The Proper Care and Feeding of Husbands*, p. 74.
6. Pearl, D. *Created to Be His Help Meet*, p. 36.
7. Handford, E. *Me? Obey Him?* p. 70.
8. Cloud, H. and J. Townsend, *Simple Secrets of a Great Marriage*, p. 34.
9. Schlessinger, L. *The Proper Care and Feeding of Husbands*, p. 38.
10. Gardner, T. *Sacred Sex*, p. 78.
11. Cloud and Townsend, *Simple Secrets of a Great Marriage*, pp. 18-19.
12. Pearl, D. *Created to Be His Help Meet*, p. 74.
13. Ludy, L. *Set-Apart Femininity*, pp. 155-156.
14. *Ibid*, p. 166.
15. E.M. Bounds, as quoted by L. Ludy in *Set-Apart Femininity*, p. 155.
16. Ludy, L. *Set-Apart Femininity*, p. 168.
17. *Ibid*.
18. Ruhnke, R. *For Better and For Ever*, as quoted by White in *Married To Jesus*, p. 102.
19. Rainey, D. "Prayer: The Secret to a Lasting Marriage."
20. Ruth Graham, as quoted by Bob Barnes, *What Makes a Man Feel Loved*, p. 25.

Chapter 16—Celebrate the Differences
1. Rogers, E. *Diffusion of Innovations: Fourth Edition*, p. 264.
2. *Ibid*, p. 265.
3. This saying was popularized in the 1940's during World War II.
4. Peace, M. *The Excellent Wife*, pp. 198-199.
5. Schlessinger, L. *The Proper Care and Feeding of Husbands*, p. 56-57.
6. Peace, M. *The Excellent Wife*, pp. 198-199.
7. Birkey, V. *God's Pattern for Enriched Living*, p. 65.
8. *Ibid*.
9. Though this prayer has often been associated with St. Francis of Assisi, it was actually written by theologian Reinhold Niebuhr.
10. Cloud and Townsend, *Simple Secrets of a Great Marriage*, p. 98.
11. Despite my frequenting both of the Goodwill branches here in Tyler, I've never been able to track down any of the hasty donations Doug later regretted. When I'd try and fail, he'd shrug, "Don't sweat it, Jennifer. Somebody else obviously needed it worse than we did!"
12. Shalit, W. *A Return to Modesty*, pp. 86-87.
13. *Ibid*, p. 153.
14. Bell, R. *Sex God*, p. 150.
15. Dobson, J. *Straight Talk to Men and Their Wives*, p. 157.
16. Crittenden, D. *What Our Mothers Didn't Tell Us*, p. 57.
17. Shalit, W. *A Return to Modesty*, p. 120.

18. Nelson, T. *Better Love Now*, p. 120.
19. Schlessinger, L. *The Proper Care and Feeding of Husbands*, p. 87.
20. Alcott, L. *Little Women,* p. 299.
21. *Ibid,* p. 297.
22. Hamilton, R. "Song for a Fifth Child."
23. Nelson, T. *Better Love Now*, p. 16.
24. Crittenden, D. *What Our Mothers Didn't Tell Us*, p. 187-188.
25. Ostyn, M. *A Sane Woman's Guide to Raising a Large Family*, p. 103.
26. *Ibid,* p. 105.
27. Barnes, B. *What Makes a Man Feel Loved*, p. 84.
28. Harley, W. *His Needs, Her Needs*, p. 78.
29. Schlessinger, L. *The Proper Care and Feeding of Husbands,* p. xvi.
30. H.J.M. Nouwen, as quoted by K. Peel in *Desperate Households*, p. 42.
31. Peel, K. *Desperate Households*, p. 42.
32. Gardner, T. *Sacred Sex*, p. 104.
33. Feldhahn, S. *For Women Only*, p. 147.
34. Handford, E. *Me? Obey Him?* p.66.
35. Cloud and Townsend. *Simple Secrets of a Great Marriage,* p. 45.

Chapter 17—Foster Friendship

1. I actually think my friend may have made this whole story up as a joke, but I'm too embarrassed to ask now. It illustrates my point, whether it really happened or not. (I also don't remember for sure whether Weasel was a *she* or a *he*. Forgive me, Terry, if I got it wrong.)
2. Brizendine, L. *The Female Brain*, p. 14.
3. Schlessinger, L. *The Proper Care and Feeding of Husbands*, p. 95.
4. I think the book, *How to Get Your Point Across in 30 Seconds or Less*, should be required reading for all wives, young and old. Of course, it took the author (Milo Frank) 121 pages to get his own point across, but never mind that.
5. Nelson, T. *Better Love Now,* p. 41-42.
6. Statistically, second marriages are much more likely to end in divorce than first marriages: According to the Forest Institute of Professional Psychology in Springfield, Missouri, "50% percent of first marriages, 67% of second and 74% of third marriages end in divorce."
7. These words are borrowed from an original song by my daughter Bethany entitled "Break These Walls", which you can hear at http://www.flandersfamily.info/music.html.
8. I'm just pulling these names out of the air, and they don't necessarily match up with actual offenses—so if you happened to go to grade school with me, you needn't bother working it out.

9. My overbite was so severe that I had to wear braces *twice* growing up—once in grade school, and again in high school and college.
10. It was true. That's what comes of playing Twister with a full bladder and being targeted for tickle torture.
11. Schlessinger, L. *The Proper Care and Feeding of Husbands*, p. 3.
12. Coody, T. *Meaningless Words*, pp. 90.
13. *Ibid, pp.90*-93.
14. Coody, T. *Meaningless Words*, p. 96.
15. Thoene, B. *Why a Shepherd?* pp. 22-23.
16. This quote is attributed to Ralph Waldo Emerson: "The only reward of virtue is virtue; the only way to have a friend is to be a friend."

Chapter 18—Control Your Tongue
1. Schlessinger, L. *The Proper Care and Feeding of Husbands*, p. 56-57.
2. *Ibid*, p. 109.
3. Crabb, L. *Men & Women*, p. 95.
4. *Ibid*, p. 50.
5. Handford, E. *Me? Obey Him?* p. 87
6. *Ibid.*
7. Nelson, T. *Better Love Now*, p. 44.
8. *Ibid*, p. 55.
9. At least, one of us was malignant. The other was in tears.
10. The statements "I hate you" and "I want a divorce"—or any variation of those sentiments—belong at the top of the list of things married couples should never say to one another. Even if such a thought enters your mind, you must not allow it to escape your lips.
11. Dietrich Bonhoeffer in *Life Together*, as quoted by Matthew White, *Married to Jesus*, p. 62.
12. Norman Wright, as quoted by B. Barnes in *What Makes a Man Feel Loved*, p. 72.
13. Coody, T. *Meaningless Words*, p. 54.
14. Leman, Kevin. *7 Things He'll Never Tell You*, p. 21.
15. Scott, S. *The Richest Man Who Ever Lived*, pp. 168-169.
16. I eventually realized that a cluttered house also puts my husband on edge. This was not as obvious a provocation as denying him sex—nor was his reaction as strong—but it's an issue, nonetheless, so I try to keep things picked up for his sake. He's a bit of a neatnik, after all. He tears every piece of trash into quarters before putting it in the trashcan, folds his *dirty* clothes before placing them in the laundry hamper, and rotates his clean socks and underwear (front to back) to ensure even wear.
17. "Haughty eyes" is first on the list of abominations in Proverbs 6:17.

Chapter 19—Forgive and Forget

1. Charnetski, C. *Feeling Good is Good for You*, p. 155.
2. Stack, D. *Martha to the Max*, p. 171.
3. Norman Wright, as quoted by Bob Barnes in *What Makes a Man Feel Loved*, p. 162.
4. Nelson, T. *Better Love Now*, p. 138-139.
5. Crabb, L. *The Marriage Builder*, p. 124.
6. Nelson, T. *Better Love Now*, pp. 131.
7. *Ibid*, p. 134-135.
8. Elizabeth Elliot, as quoted by Bob Barnes in *What Makes a Man Feel Loved*, p. 27.
9. Crabb, L. *Men & Women*, p. 66.
10. C.S. Lewis, as quoted by Kathy Peel in *Desperate Households*, p. 69.
11. Stack, D. *Martha to the Max*, p. 177-178.
12. Barnes, B. *What Makes a Man Feel Loved*, p. 149.
13. Crabb, L. *The Marriage Builder,* p. 132-133.
14. *Ibid.*
15. Elizabeth Elliot, in a personal letter to the author, dated September 30, 1986.

Chapter 20—Stay the Course

1. Handford, E. *Me? Obey Him?* p. 69.
2. Coody, T. *Meaningless Words,* p. 126.
3. Handford, E. *Me? Obey Him?* p. 58.
4. Elliot, E. *Let Me Be a Woman*, p. 47.
5. Friedman, T. *The World is Flat*, p. 168.
6. *Ibid,* p. 169.
7. *Ibid.*
8. Visit us at: http://www.flandersfamily.info.
9. Louisa May Alcott, as quoted by Kathy Peel in *Desperate Households,* p. 8.
10. Jamieson, Fausset, and Brown. *Commentary on the Old and New Testaments*, Ecc. 4:9.
11. *Ibid.*
12. Erasmus, as quoted by Debbie Maken in *Getting Serious About Getting Married*, pp. 133-134.
13. Barna, G. *Revolutionary Parenting*, p. 153-154.
14. Barnes, B. *What Makes a Man Feel Loved,* p . 174.
15. Barna, G. *Revolutionary Parenting*, p. 153-154.
16. Barnes, B. *What Makes a Man Feel Loved,* p. 179.
17. Spurgeon, C. *Morning and Evening,* Nov 26, Ecc. 9:10.
18. Peel, K. *Desperate Households*, p. 235.

19. Nelson, T. *Better Love Now*, p. 17.
20. Shalit, W. *Girls Gone Mild*, p. 278.
21. Nelson, T. *Better Love Now*, p. 168.

Afterward—The Hope of Glory
1. Stack, D. *Martha to the Max*, p. 111-112.
2. Coptic Wedding Liturgy, as quoted by Sam and Bethany Torode, *Aflame: Ancient Wisdom on Marriage*, p. 59.

Bibliography

Akerlof, George, Janet Yellen, and Michael Katz. (1996). "An Analysis of Out-of-Wedlock Childbearing in the United States." *Quarterly Journal of Economics* CXI: 277-317.

Alcott, Louisa May. (1868). *Little Women.* Abridged edition. Garden City, NY: Nelson Doubleday, Inc.

American Cancer Society. (2007). "Cancer Facts & Figures: 2007." <www.cancer.org/downloads/STT/CAFF2007PW secured.pdf>.

"Are There Cosmetic Benefits to Having Sex?" (2007). CareFair.com: Skin is In. <http://www.carefair.com/Skincare/Skin-and-Lifestyle/Having_Sex_1820.html>.

Ariely, Dan. (2008). *Predictably Irrational.* New York, NY: HarperCollins Publishers.

Baker, B. M. Parquette, *et al.* (2000). "The influence of marital adjustment on 3-year left ventricular mass and ambulatory blood pressure in mild hypertension." *Archives of Internal Medicine* 160 (22): 3453-8.

Baker, Don. (1989). *Thank You Therapy.* Wheaton, IL: Victor Books.

Barna, George. (2007). *Revolutionary Parenting: What the Research Shows Really Works.* Carol Stream, Ill: Barna Books, an imprint of Tyndale House Publishers, Inc.

Barnes, Albert. (1885). *Barnes' Notes on the New Testament.* London: Blackie and Son. Electronic Database Copyright © 1997, 2003 by Biblesoft, Inc.

Barnes, Bob. (1998). *What Makes a Man Feel Loved: Understanding What Your Husband Really Wants.* Eugene, Oregon: Harvest House Publishers.

Barrett, Erin and Jack Mingo. (2002). *Doctors Killed George Washington: Hundreds of Fascinating Facts from the World of Medicine.* Berkley, CA: Conari Press.

Bartz, Jennifer and Eric Hollander. (2007). "Is Oxytocin the Key to Understanding?" *Scientific American.com—Mind Maters.* <http://blog.sciam.com/index.php?title= the_hormone_that_helps_you_read_minds&more=1&c=1&tb=1&pb=1>.

Battaglia, Emily. (2007). "Not Tonight Dear, I Have a Headache: 4 Ways to Save Your Sexless Marriage." <http://www.lifescript.com/Life/Sex/Libido/Not_Tonight_Dear_I_Have_a_Headache.aspx?trans=1&du=1&gclid=C PanjZaO4JsCFQFqxwodQBedbA&ef_id=1350:3:c_b4202 60a4d3eea6f6e4d6c98ec1cae9c>.

Bell, Rob. (2007). *Sex God: Exploring the Endless Connections Between Sexuality and Spirituality.* Grand Rapids, MI: Zondervan.

Billings, Lyndsey, Jonathan Spero, *et al.* (2006). "Oxytocin null mice ingest enhanced amounts of sweet solutions during light and dark cycles and during repeated shaker stress." *Behavioural Brain Research,* Volume 171, Issue 1, 15 July 2006, pp. 134-141.

Birkey, Verna. (1971). *God's Pattern for Enriched Living: A Biblical Basis for a Life of Personal Enrichment for Women.* Kent, WA: Enriched Living Workshops.

Bonhoeffer, Dietrich. (1956). *Life Together.* New York, NY: Harper and Row.

Boteach, Shmuley. (1999). *Kosher Sex: A Recipe for Passion and Intimacy.* New York, NY: Doubleday.

Bouchez, Colette. (2005). "Using Your Immune System to Stay Well: Experts explain how you can tap the power of your immune system to avoid getting sick." *WebMD: Better Information. Better Health.* <http://www.webmd.com/cold-and-flu/features/using-your-imune-system-to-stay-well>.

"Breast Cancer." (2007). *Wikipedia: The Free Encyclopedia.* < http://en.wikipedia.org/wiki/Breast_cancer>.

Briggs, Laura. (2000). "The Race of Hysteria: 'Overcivilization' and the 'Savage' Woman in Late Nineteenth-Century Obsterics and Gynecology." *American Quarterly.* 52:246-73.

Brizendine, Louann. (2006). *The Female Brain.* New York, NY: Morgan Road Books.

Browning, Elizabeth Barrett. (1910). *Sonnets from the Portuguese.* Portland, ME: Thomas B. Mosher.

Bryla, Christine. (1996). "The Relationship Between Stress and the Development of Breast Cancer: A Literature Review." *Oncology Nursing Forum,* 23 (January/February 1996): 441.

Brody, S. (2003). "Alexithymia Is Inversely Associated with Women's Frequency of Vaginal Intercourse." *Archives of Sexual Behavior,* Vol. 32, No. 1, Feb. 2003, pp. 73-77(5).

_____. (2006). "Blood pressure reactivity to stress is better for people who recently had penile-vaginal intercourse than for people who had other or no sexual activity." *Biological Psychology.* Vol. 71, Issue 2, Feb. 2006, pp. 214-222.

Byron, S. (2007). "When Aging Hits Home." *Sarasota Magazine,* January issue. Florida: Gulf Coast Media. <http://www.sarasotamagazine.com/Articles/Sarasota-Magazine/2007/01/When-Aging-Hits-Home.asp>.

Campbell, Nancy. (2003). *Be Fruitful and Multiply: What the Bible Says about Having Children.* San Antonio, TX: Vision Forum Ministries.

_____. (2007). "Husbands Need Encouragement." *Above Rubies: Strenghening Families Across the World.* Franklin, TN: McQuiddy Printing Company, Issue #69.

Carmichael, Kim. (1995). "Osteoporosis: Prevention & Intervention" © Joel R. Cooper. <http://medicalreporter.health.org/tmr1295/osteo1295.html>.

Cassoni P, T. Marrocco, *et al.* (2004). "Evidence of oxytocin/oxytocin receptor interplay in human prostate gland and carcinomas." *International Journal of Oncology*, 2004 Oct; 25 (4): 899-904.

Cassoni P, A. Sapino, *et al.* (2004). "Oxytocin and Oxytocin Receptors in Cancer Cells and Proliferation." *Journal of Neuroendocrinology*, 16 (4), 362-364.

Casura, Lily. (2008). "The Cortisol Connection: Sex and Sleep, Stress, and Survival." *Healing Combat Trauma.* <http://www.healingcombattrauma.com/2008/08/the-cortisol-connection-sex-and-sleep-stress-and-survival.html>.

Charnetski, Carl and Francis Brennan. (2001). *Feeling Good is Good for You: How Pleasure Can Boost Your Immune System and Lengthen Your Life.* USA: Rodale, Incorporated.

Clarke, Adam. (circa 1800). *Commentary and Critical Notes.* Reprinted Nashville, TN: Abingdon Press. Electronic Database Copyright © 1996, 2003 by Biblesoft, Inc.

Cohen, Elizabeth. (2007). "CDC: Antidepressants most prescribed drugs in U.S." <http://www.cnn.com/2007/HEALTH/07/09/antidepressants/index.html>.

Coody, Tim. (2006). *Meaningless Words & Broken Covenants: How Our Words and the Agreements Built on Them are Becoming Increasingly Meaningless.* Mustang, OK: Tate Publishing, LLC.

Copeland, Pala and Al Link. (2004). "The Health Benefits of Sex." *The Guide to Self-Help Books.* <http://www.books-4selfhelp.com/article-health-benefits-sex.htm>.

Crabb, Larry. (1991). *Men & Women: Enjoying the Difference.* Grand Rapids, MI: Zondervan Publishing House.

_____. (1982). *The Marriage Builder: A Blueprint for Couples and Counselors.* Grand Rapids, MI: Zondervan Publishing House.

Crittenden, Danielle. (1999). *What Our Mothers Didn't Tell Us: Why Happiness Eludes the Modern Woman.* New York, NY: Simon & Schuster Paperbacks.

Clarke, Adam. (circa 1820). *Adam Clarke's Commentary and Critical Notes from the Holy Bible.* Electronic Database Copyright 2003. Nashville, TN: Abingdon Press.

Cloud, Henry and John Townsend. (2006). *Simple Secrets of a Great Marriage.* Nashville, TN: Thomas Nelson.

Cutler, Winnifred. (1991). *Love Cycles: The Science of Intimacy.* New York: Villard Books.

DeKadt. (2005). *DeKadt Facial Skin Care Anti-Aging Market Study*, 1411 females 25-64. US: Internet Study.

Deveny, Kathleen. (2003). "We're Not In the Mood." *Newsweek*, June 30, 2003, p. 40.

Dickens, Charles. (1880). *A Tale of Two Cities.* Bath, UK: Parragon Publishing.

Dobson, James. (1975). *What Wives Wish their Husbands Knew about Women.* IL: Tyndale House Publishers.

_____. (1980). *Straight Talk to Men and Their Wives.* Waco, TX: Word Books.

Eggerichs, Emerson. (2004). *Love and Respect: The Love She Most Desires, The Respect He Desperately Needs.* Nashville, TN: Thomas Nelson, Inc.

Elliot, Elisabeth. (1976). *Let Me Be a Woman.* Wheaton, IL: Tyndale House Publishers.

Evans, Randolph and James Couch. (2001). "Orgasm and Migraine." *Headache*, 41, 512-514.

Farnham, Alan. (2003). "Is Sex Necessary?" *Forbes.com— Forbes Life: Your Health.* <http://www.gorbes.com/2003/ 10/08/cz_af_1008health.html>.

Farris, Michael and Reed Elam. (2000). *A Sacred Foundation: The Importance of Strength in the Home School Marriage.* Sisters, OR: Loyal Publishing.

Farris, Vickie and Jayme. (2000). *A Mom Just Like You.* Sisters, OR: Loyal Publishing.

Feldhahn, Shaunti and Jeff (2006). *For Men Only: A Straightforward Guide to the Inner Lives of Women.* Colorado Springs, CO: Multinomah Publishers.

Feldhahn, Shaunti. (2004). *For Women Only: What You Need to Know About the Inner Lives of Men.* Colorado Springs, CO: Multinomah Publishers.

Feldman, Henry, *et al.* (1998). "Low Dehydroepiandrosterone Sulfate and Heart Disease in Middle-Aged Men: Cross-Sectional Results from the Massachusetts Male Aging Study." *Annals of Epidemiology*, 8(4), 217-228.

"Female Hysteria." (2008). *Wikipedia: The Free Encyclopedia.* <http://en.wikipedia.org/wiki/Female_hysteria>.

Bibliography

"Fertility: Less Time Than You Think." (2002). *CBSNews.com.*
<http://www.cbsnews.com/stories/2002/04/30/health/main507580.sht
ml>.

Fogari, Roberto, *et al.* (2002). "Sexual Activity and Plasma Testosterone
Levels in Hypertensive Males." *American Journal of Hypertension,*
15(3), 217-221.

Friedman, Thomas. (2006). *The World Is Flat: A Brief History of the
Twenty-First Century.* NY, NY: Farrar, Staus, and Giroux.

Gardner, Tim Alan. (2002). *Sacred Sex: A Spiritual Celebration of
Oneness in Marriage.* Colorado Springs, CO: Waterbrook Press (a
division of Random House, Inc.).

Gladwell, Malcolm. (2005). *Blink: The Power of Thinking Without
Thinking.* New York, NY: Little, Brown and Company.

Graham, Stephen. (2007). "Germans Get Incentives for Having Babies."
The Washington Post, Wednesday, January 3, 2007.
<http://www.washingtonpost.com/wp-
dyn/content/article/2007/01/03/AR2007010301490.html>.

Grant, Toni. (1988). *Being a Woman.* New York: Random House.

Grewen, Karen, Susan Girdler, *et al.* (2005). "Effects of Partner Support
on Resting Oxytocin, Cortisol, Norepinephrine, and Blood Pressure
Before and After Warm Partner Contact." *Psychosomatic Medicine,*
67:531-538.

Hamilton, Ruth Hulbert. (1958). "Song for a Fifth Child." First published
in *Ladies Home Journal.* <http://www.practical-
homeschooling.org/2009/08/song-for-a-fifth-child/>.

Handford, Elizabeth. (1972). *Me? Obey Him?* Murfreesboro, TN: Sword
of the Lord Publishers.

Harley, Willard. (1986). *His Needs, Her Needs.* Tarrytown, NY: Fleming
H. Revell.

Harrison's Principles of Internal Medicine: Thirteenth Edition. (1994).
Editors: Kurt Isselbacher, Eugene Braunwald, et al. New York, NY:
McGraw-Hill, Inc. Health Professions Division.

Henry, Matthew. (1706). *Matthew Henry's Commentary on the Whole
Bible.* McLean, VA: MacDonald Publishing Company.

Hiedemann, Bridget, Olga Suhomlinova, and Angela O'Rand. (1998).
"Economic independence, Economic status, and Empty Nest in
Midlife Marital Disruption," *Journal of Marriage and the Family* 60:
219-231.

Houghton, Craig. (2007). *Family UNplanning: A Guide for Christian
Couples Seeking God's Truth on Having Children.* USA: Xulon
Press.

Honoré, Carl. (2004). *In Praise of Slow: How a Worldwide Movement is
Challenging the Cult of Speed.* London, England: Orion Books.

"How sex makes you look and feel better." (2006). *Saga Magazine: July 14, 2006.* <http://www.saga.co.uk/magazine/relationships/couples/SexBeautyAndWellbeing.asp>.

"Human growth hormone (HGH) and anti-aging." (2005). <http://womens-health.health-cares.net/anti-aging-hgh.php>.

"Hypertension/ High Blood Pressure Guide: Symptoms and Types."(2007). *Hypertension Health Center Guide.* WebMD, Inc. <http://www.webmd.com/hypertension-high-blood-pressure/guide/hypertension-symptoms-types>.

Jamieson, Robert, A.R. Fausset, and David Brown. (1877). *A Commentary on the Old and New Testaments: Critical, Experimental, and Practical.* Originally published Hartford, CT: S.S. Scranton, 1877. Reprinted Grand Rapids, MI: Eerdmans Publishing Company, 1993. Electronic Database Copyright © 1997, 2003 by Biblesoft, Inc.

Juan, Stephen. (2006). "What are the scientific reasons for having sex?" *The Register*.® <http:www.theregister.co.uk/2006/10/06/the_odd_body_sex_and_science>.

Kaplan, Hillard, Jane Lancaster, and Kermyt Anderson. (1998). "Human Parental Investment and Fertility: The Life Histories of Men in Albuquerque." *Men in Families.* Mahwah, NJ: Lawrence Erlbaum Press.

Kirch, Irving. (1998). "Antidepressants Proven to Work Only Slightly Better Than Placebo." *Prevention and Treatment,* June 1998.

Knox, S. and K. Uvnas-Moberg. (1998). "Social isolation and cardiovascular disease: an atherosclerotic pathway?" *Psychoneuroendocrinology,* 1998; 23: 819-35.

Kovacs, Gábor, Zoltán Sarnyai and Gyula Szabó. (1998). "Oxytocin and Addiction: A Review." *Psychoneuroendocrinology,* 1998; 23: 945-62.

Lamer, Timothy. (2007). "Unfocused families—Fertility: Changing attitudes about children could have major economic consequences." *WORLD.* July 21, 2007: p. 27.

Lê, M., *et al.* (1989). "Characteristics of Reproductive Life and Risk of Breast Cancer in a Case-Control Study of Young Nulliparous Women." *Journal of Clinical Epidemiology,* 42 (12), 1227-1233.

Leitzmann, Michael, *et al.* (2004). "Ejaculation Frequency and Subsequent Risk of Prostrate Cancer." *JAMA.* 2004, April7. Vol. 291. No. 13. pp. 1578-1586.

Leman, Kevin. (2007). *7 Things He'll Never Tell You...but you need to know.* Carol Stream, IL: Tyndale House Publishers, Inc.

Liebau, Carol Platt. (2007). *Prude: How the Sex-Obsessed Culture Damages Girls (and America, Too!).* New York, NY: Center Street, a division of Hachette Book Group USA, Inc.

Littauer, Florence. (1989). *Personalities in Power.* Lafayette, LA: Huntington House Inc.

Ludy, Eric and Leslie. (2007). *Meet Mr. Smith: Revolutionize the Way You Think About Sex, Purity, and Romance.* Nashville, TN: Thomas Nelson Publishing.

_____. (2006). *The First 90 Days of Marriage.* Nashville, TN: Thomas Nelson Publishing.

Ludy, Leslie. (2008). *Set-Apart Femininity: God's Sacred Intent for Every Young Woman.* Eugene, Oregon: Harvest House Publishers.

Maines, Rachel. (1999). *The Technology of Orgasm: "Hysteria," the Vibrator, and Women's Sexual Satisfaction.* Baltimore: The Johns Hopkins University Press. ISBN 0-8018-6646-4.

Maken, Debbie. (2006). *Getting Serious About Getting Married: Rethinking the Gift of Singleness.* IL: Crossway Books.

Margolis, Jonathan. (2004). *O: The Intimate History of the Orgasm.* New York, NY: Grove Press.

Medical Patent News. (2005). "Nastech Pharmaceutical awarded new breast cancer patent." <http://www.news-medical.net/?id=10532>.

Mitchell, Kathy and Marcy Sugar. (2006). "Annie's Mailbox." *Creators Syndicate.*

Mulhauser, Greg. (2006). "Experts Warn About Growing Use of Prescription Sleeping Pills." *Psychology, Philosophy, and Real Life.* <http://counsellingresource.com/features/2006/ 02/09/sleeping-pill-risks/>.

Naitoh, John, Rebecca Zeiner, *et al.* (1998). "Diagnosis and Treatment of Prostate Cancer" *American Family Physician,* Vol. 57/ No.7 (April 1, 1998). Published by the American Academy of Family Physicians.

Nelson, Tommy. (2008). *Better Love Now: Making Your Marriage a Lifelong Love Affair.* Nashville, TN: B&H Publishing Group.

Ornish, Dean. (1998). *Love & Survival: The Scientific Basis for the Healing Power of Intimacy.* New York, NY: HarperCollins Publishers, Inc.

Ostyn, Mary. (2009). *A Sane Woman's Guide to Raising a Large Family.* Layton, UT: Gibbs Smith.

Owen, Jr., Samuel A. (1990). *Letting God Plan Your Family.* Wheaton, IL: Crossway Books.

"Oxytocin." (2007). *Wikipedia: The Free Encyclopedia.* < http://en.wikipedia.org/wiki/oxytocin>.

Peace, Martha. (1999). *The Excellent Wife: A Biblical Perspective.* Bemidji, MN: Focus Publishing.

Pearl, Debi. (2004). *Created To Be His Help* Meet. Pleasantville, TN: No Greater Joy Ministries, Inc.

Pearl, Michael and Debi. (1997). *No Greater Joy: Volume One.* Pleasantville, TN: No Greater Joy Ministries, Inc.

_____. (2007). *Jumping Ship: What to Do So Your Children Don't Jump Ship to the World when They Get Older.* Pleasantville, TN: No Greater Joy Ministries, Inc.

Peel, Kathy. (2007). *Desperate Households.* Carol Stream, IL: Picket Fence Press, an imprint of Tyndale House Publishers, Inc.

Physician's Desk Reference. (2007). Online Resource. <http://www.pdr.net/druginformation/DocumentSearchn.aspx?documentId=60861170&drugname=Ortho%20Tri-Cyclen%20Lo%20Tablets#PDRWAR01>.

Physician's Drug Handbook: 11th Edition. (2005). Philadelphia, PA: Lippincott Williams & Wilkins.

"Prescription Sleeping Pill Use Tied To Cancer." (2008). *Medical News Today.* <http://www.medicalnewstoday.com/articles/118586.php>.

Pressfield, Steven. (2002). *The War of Art: break Through the Blocks and Win Your Inner Creative Battles.* New York, NY: Grand Central Publishing.

Pride, Mary. (1989). *All the Way Home: Power for Your Family to be Its Best.* Westchester, IL: Crossway Books.

_____. (1985). *The Way Home: Beyond Feminism Back to Reality.* Westchester, IL: Crossway Books.

Provan, Charles. (1989). *The Bible and Birth Control: Psalm 127:4.* Monongahela, PA: Zimmer Printing.

Rainey, Dennis. (2001). "Prayer: The Secret to a Lasting Marriage." Little Rock, AR: FamilyLife.com. <http://www.christianity.com/christian%20living/features/11545181/>.

Rawlings, Marjorie. (1938). *The Yearling.* Copyright renewed by Charles Scribners, 1966. New York, NY: Aladdin Paperbacks, imprint of Simon & Schuster.

Robinson, D. and Wei, F., *et al.* (2002). "Oxytocin mediates stress-induced analgesia in adult mice." *Journal of Physiology*, 2002, Apr 15; 540 (Pt 2): 593-606.

Robinson, Marnia and Gary Wilson. (2005). "The Big 'O' Isn't Orgasm." *Reuniting: Healing with Sexual Relationships.* <http://www.reuniting.info/science/oxytocin_health_bonding>.

RoC® Ten Years Back. (2006). *Omnibus Survey*, 1022 women 18+. US.

Roche, Niall. (2008). "Exactly How Does a Lack of Sleep Affect the Body?" *EzineArticles.com.* <http://ezinearticles.com/?Exactly-How-Does-a-Lack-of-Sleep-Affect-the-Body?&id=1417955>.

Bibliography

Rogers, Everett. (1995). *Diffusion of Innovations: Fourth Edition.* New York, NY: The Free Press.

"Romance Writers of America's 2005 Market Research Study on Romance Readers." (2005). <http://eweb.rwanational.org/eWeb/docs/05MarketResearch.pdf>.

Ruhnke, Robert. (1996). *For Better and For Ever.* San Antonio, TX: Marriage Preparation Resources.

Saisan, J. and Kemp, G., *et al.* (2008)."Sleeping Pills, Sleep Aids and Medications: Prescription, OTC and Natural Sleep Aids; What You Need to Know." *Help Guide.org.* <http://www.helpguide.org/life/sleep_aids_medication_-insomnia_treatment.htm>.

Sardone, Susan. (2007). "Love Quotations: Philosophical Quotes from philosophers and wise thinkers on the nature of love." <http://honeymoons.about.com/cs/wordsofwisdom/a/philosophquotes.htm>.

Schlegel, Katharina von. (1752). "Be Still My Soul," translated into English by Jane Borthwick, 1955. © Breitkopf & Hartell. Wiesbaden.

Schlessinger, Laura. (2004). *The Proper Care & Feeding of Husbands.* New York, NY: HarperCollins Publishers.

_____. (2007). *The Proper Care & Feeding of Marriage.* New York, NY: HarperCollins Publishers.

Scott, Steven. (2006). *The Richest Man Who Ever Lived: King Solomon's Secrets to Success, Wealth, and Happiness.* USA: Doubleday, a division of Random House, Inc.

Seckel, B. (2005). *Save Your Face: The Truth About Facial Aging, Its Prevention, and Cure.* Massachusetts: Peach Publications.

"Sexercise Yourself into Shape". (2006). *BBC News.* <http://news.bbc.co.uk/2/hi/4703166.stm>.

Shalit, Wendy. (2007). *Girls Gone Mild: Young Women Reclaim Self-Respect and Find It's Not Bad to Be Good.* New York, NY: Random House.

_____. (1999). *A Return to Modesty: Discovering the Lost Virtue.* New York, NY: Simon & Schuster, Inc.

Shapiro, D. (1983). "Effect of Chronic Low Back Pain on Sexuality." *Medical Aspects of Human Sexuality,* 17, 241-245. As cited in Whipple, Koch, *et al.,* 2003.

Shivanandan, Mary. (1999). *Crossing the Threshold of Love: A New Vision of Marriage.* Washington, DC: The Catholic University of America Press.

Shaw, Gina. (2007). "The New Low for High Blood Pressure." *Hypertension Health Center Guide.* WebMD, Inc.

<http://www.webmd.com/hypertension-high-blood-pressure/guide/new-low-for-high-blood-pressure>.

Spafford, Horatio. (1873). "It Is Well with My Soul." *The Celebration Hymnal: Songs and Hymns for Worship.* Copyright © 1997. USA: Word Music/ Integrity Music.

Spurgeon, Charles Haddon. (circa 1880). *Morning and Evening: Daily Readings.* PC Study Bible formatted electronic database. Copyright © 2003: Biblesoft, Inc.

Stack, Debi. (2000). *Martha to the Max: Balanced Living for Perfectionists.* Chicago, IL: Moody Press.

Tan, Amy. (1989). *The Joy Luck Club.* London, England: Penguin Books.

Thoene, Bodie and Brock. (2007). *Why a Shepherd? More Than Just a Name... It is the Reason He was Sent.* Vista, CA: Parable.

Thomas, Cal. (1994). *The Things That Matter Most.* New York, NY: HarperCollins Publishers.

Thomas, Jennifer. (2001). "Frequent Sex May Help You Look Younger." *HealthScout.* <www.healthscout.com>.

Tiger, Lionel. (1999). *The Decline of Males.* New York: Golden Books.

Tobe, Sheldon, Alexander Kiss, *et al.* (2005). "Impact of Job and Marital Strain on Ambulatory Blood Pressure: Results from the Double Exposure Study." *American Journal of Hypertension.* Vol.18, Issue 8, August 2005, pp. 1046-51.

Torode, Sam and Bethany. (2005). *Aflame: Ancient Wisdom on Marriage.* Grand Rapids, MI: Wm. B. Eerdmans Publishing Company.

_____. (2002). *Open Embrace: A Protestant Couple Rethinks Contraception.* Grand Rapids, MI: William B. Eerdmans Publishing Company.

Trader, Lois. (2007). "Prescription Sleeping Pills: Who Really Gets a Good Night Sleep without Some Sort of Sleep Aid?" *Suite101.com: The Genuine Article. Literally.* <http://common-patient-ailments.suite101.com/article.cfm/prescription_sleeping_ pills>.

Trapp, Maria Augusta. (1949). *The Story of the Trapp Family Singers.* Reprinted 2002. New York, NY: Perennial (An Imprint of HarperCollins Publishers).

Trueblood, Elton and Pauline. (1933). *The Recovery of Family Life.* New York, NY: Harper and Brothers.

Tur-Kaspa, Ilan, *et al.* (1994). "How Often Should Infertile Men Have Intercourse to Achieve Conception?" *Fertility and Sterility,* 62(2), 370-375.

Veith, Gene Edward. (2003)."Population Implosion." *World Magazine.* February 15, 2003.

Waite, Linda, Don Browning, *et al.* (2002). "Does Divorce Make People Happy? Findings from a Study of Unhappy Marriages." New York, NY: Institute for American Values.

Waite, Linda and Maggie Gallagher. (2000). *The Case for Marriage: Why Married People are Happier, Healthier, and Better Off Financially.* New York, NY: Doubleday.

Watters, Steve and Candice. (2009). *Start Your Family: Inspiration for Having Babies.* Chicago, IL: Moody Publishers.

Weeks, David and J. James. (1998). *Superyoung: The Proven Way to Stay Young Forever.* London: Hodder and Stoughton.

Whipple, Beverly, Patricia Koch, *et al.*, contributors. (2003). "The Health Benefits of Sexual Expression." *Planned Parenthood White Paper.* New York, NY: Katharine Dexter McCormick Library.

White, Matthew. (2007). *Married To Jesus: Experience a Marriage Based on the Relationship Between Christ and His Church.* (Self-published).

Wilcox, Bradford and John Bartkowski. (1999). "The Evangelical Family Paradox: Conservative Rhetoric, Progressive Practice." *The Responsive Community* 9 (Summer): 34-39.

Wilcox, Bradford. (2000). "American Family Facts: Statistical information on the moral and economic health of American families." *Southeast Christian Church Website* < http://www.southeastchristian.org/study/family.aspx?id= 1648>.

Williamson, G. (1970). *The Shorter Catechism: Volume 1.* Phillipsburg, NJ: Presbyterian and Reformed Publishing Co.

Wills, Janice. (2007). "Husbands Need Encouragement." *Above Rubies: Strengthening Families Across the World.* Franklin, TN: McQuiddy Printing Company, Issue #69, p. 5.

Thanks for taking time to read my book, *Love Your Husband/ Love Yourself.* I pray that you and your husband will be abundantly blessed as you both embrace God's purpose for passion in marriage!

If you would like to read more, I encourage you to visit my family website (*www.flandersfamily.info*), subscribe to my blog (*http://lovinglifeathome.com*), or follow me on Facebook (*www.facebook.com/love.your.husband.yourself*).

If you have comments, questions, or other feedback, you may write me at *flandersfamily@flandersfamily.info.* I'm not able to respond to all inquiries personally, but I do read all of my mail and try to address questions of general interest online.

Blessings,

Jennifer Flanders

Made in the USA
Lexington, KY
03 November 2019